# THE PROBLEM OF ORDER

# THE PROBLEM OF ORDER
Elizabethan Political Commonplaces and
an Example of Shakespeare's Art

*by*

ERNEST WILLIAM TALBERT

*Chapel Hill*

THE UNIVERSITY OF NORTH CAROLINA PRESS

Copyright © 1962 by

The University of North Carolina Press

*Manufactured in the United States of America*

PRINTED BY THE SEEMAN PRINTERY, DURHAM, N. C.

# Preface

THE PRESENT ESSAY was designed as part of a study of Shakespeare's early plays, and although it emerged as a discrete unit, it has been written especially for those interested in sixteenth-century English literature. I hope they will find it useful. Although readers of the last chapter may wish at times to have Shakespeare's *Richard II* open before them, criticism by turning to the appropriate texts has also been the aim of the author.

I wish to acknowledge my indebtedness to the Alumni Annual Giving funds of the University of North Carolina, administered by the University Research Council, for aid in the publication of this book and to the Ford Foundation for a grant under its program for assisting American university presses in the publication of works in the humanities and social sciences.

E. W. T.

# Introduction

THIS STUDY is concerned less with the Elizabethan ideal of order than with the way in which some of Shakespeare's contemporaries viewed the problem of order in a body politic. At first glance it may seem to be supererogatory, especially in view of E. M. W. Tillyard's examination of Shakespeare's two tetralogies, for certainly no one can deny the validity of his Elizabethan world-picture. If the student of sixteenth-century literature can be certain of anything, he can be sure of the fact that it would be very difficult for an Elizabethan to escape the doctrine of the official sermon on obedience. Therein man's social and political life was placed in a framework of harmony, order, and degree, and a prospect of ultimate blessedness was opened up to those who performed their duty in the state of life to which it had pleased God to call them. From such a point of view, understandably emphasized by an authoritarian state, civil disobedience was a heinous sin:

> Though kinges forget to gouerne as they ought,
> Yet subiectes must obey as they are bounde.
>
> (*Gorboduc*, V, i, 50-51)

Yet if we can judge by their speeches in Parliament, Elizabethans were fond of reminding themselves that not all nations, and, indeed, not all Englishmen, had been fortunate enough to live under Elizabeth.[1] In addition to a world-picture, there also existed more specific pictures of various states and common-

---

1. J. E. Neale, *Elizabeth I and Her Parliaments, 1559-1581* (London, 1952), p. 360 and *passim*.

weals, including one of Elizabethan England. Whether they illustrated order or disorder, those pictures were frequently developed or analyzed in accordance with the political commonplaces of the age, that is, in accordance with ideas that propagandists of all sorts were inclined to use. Connected less obviously with any ideal of order than with the Elizabethan picture of contemporary England or of earlier and different states, such ideas might lead to an emphasis upon the importance of the whole body politic and upon the necessary duties, not simply of the ruled, but also of the ruler. They might lead to a recognition of a necessity to choose between evils, or they might be enunciated in an exposition of the virtue of checks and balances or be called true commonplaces even when they were said to be falsely applied.

The chapters that follow first sketch the appearance and some of the contexts of the political commonplaces of the later sixteenth century and indicate a process of thought that seems to have been conventional when Elizabethans turned their attention to the problems and the ills of a body politic. It is hoped that such a sketch will complement what has come to be known as the Elizabethan world-picture.

From such a discussion there emerges a much more complex background for the interpretation of Elizabethan literature than that provided by ideas that focus upon the ideal of order. An elucidation of the necessity for checks and balances in a body politic, for example, when joined with some precepts about the conduct of princes could be but a step removed from an equivocal portrayal of rulers and their great lords. This consideration, then, is illustrated in the final chapters, which also examine the fact that one aspect of the problem of order might seem to make censorship necessary.

More specifically, the second portion of this essay considers Samuel Daniel's defense of *Philotas* and the way in which Shakespeare dramatized the deposition of Richard II. In the first instance, an analysis of a play believed to be "seditious," as well as the author's defense of his art, elucidates what might be acceptable to the authorities; for it was argued successfully before the Privy Council that a drama was not propaganda, that something more complex than an inculcation of order was thoroughly conventional and did not refer to the contemporary, or nearly contemporary, scene. Such a situation is then related to the publication and performance of *Richard II* and to the way in which Shakespeare referred elsewhere to the deposition of Richard. In this final chapter it can be seen from a detailed analysis of his art how Shakespeare took the step referred to above and fused disparate emphases in current thought about the body politic. Thereby his representation of Richard's deposition, by its very equivocality, interprets much more concisely than does the writing of the other authors here considered an important aspect of the political thought of its age.

# Contents

*Preface* v

*Introduction* vii

## Part One

### CURRENT THOUGHT ABOUT THE BODY POLITIC

I. Some General Considerations 3

II. Sir Thomas Smith and Richard Hooker 21

III. Sedition and Pageantry 65

IV. Sir Philip Sidney 89

## Part Two

### CENSORSHIP AND A DRAMATIST'S CAPABILITIES

V. Clinias or Dramatist? 121

VI. Shakespeare's Deposition of Richard II 146

*Notes* 201

*Index* 237

Part One

# Current Thought about the Body Politic

# I

# Some General Considerations

IN THE PRESSURE of Elizabethan circumstances one encounters political thought rather than political theory, and such thought is, as always, thoroughly chameleonic. In the political thinking that was their heritage, for example, Elizabethans could have found the most diverse political attitudes buttressed by an appeal to authority. The Bible could be twisted upon itself. It could be made to exalt or disparage rule by a single person. It could be used to inculcate obedience to civil authorities or, by inference, to incite the godly to resistance. It spoke of regal power as being ordained of God, of rendering unto Caesar the things that were Caesar's, but it spoke also of covenants between the ruler and the ruled, made "between the Lord and the king and the people, that they should be the Lord's people; between the king also and the people." Even from Roman law, as embodied in Justinian's *Corpus,* could be derived two opposite theories of government. Although one of the favorite texts stated that what pleased the ruler had the force of law (*Quod principi placuit legis habet vigorem*), it was immediately followed by a phrase that might be regarded as expressing the doctrine of consent, of a popular grant of regal power: *utpote cum lege regia, quae de imperio eius lata est, populus ei et in eum omne suum imperium et potestatem conferat.* Although *lex regia* was usually interpreted in a Hobbesian manner so that it amounted to a total and inevitable alienation of popular power, the phrase, nevertheless, which referred to the people's conferring "imperium" upon a ruler could be construed as congruent with thought that might later lead to a theory of governmental contract.[1]

It might seem that this last tendency would be likely to occur when writers emphasized St. Augustine's contention that all secular power had its origin in Sin and hence needed to be controlled; but the polemical use of this political thought reminds one of some of the consequences of the Investiture Struggle. To Duns Scotus, seeking to strengthen the church in its struggle with secular rulers, the exercise of civil power was surrounded with popular and religious restrictions; and the conciliarists, endeavouring to correct abuses of the papacy, would attempt to adapt the same principle and turn it against the church. Thus both papal and regal power would be represented as a manifestation of God's power, and, similarly, an emphasis upon the sinful origin of government could turn in opposite directions, could argue that the governmental function consisted primarily in protecting life and liberty, or could advocate man's obedience to an absolute, or even a tyrannical, governor as part of God's punishment for sin. Although the idea was growing that a king was vice-regent of God and ruled independent of ecclesiastical institutions, and of popular will or consent, the general opinion of the late middle ages was that "no one form of government is more divine than another, that the advantages of Monarchy are relative, not absolute, and that there may be times and circumstances in which Republican Constitutions would deserve preference." Accordingly, even advocates of royal absolutism might concede that "the right of deposing the Ruler in a case of necessity could be conceded to the People without any surrender of the maxim 'Princeps maior populo.'" In the early sixteenth century, in support of this last thought, there might appear a reflection of the Germanic theory of kingship, which postulated a minimum requirement of the people's assent to a king's accession and often allowed the people, or at least their leaders, the right of election and the right of imposing conditions upon the one chosen.[2]

For matter specifically related to the English state, propagandists anxious to influence events might find useful, for example, certain features in the writings of Fortescue, to whom

Sir Walter Raleigh referred as "that notable Bulwarke of our lawes."³ When Fortescue looked at the condition of England in the late fifteenth century, he believed that it would be well to strengthen the royal power; yet he would repeat a conventional idea that supreme authority rested in divine and natural law, by which the king should rule. He would also write that the English ruler was limited by Parliament. Regardless of how Fortescue himself handled such concepts, from an emphasis upon divine and natural law alone, a dominant governmental function might be given the prince who was "appointed to protect his subjects in their lives, properties and laws"; to this end, he had "delegation of power" from the people and "no claim to any other power."[4]

From such a conclusion, emphasizing divine and natural law, Reginald Pole might well have defended More and Fisher and attacked Henry's royal supremacy. By a clear reflection of the Germanic theory of kingship, however, Pole argues that regal power was conferred upon Henry by the people along with the crown at the coronation and that the people's right to rebel, if their grievances were not redressed, was inherent in that coronation ceremony.[5]

On the other side of the religious fence, and with a third, but nonetheless congruent, emphasis, John Major, the Scottish teacher of the reforming John Knox and of George Buchanan, wrote in his *History of Greater Britain* that the ruler holds his right as king "of a free people," that he cannot "grant that right to anyone against the will of the people," that inasmuch as he holds his power from the people, or from the chief men acting for the people, they have the right, when necessary, to "transfer from one race to another the kingly power," thereby depriving a king and his posterity "of all authority."[6]

With no enunciation of this last conclusion, but in the reign of Elizabeth, similar ideas appear, though the emphasis will be thrown upon the English Parliament. Soon after Elizabeth's accession, for example, Lawrence Humphrey and John Aylmer, the future Bishop of London, would affirm the right of Parliament to restrict and regulate the exercise of royal power in a manner that reminds one of an earlier passage in Fortescue's works. At her coronation Elizabeth listened to an oration written by John Hales, but delivered by a nobleman, wherein the speaker advised her of her duties, gave high praise to those who had written and fought against Mary, and informed her of the powers of Parliament and its liberties "according to the ancient Laws and Customs of the Realm." As late as 1564, Cartwright, less orthodox than the Englishmen just noted but at that time in favor with the authorities, delivered an oration to Elizabeth at Cambridge and expressed the idea that a "mixed" state—a rule shared by the Aristotelian one, few, and many—was preferable to a monarchy, largely because it provided such safeguards as parliamentary action.[7]

Such tendencies in political thought, however, might be smothered by concepts comparable to that of the Tudor myth, which emphasized the unlimited obedience due the house that united warring factions and fulfilled the prophecy of Merlin. Or pure expediency and the events of time might underlie such a situation as that in 1535, when William Marshal under the patronage of Thomas Cromwell translated Marsiglio of Padua's *Defensor Pacis*—one of the earliest and probably the greatest of the conciliarists' treatises—and omitted the chapter dealing with correction of a secular ruler as having "nothing appertaining to this realm of England."[8] With the exception of the reign of Mary, the Tudor art of government was such that very few "disloyal" voices, aside from those of Catholic polemicists, were raised in behalf of the doctrine that a ruler was limited by divine and natural law and by a delegation of power from the people, and was, consequently, subject to deposition when he violated such restrictions. Utilized in a polemical spirit, however, such ideas might have for some Catholics the peculiar force of being similar to a process of thought which could be found in St. Thomas Aquinas' great work. There the following sequence appears: (1) since royal power has a popular origin, the people have a right to restrain or abolish it when the ruler abuses his power; (2) even though the people may have submitted to a ruler in perpetuity, a deposition is not unlawful since the prince broke faith first; (3) if any check is necessary, it should be exercised by public authority, not by private action.[9]

To Aquinas, this public authority was apparently some power to which the king was subject other than that exercised in establishing the original royal power; and his conclusions seem to reflect, consequently, the many defenses of a pope's right to depose a tyrant. Yet kindred ideas, without any implication of Papal Supremacy, might crop up in Elizabethan political thought; and though in their bare logical force they were submerged by Tudor competency, they might emerge with other concepts that thoroughly qualified their potentially "seditious" nature. Aquinas' emphasis upon public authority *per se* could be incorporated easily into defenses of Elizabethan polity and of moving by the slow but public force of Parliament, a body which included the ruler, the nobility, and the commons of the realm.

Since, as the last statement indicates, the vast bulk of the English nation, or of any nation, would of necessity be made up of the commons, or the Aristotelian "many," and since the possibility that the "many" might become a mob was widely known and strongly feared, a somewhat more detailed discussion of the political thought prevalent in England from *ca.* 1550 to *ca.* 1600 could well begin with the first precepts about society and the state that the young Edwardian and Elizabethan had to learn. If an Edwardian attended "pettie" school, and always when he studied the *Book of Common Prayer,* he learned his duty to his fellowman from the Ten Commandments and, specially, from the Golden Rule:

My duety towards my neighbor is, to love him as myself.
And to do to all men as I would they should do to me.

In an eminently practical manner, this generalization would be elucidated in some detail until the child recited that he was commanded by his Creator to do his "duetie in that state of lyfe, unto which it shall please God" to call him, not simply to "loue, honour, and succour" his parents, but also to "honour and obey the king and his ministers," to submit himself to "governors, teachers, spiritual pastors, and masters," thereby conducting himself "lowly and reverently" toward all his "betters." If the young Edwardian attended grammar school, those precepts would be reinforced by the Ponet catechism, which the student might be expected to memorize in Latin.[10]

Although catechisms associated with the name of Bishop Ponet did not survive into the reign of Elizabeth, Dean Nowell probably utilized them when he prepared his fuller catechisms and strongly reinforced the political indoctrination of the *Book of Common Prayer*. When, for example, the teacher asked whether the fifth commandment applied to fathers and mothers in a literal sense only, the student was expected to extend the word "parents" to all who had any authority:

*M.* Doth the law extend only to parents by nature?
*S.* Although the very words seem to express no more: yet we must understand that all those to whom any authority is given, as magistrates, ministers of the church, school-masters; finally, all they that have any ornament, either of reverent age, or of wit, wisdom, or learning, worship, or wealthy state, or otherwise be our superiors, are contained under the name of fathers; because the authority both of them and of fathers come out of one fountain.

This "fountain" of authority was then derived from the law of God, and the figurative meaning of "parent" was emphasized in contrast with the literal one:

*M.* But is it much more heinous for a man to offend or kill the parent of his country than his own parent?
*S.* Yea, surely. For if it be for every private man a heinous offense to offend his private parents, and parricide to kill them; what shall we say of them that have conspired and borne wicked armour against the commonweal, against their country, the most ancient, sacred, and common mother of us all, which ought to be dearer unto us than ourselves, and for whom no honest man will stick to die to do it good, and against the prince, the father of the country itself, and parent of the commonweal; yea, and to imagine the overthrow, death, and destruction of them whom it is high-treason once to forsake or shrink from? So outrageous a thing can in no wise be expressed with fit name.[11]

Such catechistical precepts insisting upon obedience would be amplified by other texts in the schools, by portions of Cicero's *De Officiis,* for example, and by constant and innumerable reminders. For those not in the schools, precepts in the *Book of Common Prayer* would be reinforced by sermons on obedience and loyalty, most forcefully perhaps by the official one already mentioned; and all Elizabethans were confronted constantly with reminders that they were expected to do no more than did all creation. In liturgy and elsewhere, the overflowing, inexhaustible, asensual fecundity that was God's love was referred to as manifesting itself in the immense plenitude that confronted the senses, a carefully ordered plenitude that sprang from a Onehood which should be obeyed. Of this the preacher reminded his congregation when he spoke to them the *Sermon of Obedience,* which was the official *Exhortation concerning good Ordre and Obedience to Rulers and Magistrates.*

Almightie God hath created and appoyncted all thynges, in heaven, yearth, and waters, in a most excellent and perfect ordre. In heaven he hath appoynted distincte Orders and states of Archangelles and Angelles. In the yearth he hath assigned Kynges, princes, with other gouernors under them, all in good and necessarie ordre. The water aboue is kepte and raineth doune in dewe time and season. The Sonne, Moone, Sterres, Rainbowe, Thundre, Lightenyng, cloudes, and all birdes of the aire, do kepe their ordre. The Yearth, Trees, Seedes, Plantes, Herbes, and Corne, Grasse and all maner of beastes kepe theim in their ordre. All the partes of the whole yere, as Winter, Somer, Monethes, Nightes and Daies, continue in their ordre. All kyndes of Fishes in the sea, Rivers and Waters, with all Fountaines, Sprynges, yea, the Seas themselves kepe their comely course and ordre. And Man himself also, hath all his partes, bothe within and without, as Soule, Harte, Mynd, Memory, Understandyng, Reason, speache, with all and syngular corporall membres of his body, in a profitable, necessarie and pleasaunt ordre. Euery degree of people, in their vocacion, callyng, and office, hath appointed to them their duetie and ordre. Some are in high degree, some in lowe, some Kynges and Princes, some inferiors and subjectes, Priestes and Laymen, Masters and Servauntes, Fathers and Children, Husbandes and Wifes, Riche and Poore, and euery one haue nede of other, so that in all thynges is to bee lauded and praised the goodly ordre of God, without the whiche, no house, no citee, no common wealthe, can continue and endure. For where there is no right ordre, there reigneth all abuse, carnall libertie, enormitie, synne, and Babilonical confusion. Take awaie Kynges, Princes, Rulers, Magistrates, Judges, and suche states of God's ordre, no man shall ride or go by the high way unrobbed, no man shall slepe in his awne house or bed unkilled, no man shall kepe his wife, children, and possessions in quietnesse, all thynges shall be common, and there muste nedes folowe all mischief and utter destruccion, bothe of soules, bodies, goodes and common wealthes.[12]

The heads of traitors and other criminals also reminded Elizabethans of the punishment that a violation of order received.

It is true that a Laneham, viewing Leicester's entertainment of Elizabeth, might become enchanted with the correspondences that could be drawn out of "two."[13] But for men of his class, inveterate seekers of correspondences though they were—and in that they but followed their betters—an emphasis upon the Oneness that was thought to control multiplicity, and out of which multiplicity flowed, was an axiom that to them might seem to be manifested daily. In that, they again would have followed their betters.

> And if thou notest that which is revealed
> By Daniel, thou wilt see that in his thousands
> Number determinate is kept concealed. . . .
> The high behold now and the amplitude
> Of the eternal power, since it hath made
> Itself so many mirrors, where 'tis broken,
> One in itself remaining as before.
>
> That which can die and that which dieth not
> Are nothing but the splendor of that Idea
> Which by His love our Lord brings into being.
>
> . . . .
> That living Light
> Through its own goodness reunites its rays
> In new subsistences as in a mirror,
> Itself eternally remaining One.
> Thence it descends to the last potencies,
> Downward from act to act becoming such
> That only brief contingencies it makes.[14]

The figure of the mirror that Dante uses was a conventional one, and even more frequently, perhaps, in commentaries upon the idea of order, would appear the concept of a rough scale of being. This last idea, with congruent analogies, appeared constantly in literature, and has been so enlarged upon in recent years that only the briefest of surveys is necessary here.

A vast inanimate division was thought to be lowest in the scale of being; it comprised the elements, liquids, and metals, all of which had only existence.¹⁵  In the middle were animate beings: (1) the vegetative, which had existence and life; (2) the sensitive, which had existence, life, and feeling; and (3) the rational, which had existence, life, feeling, and understanding. In the top major division were the angelic orders, beings purely rational or spiritual.  Within each rank in each division or subdivision, gradation upward was preserved.  Fire was the highest and most excellent of the elements; gold, the highest of the metals; the oak, highest of trees; the dolphin or the whale, highest of fish; the lion or the elephant, highest of beasts; the eagle, highest of birds; the ruler, highest and most excellent of men; and through the orders of angels such rank was preserved.  Thus on the earth there was "no worm that crawls upon the ground, no bird that flies on high, no fish that swims in the depths" that did not have a place in the order that God provides.

In this chain of being, though rank may be set on rank in one sense, in another sense rank merges with rank; for each has some attribute in common with the next higher.  Man looks both ways, up and down.  His body, for example, has three centers: liver, heart, and brain.  The liver, ruler of the "vegetative" portion of man, converts food into the four liquid substances known as the humors, the attributes of each corresponding with two of the elements. The humors generate vital heat and with the "natural spirits," also created in the liver, they are said to move along the veins until they reach the heart.  There they are acted upon by heat and air from the lungs to become "vital spirits" and to be carried through the arteries along with a "nobler" kind of blood; for the heart is the seat of the passions and the ruler over the "sensitive" portion of man.  Some of the "vital spirits" when they reach the brain are converted into "animal spirits," which execute the acts of the brain through the nerves and partake of both the body and the soul; for the brain is the king of the whole body and the seat of man's rational and immortal part.  Like the body, it is given a three-fold hierarchy. The lowest contains the five senses.  The mid-portion contains the common sense, the fancy, and the memory.  The highest portion is the seat of reason, where the understanding sifts reports from the middle kingdom and presents to the will the evidence for a just decision. In his reason and soul, man is like the angels, though the angels know instinctively what man must acquire by his discursive reason. In other respects, he is akin to the beasts.

Montaigne and others might question such a simplified scale; but medieval and Renaissance lovers of correspondences, viewing the corresponding planes therein, linked section of plane with section of plane. Thus portions of the celestial world (the macrocosm) were made analogous with portions of the social world (made up of men, each a microcosm) and with portions of the natural world. The sun among the planets was linked with the king among men, with the head in the body, with the lion among beasts, with the eagle among birds. Justice led all the virtues, being the prime virtue of the king. This order and harmony in corresponding planes might naturally be associated with the concept of musical harmony or choreography and, linked with ideas about the movements of the planets and the music of the spheres, be extended to the social world.

A familiar passage from Macrobius on Homer's golden chain can serve to summarize once more the basic concept of Oneness that was thought to produce and control multiplicity. Starting with the conception of the *single* radiance of a trinity, Macrobius likewise utilizes the figure of the mirror and speaks of the "connection of parts" from "the Supreme God" down to the "last dregs of things" at the "very bottom of the series."

> Since from the Supreme God Mind arises, and from Mind, Soul, and since this in turn creates all subsequent things and fills them all with life, and since this single radiance illumines all and is reflected in each, as a single face might be reflected in many mirrors placed in a series; and since all things follow in continuous succession, degenerating in sequence to the very bottom of the series, the attentive observer will discover a connection of parts, from the Supreme God down to the last dregs of things, mutually linked together and without a break. And this is Homer's golden chain, which God, he says, bade hang down from heaven to earth.[16]

To violate such order, to attempt to break that golden chain in any way would be, consequently, a vicious sin.

To anyone concerned with the political thought of the period, however, the world-picture outlined above, with a constant emphasis upon obedience, is far too simple. Man linked the animate with the angelic world; he was the nodal point in the scale of being, but the force of the drag downward was always strong. He *did* exist among the "dregs of things." He lived as a son of Adam, and in addition to his struggle with a body subject to the passions of beasts, he was thought to be influenced by the planets and the stars that separated him from the Heavenly Empyrean; or he was considered the battleground on which the legions of fallen angels waged war against their Creator.

For his guidance, of course, he had the positive laws of his realm and a sort of international law of nations, and particularly natural law. This last law, frequently elucidated in discussions of the law of reason, and vice versa, although it might be the subject of complex discussions, might also be considered capable of being summed up in the words of the Golden Rule; for since the Incarnation, man also had the Word, or the Law, of God, given him because of the weakness that caused his original violation of lawful order and all of his subsequent aberrations.[17]

Yet in spite of such laws, and in spite of the freedom of man's will, supernatural and celestial forces were potent and the springs of conduct were constantly agitated. The social world of which man was a part also suffered all too frequently in a corresponding manner. Through Fate, Decay, or Sin, for example— and the three might be made identical—the estates of the body politic could become distempered, could become ill unto death, or approach a total eclipse.

Consider the simple basic analogy inherent in the phrase "body politic," an analogy drawn from the two worlds peculiarly man's: his physical body and his social-political state. Analogies between man's body and any kingdom appeared in speeches delivered in Elizabeth's House of Commons so frequently that at times they seem to be little more than "fillers";[18] but in the speeches wherein they occur to introduce, and even to buttress, arguments, they were not always used to inculcate a simple obedience, as they might be when they were turned against an unruly multitude represented as the vicious passions or the diseased members of a commonweal. In this world, as Richard

Hooker argued eloquently in prose, seldom if ever is there only good even in the most careful choice.[19] As a poet would write,

> Where as our humaine actions all are mixt,
> Men liue in motion, so do theyr designes;
> Nothing is simply good, or firmly fix'd.
> All haue defects: Nature it selfe declines,
> Darknes oft clouds the clearest Sun that shines.
> Our purest streames are not without their mud
> And we mistake, what oft we take for good.[20]

That the Sun might be clouded, that the reason of the body politic might mistake what it took for good, temporarily at least, can be implicit in the very nature of the omnipresent analogies between body and commonweal; and such attitudes are at times apparent in the comments or speeches of those who were alarmed over what seemed to be Elizabeth's hesitation.[21]

The conventional and the accepted works both ways, as any propagandist knows. If the ruler-sun were clouded, if the reason in the head of the body politic were mistaken, errors liable to result should be made clear to the prince and should be avoided as far as was possible. The ruler had a duty to listen to good advice and to act upon it. He, too, had obligations. Though difficult and almost innumerable, they were inescapable, and this, too, all Elizabethans knew, whether they were critical or uncritical, subversive or loyal.

As a consequence, one also finds another process of thought indicated when one turns back to precepts with which the young Elizabethans were indoctrinated. Although they in time might perceive its ramifications, it was basically concerned with a duty downward rather than upward. Erasmus, for example, admired the *De Officiis* because of its equity and also, in J. Brinsley's words, because of "the conscience he [Cicero] requireth especially in gouernours."[22] Theoretically, from those studying such texts subalterns in rule would grow, whether lay or ecclesiastical. Thus, in the Nowell catechism, though it was heavily outweighed by precepts on the duty of the ruled, even in the section from which quotations have been given, the child recited one sentence on the duty of rulers: "For by the name of parents, we are charged not only to yield and obey to magistrates, but also to honour and love them. *And likewise, on the other part, superiors are taught so to govern their inferiors, as a just parent useth to rule over good children.*"[23]

The state of life to which God had called rulers demanded that they imitate God's goodness and extend to the ruled what the *Timaeus* called an unenvious love. As Aquinas phrased it, if all were equal, none could "act for the advantage of another": "the creature approaches more perfectly to God's likeness if it is not only good but can also act for the goodness of other things."[24]

As part of their duty, if quiet were to be achieved in the commonweal (and their own positions maintained), the ruler and his subalterns might have to enforce for the benefit of their "good children" restraints of one sort or another upon the ambitious in their own class of spiritual or temporal noblemen, or they might have to root out those who owed their allegiance to Rome or who tended to be "schismatic." In either instance they might have to punish those of the many who by nature or lack of training might follow false leaders. As Burghley phrased it, however, in advice to Elizabeth about another matter, and perhaps with a glance in Machiavelli's direction, "it is the poison of all government, when the subject thinks the prince doth anything out of fear than favour."[25] Even when it be phrased in such a manner, it is apparent that a prince's beneficent vigor should be exercised constantly.

In addition, as it has been indicated, no matter how St. Augustine, St. Thomas Aquinas, or Petrarch might argue Fortune out of the universe, this "female Jove," the last of all the gods, continued to seem real, above all to men actively concerned with the health of their particular commonweal. Retreat from the disjunction of things into loyalty and obedience was usually all that was asked, or demanded, of the Lanehams and the vast majority of those who learned the Anglican catechism. But extending a spiritual devotion into the realm of the mixed and the multifarious, however satisfying it might be to Archbishop Cranmer, to Bishop Ponet, to Leicester, or to Burghley, would be less likely to bring them success as rulers, magistrates, and counselors of a king than using such conventional and practical remedies against Fortune as justice, temperance, wisdom, and courage. By such virtues the evils resulting from "mixt" "humaine actions" and muddied streams might be met.

Thus part of the duty that such people as Burghley had to perform demanded that they provide the head of the state with the means of making good judgments. "Mr. Vice Chamberlain [Hatton] who returned to this court on Saturday last hath dealt very plainly and dutifully" with the Queen about the question of relieving the Netherlands, a circumstance "which hath been accepted in so evil part as he is resolved to retire for a time."[26] From the days of Plato on, it was argued that a suitable education must be provided those who would become rulers and lesser governors. This education, as far as the ruler was concerned, was conceived of, in part, as being given to him constantly in the form of good counsel. The past history of England, or of any state, it was argued, showed the necessity not simply for a sound politic body but for a sound politic head and sound politic physicians as well.

The simple "Do unto others," then, could be turned directly or indirectly against subaltern rulers or even a prince. As has been indicated, the way in which a rough scale of being might validate a loyalty upward could logically carry with it the necessity for a loyalty downward, for a voluntaristic metaphysical pathos, which by its very nature would include the cardinal virtues —for extending, in brief, an approximation of God's unenvious love to those less good, less perfect, less high—and, what is more important in this respect, to an anticipation by the ruled of such a Christian action. God's ways in handling the affairs of men might be inscrutable, but any human ruler's actions would be much more obvious.[27]

In the Parliament of 1586-87, "Mr. Job Throckmorton spake sharply of princes and after [was] rebuked . . . by Mr. Vice-Chamberlain." Although arguing in the main within the premises of God's immediacy in human affairs and His punishment of a nation for their sins, and hence along the lines that England should reform and trust in God who has shown Himself to be

English, Throckmorton had attacked the Kings of Spain, France, and Scotland, the last of whom, at the moment, had been commended by Dr. Allen, the Catholic propagandist. The point of his oration, however, was that the finger of God directed England to the Low Countries, where the Queen might "succour the afflicted for the cause of religion." The Netherland's offer of the sovereignty to Elizabeth was valid: not only had the King of Spain lost the right of his sovereignty there "by tyranny and blood, or rather, if ye will, by the just judgement of God," but those countries were never an "absolute government."[28]

The merging of religion with distinctions between a king and a tyrant, and between "absolute" and non-absolute governments, is as interesting as Throckmorton's oratory is compelling. That it was popular, in spite of Hatton's rebuke and Throckmorton's later punishment—when James VI protested such lewd blasphemy—is witnessed by the fact that the Commons planned to petition the Queen through their speaker Puckering that she accept the sovereignty offered her. With the tactful statement that her royal estate was not to be directed by Commons but managed by herself, they nevertheless went on to promise that in the event of her acceptance they would "follow and feed this holy war with a yearly benevolence, to be levied among the wealthier persons of the Realm." At this point, Elizabeth probably commanded the Commons not to meddle with her prerogative.[29]

The subsequent story of resilient Commons and a determined queen can be read elsewhere, but one is certainly justified in repeating an earlier statement. Other men less religiously agitated than Throckmorton and existing, in part at least, at the "very bottom of the series" might well pay less attention at times to God's immediacy than to a man's, even a ruler's, conduct. Even because they might grant the great difficulty of attempting through wisdom and power to combat Fortune and the flux of evil that arose from those same "last dregs of things," they might well argue that the wisdom of an English ruler should seek the wisdom of others. Nor need that wisdom come from privy councilors alone; for some states, including England, were thought to be so constituted that good counseling, both religious and temporal, was embodied in their basic institutions. As every reader of history knows, this concept of counseling a ruler, as far as the English Parliament was concerned, could and did pass into a legislative concept.

In accordance with the thought of Aylmer or Humphrey or Hales, the Commons of Elizabeth I were liable to show great concern about their legal and "historical" prerogatives, and they heard the vaguest and most inaccurate of historical precedents alleged by speakers who—like "Norton, the scold"—would "act, insist, speak, read" on matters they considered essential for England's good.[30] This they did at times in spite of Elizabeth's possible displeasure or downright anger at what she might consider to be infringements of her prerogative. Of them all, Peter Wentworth was undoubtedly the most fearless, even of the Puritan group; and his motion about liberty of speech in 1576, as well as his speech about parliamentary liberty in 1587, place him among England's celebrities. His questions in the Parliament that also heard Job Throckmorton speak "sharply of princes" have been likened, in the English secular sphere, to the theses Luther posted on the church door at Wittenberg; but other individuals, not so inflamed with Puritan zeal, who were, nevertheless, both learned and vocal, realized that the valuable rules of politics, as Aristotle wrote, had been discovered "several times over." Particularly in matters touching religion did many of them believe that England already had learned the hard way, and they might argue that the state through Parliament should help the ruler along the mazes of human error—especially when such a path must be travelled by a woman in accordance with the dictates of a necessity not always determined by any simple ethical dichotomy.[31]

As it was stated at the beginning of this chapter, in the arena of Elizabethan politics the stresses and strains of the immediate, or of what was considered immediate, were dominant. As a consequence, phrases comparable to Coke's later statements about a charter of liberties or similar to his definition of Parliament need to be viewed in such a light. Moreover, Elizabethans could speak in one breath of their ruler's "absolutism" and of Parliament also. Thus when learned Elizabethans defined Parliament in words similar to those later used by Coke ("the king's majesty sitting there as in his royall politick capacity, and . . . the three estates of the realm: . . . the lords spirituall . . . the lords temporall . . . the commons"),[32] the emphasis, in all probability, would be upon the irrefragable unity of such a body. It stood for the whole commonweal of England: the one, the few, and the many.

As phrased by Barbaro in 1551, the function of England's estates was to "render the absolute and royal power legitimate,"[33] and the evolution of history gave increasing validity to what seems at first glance to be vague phraseology. Although Parliament was often simply ancillary to the Privy Council, in the latter part of the fifteenth century election to the House of Commons began to be considered a way to rise in the world. The idea of the force of parliamentary law, recognized as early as 1376 by Chief Justice Thorpe, was also becoming increasingly strong. Yet, as explicitly stated in Coke's definition, the ruler was considered an indispensable part of Parliament. Henry VIII, for example, when utilizing the favorite analogy of body and realm, would tell his estates that according to his judges he stood highest when in Parliament, when knit as head with the members of his realm to produce one body. Nor can such a comment be explained simply as Tudor aplomb; it is basic to the later Elizabethan concept.[34]

With only a slight shift from Henry's emphasis upon his "height," one of Elizabeth's privy councilors, who was also an ambassador and a member of Commons, could write that Parliament in its sphere was "most high," since there, cooperating with one another, were both ruler and representatives of all the ruled. The phrase is Sir Thomas Smith's and is one of the most characteristic in his discussion of the Elizabethan state. Although it may be equivocal when related to the question of whether the ruler or representatives of the ruled were dominant, Elizabeth and her advisors saw to it that nothing would develop to cast any strong doubts about the Queen's "unenvious love" or to jeopardize seriously that unity whereby the head could not exist without the body nor the body without the head. This they did in spite of the fact that in her parliaments forceful objections frequently appeared connected with religion, the Queen's marriage, and various aspects of finance—objections about which the intelligent in the country at large, and particularly in the London populace, must have known something.[35]

As the preceding brief discussion indicates, the logic in back of statements that at first glance may seem theoretically opposed to one another frequently can be perceived by a consideration of the immediate historical event. Nor should one be surprised that ideas conventionally related to the duty of English rulers and found in orthodox treatises meant to defend the vigorous Elizabethan "middle-way" can be found also in inflammatory treatises of both the right and the left, for they apparently had an emotional acceptance that made them valid for contemporary propagandists of all sorts. Thus a writer whose concept of Parliament has just been mentioned provides a discussion of the English state which is singularly appropriate for specifying and enlarging upon some of these commonplaces. This is true in spite of the fact that he avoids a religious emphasis and avoids also an aspect of the Elizabethan heritage that related positive law to divine and natural law and might even judge the former by the latter.[36] In the following chapter, then, Sir Thomas Smith's orthodox *De Republica Anglorum* will be used as a basis for referring to comparable matter elsewhere. It will then be complemented by a similar treatment of a magnificent defense of the Elizabethan middle way, namely, Richard Hooker's *Laws of Ecclesiastical Polity.*

II

# Sir Thomas Smith and Richard Hooker

ALTHOUGH SIR THOMAS SMITH in 1565 made no claim for the completeness of his *De Republica Anglorum,* published posthumously in 1583, its usefulness in the late sixteenth century is indicated by the fact that when Harrison published his *Description of England* in 1587, he drew the additional chapter dealing with Parliament from Smith's treatise. Equally revealing is the fact that in 1592, Smith's treatise was recommended for study by one "R. B.," presumably Robert Beale, secretary, as well as clerk, to the Privy Council and a brother-in-law of Sir Francis Walsingham. Although R. B. cautions Sir Edward Wotton that the book contains "many defects," he considers it to be a treatise whereby "a Secretarie" may "seeke to understande the State of the whole Realm." Indeed, Smith's own words, as well as some of his official and private activities as ambassador to France, indicate that the little book was designed, in part at least, to explain what Smith may well have believed to be understood imperfectly by writers like Bodin, namely, "the forme and manner of the government of England."[1]

When Smith was writing his tract, Bodin was preparing a work for publication that would argue the "mixed" state out of existence, in spite of the fact that it had the sanction of Aristotle; and in doing so, he drew illustrative but derogatory material from England's annals.[2] On this count alone, given Smith's interest in such matters, one can perhaps find a reason for writing the *De Republica Anglorum.* Smith gives a solution to the questionable validity of the mixed state only incidentally, however; for the basic argument of his treatise is designed, quite obviously, to indicate that the polity of England is a thoroughly laudable one, and to achieve his purpose Smith writes in a manner which he "imagines" Aristotle wrote of many Greek commonwealths. Thus, he hopes that those interested will discuss what he has written and consider, for example, whether English "law" is superior to that found on the Continent.[3]

Equally obviously, the polity of England, to Smith, shows a particular elaboration of a fundamental concept about government which the Renaissance found in both Plato and Aristotle and which can be found also in the writing of Erasmus and others, namely, that the performance of mutual duties and responsibilities is an essential feature of any commonweal. This major point is based, as one might expect, upon Smith's brief definition of a commonweal. Such a body he contrasts, in an Aristotelian manner, first with a mob, that is, with a large group of individuals in no way permanent, and then with a large group of individuals living relatively permanently under the rule of one person, but living as bondsmen. In this latter society, there is "no communion" between the ruler and the ruled; "the wealth of the Lord is only sought for, and not the profit of the slave or bondman." This sort of rule seems applicable to the Turks; and in that nation, if the ruler considers only himself and his sons to be freemen, "a man may doubt whether his administration be to be accompted a common wealth or a kingdome, or rather to be reputed onely as one that hath under him an infinite number of slaves or bondmen among whom there is no right, law nor common wealth compact, but onely the will of the Lorde and segnior." Such a society would not be considered by "the olde Greekes" as any type of public rule, or "policy," for "A common wealth is called a society or common doing of a multitude of free men collected together and united by common accord and covenauntes among themselves, for the conservation of themselves aswell in peace as in warre."[4]

As it should already be apparent, such a related group of ideas was thoroughly conventional and probably had many ramifications for the educated simply in their enunciation; for the ruler of Smith's commonweal would be imitating the rule of God. As Erasmus, for instance, had written, "God gave the angels and man free will so that He would not be ruling over bondsmen and so that He might glorify and add further grandeur to His kingdom."[5]

Louis Le Roy takes a similar point of view. This French writer was one of those whom Smith knew while in France, and Le Roy's edition of Aristotle's *Politics* with commentary was the work which Gabriel Harvey noted as being on nearly every English scholar's desk along with a copy of Bodin's *Respublica*.[6] At any rate, when Le Roy glosses Aristotle on the nature of rule, he writes a full Platonic commentary that includes a discussion of the "virtuous" influence of light and heat and some distinctions between king and tyrant. There, too, appear constant and relatively long analogies between body, family, and state; and, in the comment on Aristotle's discussion of bondsmen, there appears a full treatment of the distinction between "masterly" and "political" rule, only the latter being applicable, of course, to what Smith defines as a commonweal. In contrast with Smith's treatise, however, Le Roy's discussion includes excellent references to outstanding authorities, to Plato on the "Understanding," for example, and to works by Neo-Platonists, including a citation of the passage referred to above from Macrobius and other citations and summary statements from such writers as Ficino and Pico della Mirandula.[7]

For the learned, then, such material from Erasmus and Le Roy might well have provided a context for Smith's definition of a commonweal drawn essentially from Aristotle; and, indeed, in one sense at least, Smith's *De Republica* grew out of the advanced academic curriculum.[8] Smith himself had begun his own career at Cambridge a few years after Erasmus had been at Queens' as Lady Margaret Professor. With John Cheke at St. Johns, Smith became the center of a group of young Protestants with a strong humanistic interest. In this circle were such students as Ponet, John Aylmer, Roger Ascham, Thomas Becon, William Bill, William Grindal, and William Cecil. Also at Cambridge was Edwin Sandys, who may have been associated with the group, as may have been Walter Haddon, who, though enrolled at King's, was a Greek pupil of Smith's. All were to become leaders of England; all, if they were not present when Smith introduced the Erasmian pronunciation of Greek in lectures on Aristotle's *Politics,* probably had first studied that basic treatise and its earlier commentaries while at the university. In the light of such a background, as well as in the light of the general considerations sketched in the previous chapter, Smith's basic definition neatly exemplifies an attitude which, regardless of its immediate derivation, would be considered sound by Elizabethans and, indeed, by any Christian society.

Bodin, for example, would not object greatly to such a basic point of view;[9] nor would he object to the triple classification which Smith lifts from Aristotle's enumeration of types of government: that is, rule by one, rule by the few, and rule by the many. In the *De Republica Anglorum,* Smith then notes, also in the manner of Aristotle, that each of the three methods of governing may show a rule that is good and just and one that is evil and unjust. Rule by one, therefore, involves rule by a king as opposed to rule by a tyrant. Rule by a few involves the rule "of the best men" as opposed to the rule "of the richer and stronger sort." Rule by many involves rule by the multitude as a commonweal in contrast to rule by the "popular or rascall and viler sort" who usurp power simply because they are greater in number.[10] Smith, however, makes no attempt to argue that any one of the three "good and just" governmental types is superior to the others, for the "common wealth or policie must be according to the nature of the people."[11]

This last maxim was again thoroughly conventional, but in an exaggerated form it would be developed with a vengeance by Bodin when in his *Methodus* he referred to many nations and included the English as a race zealous in resisting authority.[12] Others, of course, might refer to them more favorably. Earlier in the century (1520), John Major, for example, had given the idea an entirely different emphasis when he wrote that in England "the people are more hotly jealous of their rights than in many other kingdoms, and rise against their kings should these make any unreasonable demands."[13] Later in the century, De Spes, Mendoza, and other foreign observers comment upon the

Englishman's nationalism and hatred of being ruled in any way by a foreigner.[14] Smith's statement about "the nature of the people," however, is specified in this portion of his discussion only briefly and generally. Elsewhere he will enumerate other characteristics and emphasize the loyalty of the English to their native ruler. Here he remarks only that some nations will not accept any form of rule by one, no matter how well it be administered, while other nations must be ruled by one prince or with private strife and foolish ambition they will "consume one another and bring themselves to nothing."

This aspect of contemporary thought, which recognizes the necessity for different forms of government and reminds one of the general attitude in the late middle ages, appears also in Smith's concatenated definition of "rule," "justice," and "law": "To rule, is understoode to have the highest and supreme authoritie of commaundement. That part or member of the common wealth is saide to rule which doth controwle, correct, and direct all other members of the common wealth. *That part which doth rule, define and commaund according to the forme of the governement, is taken in everie common wealth to be just and law....*"[15]

Within his definition of a commonweal, consequently, justice and law is action effected by the form of government that agrees with the nature of the people. Two consequences logically follow: both elucidate once more the purpose and nature of Smith's work. Before justice and law in England can be understood, the form of English government must be understood; and since in peace the English Parliament is "most high," it effects both change and continuity in the state. Smith gives Parliament (that is, king and representatives of the estates) not only the right to alter the "forme" of the succession but also an unquestioned right over private property.[16] These aspects of Smith's thought, found with varying emphases in speeches by members of Elizabeth's parliaments, as well as Smith's treatment of deposition, will be mentioned later.

At the moment, since it involves an appreciation of his triple method of rule, Smith's treatment of governmental change should be noted. Instead of developing by "provining and propagation," as in the hypothetical beginnings of a state, some rule may result from conquest, and Smith cites the Saxons in Great Britain. It is interesting to note, however, that in this respect he also cites briefly one aspect of the Germanic theory of kingship, namely, that, when their chief was dead, the Saxons elected a "head or king" by consultation of the nobler sort. He then notes that such a situation may cause a commonwealth to "divide into more heads," as with the Lombards and, again, the Saxons.[17]

Smith also discusses, with an appreciable fullness by referring to the Roman state, a second type of major change which may occur without foreign conquest. Rule by kings occurred in the reigns of Romulus, Numa, and Servius. Rule by tyrants, in the reigns of Tarquin, Scylla, and Caesar. Rule by a few of the "best" men occurred under the first consuls. Rule by the usurping few, under the senators after Tarquin and before the Tribunate, under the Decemviri, and "more perniciously" under the triumvirate of Caesar, Crassus, and Pompey, as well as the triumvirate of Octavius, Antony, and Lepidus. Beneficent rule by the many occurred after the expulsion of the Decemviri "and long after, especially after the law was made, either by *Horatius* or (as some would have it) *Hortentius, quod plebs sciverit, id populum teneat."* Usurping rule by the many appeared a little before Scylla's reign and a little before Caius Caesar's reign. In fact, this last type of rule by the many produces rule by tyrants, for vicious rule can effect a further change.[18]

Especially revealing in this discussion is Smith's reference to the Venetians, as part of his discussion of the Swiss government. The Swiss took at first for their government "a common rule and popular estate [that is, beneficent rule by the many] and do yet at this day, or else admit the rule of a certaine fewe, excluding the multitude and communaltie, as the Paduans, Veronenses, and Venetians have accustomed."[19] Although, in this instance, he is concerned primarily with his basic maxim that a commonwealth or "policie" must accord with the nature of the people, the fact that Smith classifies the Venetian government as an aristocracy is somewhat unusual; for in the late sixteenth century, Venice might be thought of as being a modern example of the type of rule that Aristotle found in Sparta, namely, that effected by the mixed state.[20]

That Smith does not refer to the mixed state as a fourth type of government may result, however, from his knowledge of Bodin; for sovereignty to Bodin was indivisible, and in his *Methodus* he had examined those governments thought to be mixed, arguing that in each instance sovereignty actually resided in one of the three components of the state.[21] Smith handles the matter briefly, but proceeds upon a basis almost exactly antithetical. Using the conventional analogy between the body politic, the natural world, and the world of man, he turns to another commonplace and asserts that just as no one element and no one complexion exists in its pure essence, so no one of the three forms of government exists without a mixture of another form. Although the name given to any form of government is derived from that element which is most powerful, all governments are "mixed."[22] In such a manner, Smith, like Bodin, excludes a fourth type of government; but at the same time Smith perhaps attempts to clear the ground to contradict any assertion that might refer to the English government as ineffective because of limitations placed upon the king's sovereignty.

The process of Smith's thought as he develops it from this cleared ground might be represented as follows. Since all governments are mixed, only the previous triple division will be valid in discussing any one particular form of government. Since England has always been governed by monarchial rule and is now governed by only one king, England's representing an effective rule, justice, and law depends upon whether her ruler is a king or a tyrant.[23] Thus Smith's differentiation between those two types of rulers becomes crucial to his elucidation and his defense of the English state; and one finds, again as it might be expected, that to all intents he equates a tyrant with a king who in peace has "absolute" power. The wise Romans did not grant a dictatorship for more than six months; for as Plato knew, the frailty of man is such that any absolute and uncontrolled authority for any length of time makes him dangerous and potentially vicious:

Other [sic] do call that kind of administration which the Greekes do call παμβασιλείαν, not tyranny, but the absolute power of a King, which they would pretende that everie King hath, if he would use the same. The other they call βασιλείαν νομίχήν or the Royall power regulate by lawes: of this I will not dispute at this time. But as such absolute administration in time of warre when all is in armes, and when lawes hold their peace because they cannot be heard, is most necessarie: *so in time of peace, the same is verie daungerous, aswell to him that doth use it, and much more to the people upon whom it is used: whereof the cause is the frailtie of mans nature, which (as Plato saith) cannot abide or beare long that absolute and uncontrowled authoritie, without swelling into too much pride and insolencie.*

. . . of it selfe at the first [Τυραννίς] was not a name odious: But because they who had such rule, at the first, did for the most part abuse the same, waxed insolent and proude, unjust and not regarding the common wealth, committed such actes as were horrible and odious, as killing men without cause, abusing their wives and daughters, taking and spoyling all mens goods at their pleasures, and were not shepheardes as they ought to be, but rather robbers and devourers of the people, whereof some were contemners of God . . . that kind of administration and maner also, at first not evill, hath taken the signification and definition of the vice of the abusers, so that now *both in Greeke, Latine, and English a tyrant is counted he, who is an evill king, and one who hath no regard to the wealth of his people, but seeketh onely to magnifie himselfe and his, and to satisfie his vicious and cruell appetite, without respect of God, of right or of the law because that for the most part they who have had that absolute power have beene such.*[24]

Such a tendency in English political thought was to be developed fully in the succeeding century, but the germ for such a development is here, as well as in such a gloss as that on the Geneva Bible that states opposite I Kings 12: 9: "There is nothing harder for them that are in autoritie, then to bridle their affections, and followe good connsell."[25] A "radical" gloss alone need not be cited. Witness a detail in the humanistic, if not the religious, tradition which Smith was heir to, as it might be seen much earlier in the century when Vives prescribed More's *Utopia* as a text to be studied by the Princess Mary. For More, with Machiavelli and Contarini, was to be named by Bodin as one who had taken up the ancient theory of the superiority of the mixed state and diffused it;[26] and it would be argued, as in Cartwright's speech in 1564, that the superiority of this state resulted from the institutional checks upon the monarch which were embodied in a rule effected, not simply by the one, but by the few and the many as well.[27]

Elsewhere in Elizabethan thought were ideas comparable to that of the Geneva gloss and of Smith's reference to Plato. They could become rebellious and in other circumstances be used to advocate resistance and even revolt. In their germinal form, they may appear in some of the speeches in Elizabeth's House of Commons as part of the heritage that the Stuarts were unwilling to receive. The first of that line on the English throne would bow, of course, in the direction of the thought expressed in the first portion of the Biblical gloss when he began his *Basilicon Doron*: "As *Hee can not bee thought worthie to rule & command others, that cannot rule and dantone his owne proper affections & vnreasonable appetites;* so can he not be thought worthy to gouerne a Christian people, knowing and fearing God, that in his own person and hart feareth not, and loueth not the Diuine Majestie."[28]

Obviously, however, for the late sixteenth century, this statement by James, the second part of the thought in the Biblical gloss, and the context of any parliamentary idea that might be germinally rebellious, instead of being anti-monarchial, would emanate rather from the spirit of the vast corpus of treatises *de regimine principum*.[29] Discussions appeared therein, stretching back at least to Plutarch, which pointed out the necessity for accepting counsel even though it be displeasing and which helpfully elucidated the differences between self-seeking flattery and good advice.[30]

The course of Smith's argument, however, develops out of other distinctions that he makes between the good and the evil ruler. In this respect he considers three basic features of rule by one: the way in which the ruler obtains authority, the way in which he administers authority, and the aim of his administration. In this discussion, Smith opposes a king's direct succession or election with the will of the people to a tyrant's use of force to acquire rule despite the people. A king's concern for law and equity in the administration of rule, he opposes to a tyrant's making and breaking of laws without the advice or consent of the people. The king's concern for the good of the ruled, as well as of himself, Smith opposes to the tyrant's concern only for himself, his faction, and his kindred. Octavius and, perhaps, Scylla he calls tyrants by entry but kings by administration. Nero, Domitian, and Commodus are kings by entry but tyrants by administration. Other emperors after Caesar and Octavius are kings by entry and aim but tyrants by administration. In the last category, he also places the Pope of Rome, who grounds his power upon Christ and pretends to be his successor; "yet the generall Councels make a strife with him, to make the Popes power either *Aristocratian* or at least *legitimum regnum*, and would faine bridle that *absolutam potestatem*."

The kings of France and certain princes of Italy also abrogate previous laws and impose "tributs and impositions" by their own will, or by the "private Counsell and advice" of friends and favorites only. Louis XI is then singled out as one whose tyrannical administration wrested France from a "lawful and regulate raigne" to an "absolute and tyrannicall power and government."[31]

In contrast, the English king has the power that may be called absolute only in some dozen instances, eight of which seem relatively important for our purpose here.[32] Yet that power is sufficient for the English government to be excluded from those conventionally thought of as mixed. The king alone has the right to appoint the "chiefe and highest" officers of the land "be it of judgement or dignitie, temporall or spirituall"; he has the right to dispense with certain laws; and he has the right of certain prerogatives. Both of these last rights are found in books of common law.[33] He has unqualified authority in questions of war and peace; he has the same power in other matters related to foreign affairs; and he has absolute power in three other situations: during wartime, on the field, and on other occasions subject to martial law. In this last instance, however, Smith adds a *caveat* when he refers to the use of martial law within the realm before "any open warre in sudden insurrections and rebellions." Such a practice is not allowed of "wise and grave men," who have consideration "of the consequence and example, asmuch as of the present necessitie, especiallie, when by anie meanes the punishment might have beene doone by order of lawe." Indeed, in exercising all of his preceding rights, the English king is counseled.

In other respects, Parliament is absolute; "The most high and absolute power of the realme of Englande, consisteth in the Parliament." What is done by Parliament "is the Princes and whole realmes deede: whereupon justlie no man can complaine, but must accommodate himselfe to finde it good and obey it," for it "representeth and hath the power of the whole realme both the head and the bodie." "For everie Englishman is entended to bee there present, either in person or by procuration and attornies, of what preheminence, state, dignite, or qualitie soever he be, from the Prince (be he King or Queene) to the lowest person of Englande. And the consent of the Parliament is taken to be everie mans consent."[34] Because of Parliament "no other meanes" are "accounted vailable to make any new forfaiture of life, member, or landes of any English man, where there was no lawe ordayned for it before."[35]

Smith, consequently, lists some nine powers that belong to Parliament: to dispense with old laws and establish new; to change the rights and possessions of private men; to legitimize bastards; to establish the form of religion; to alter weights and measures; to give "formes of succession to the crowne"; to define doubtful rights about which no law has been made; to determine subsidies, tailles, taxes, and impositions; to give "most free pardons and absolutions," or to restore "in blood and name," or to condemn or absolve those "whom the Prince will put to that triall. . . ."[36] Related to his discussion of the English king's limitation by this major aspect of what has been defined as law and justice are Smith's comments on the loyalty of the English and his insistence upon their reverence for their kings, particularly in Parliament.[37]

From such considerations of legitimate English rule, as well as from the fact that no English king acknowledges another prince on earth to be his superior, Smith writes, as some previous historians had, that John's resignation of the English crown was invalid:

Although king *John* (by the rebellion of the nobilitie ayded with the daulphin of Fraunce his power) to appease the Pope who at that time possessing the consciences of his subjectes was then also his enemy and his most greevous torment (as some histories do write) did resigne the crowne to his legate *Pandulphus,* and tooke it againe from him as from the Pope by faith and homage, and a certain tribute yearly. *But that act being neither approved by his people, nor established by act of parliament, was forthwith and ever sithens taken for nothing, either to binde the king, his successors or subjectes.*[38]

The fallibility of kings, should they have absolute power, is thus restricted by what Smith calls the law and justice of England. Conversely, the king's position in Parliament and his power of veto are checks upon the fallibility of other components of a commonweal, as is the king's right by law to dispense with certain laws and his use of his prerogatives set down in books of common law. When, for example, one obviously guilty of treason had been dismissed in a previous reign, the twelve of the "enquest" who freed him were not simply threatened with Star Chamber or the Privy Council but were imprisoned; and in another similar case, they were "put to open ignominie and shame." Although such an exercise of regal power was not commended even at the time, since "many accounted [it] verie violent, tyrannical, and contrarie to the libertie and custome of the realme of England," and although it is "very seldome in use," yet the "enquest" may be so corrupted temporarily "that the Prince may have cause with justice to punish them: For they are men, and subject to corruption and parcialitie, as others be."[39]

Probably such "corruption and parcialitie" was too apparent to Smith, not simply as ambassador, but also as privy councilor and as member of parliament. Viewed philosophically, it just might be related to concepts in current thought that involved the idea of change, diversity, and general mutability. Witness Smith's statement about changes in a "politique bodie" and about man in the aggregate: "For the nature of man is never to stand still in one maner of estate, but to grow from the lesse to the more, and decay from the more againe to the lesse, till it come to the fatall end and destruction, with many turnes and turmoyles of sicknesse and recovering, seldome standing in a perfect health, neither of a mans bodie it selfe, nor of the politique bodie which is compact of the same."[40]

The basic idea, as the conventional analogy indicates, was so well known and is so general in nature as to almost preclude any glossing; yet some of its particular aspects might well have formed, for Smith's educated readers, a background that would be constantly applicable to his discussion of the nature of rule. Sometimes, in contrast with Smith's emphasis here, change and mutability might be considered, in general, to be for the better; and so Le Roy argued, believing that the moderns surpassed the ancients.[41] Or in the direction of Le Roy, and in the partially Platonic terms that Spenser uses, the power of mutability might be regarded as but one aspect of a progress toward perfection in cyclical change:

> . . . all things stedfastnes doe hate
> And changed be: yet being rightly wayd
> They are not changed from their first estate;
> But by their change their being doe dilate:
> And turning to themselves at length againe,
> Doe work their own perfection so by fate. . . .
>
> (*FQ*, VII, vii, lviii)[42]

Even this last emphasis, however, would not be strictly applicable to the *De Republica Anglorum* which is briefly concerned, rather, with the "mutability of mens wittes": ". . . for never in all pointes one common wealth doth agree with an other, no nor long time any one common wealth with it selfe. For al chaungeth continually to more or lesse, and still to diverse and diverse orders, as the diversity of times do present occasion, and the mutability of mens wittes doth invent and assay newe wayes, to reforme and amende that wherein they do finde fault."[43]

More nearly akin to the quotations from the *De Republica Anglorum,* consequently, and reflecting perhaps a knowledge of Machiavelli's works, would be such a hard-headed though pessimistic attitude as that expressed by Raleigh: ". . . there is not in nature a point of stability to be found; everything either ascends or declines: when wars are ended abroad, sedition begins at home, and when men are freed from fighting for necessity, they quarrel through ambition."[44] The prevalence of such an attitude goes far toward explaining why Smith is concerned with pointing out how the English state provides effectively for contingencies that arise from the times or the men and that, unless controlled, are liable to produce a vicious rule and even effect a change from one form of government to another.[45]

His statement, however, that the nature of men, in their own bodies and in their politic bodies, "is never to stand still in one maner of estate, but to grow from the lesse to the more, and decay from the more againe to the lesse, till it come to the fatall end and destruction" may well have seemed to some of Smith's contemporaries to accord roughly with another concept specially applicable to states. As might have been noted when Le Roy's commentary was referred to, during the middle ages and the Renaissance, the idea of the decay of states had been dilated and elucidated by astrological writers who in turn had been refuted. The congruent idea of the constant flux of things runs, of course, through much ancient poetry and philosophy and is continually apparent in the Renaissance, while the concept of a world soul and the belief that the world itself was decaying also appear in the latter part of the sixteenth century.[46] Thus the force of a mutability greater than the relatively simple change represented in Ovid's *Metamorphoses* was a constant theme, with or without a reference to the precession of the equinoxes.

More specifically, this could be true when writers referred to another idea that might be related pessimistically to change; for mutability was sometimes thought of as producing an age far removed from Saturn's golden reign. Man, consequently, might be represented as existing in an unvirtuous present that could be controlled forcefully in mundane things only by God's justice lent to princes (see Spenser's *The Faerie Queene*, V, "Proem," iv, x). Or from a position emphasizing mutability, but turned in another direction, the necessity for the prince's exercise of a Machiavellian force and art might be stressed. Or this unvirtuous present, which results from the fearsome power of mutability, whose effect seems to break Homer's golden chain (that is, the divine mind that produces order), might be conceived of as only one phase of a perpetual continuation in cyclical diversity.[47]

Regardless of its ultimate derivation, this last process of thought might seem compatible also with Smith's description of the changing Roman state, as well as with the general idea that forms of government succeed one another. With varying emphases the concept of a cyclical change applicable to states appears in the writings of Plato, Aristotle, and Cicero, in the works of the ancient historian Polybius and of Renaissance writers like Machiavelli and Contarini.[48]

In this respect, the name of Bodin probably would be important once more. Written not simply to invalidate the concept of a mixed state, Bodin's *Methodus* attempts to understand change in history in order to provide the means for controlling change. While arguing that monarchy is the best form of government and that mixed states do not exist, Bodin also asserts that, with care, one can perceive certain constant features that operate to effect the mutability of states. Aside from such obvious patterns of change as the disruption caused by the lust of man or the succession of a just rule after the overthrow of a tyrant, one of those constant factors, already briefly noted, is the nature of the nation being governed; and in his treatise Bodin attempts to link the nature of a race with its country's geographical position and with the operation of a cyclical change which, while concomitant with men's actions, is, to a degree at least, independent of them. The recurrence of such cycles, their nature, and their variation, he works out on the basis of a Pythagorean number theory which must have caused many aching heads among those who would follow his discussions; but thereby the concept of change in states might become determinable, in part, without turning simply to the science of astrology. An extra-human, even a mathematical, bridle is postulated as controlling, in part at least, that "female Jove" Fortuna.[49] If such a tendency were pushed to its logical Christian extreme and to an approximate rest in a Sabbaoth God, and if the mathematical expression of cycles were understood sufficiently, at least

God's ways might appear less inscrutable, and, indeed, more beneficent, because of the intellectual virtuosity given man.

In the immediate circumstances of practical politics, however, be it reflected in the purposeful romance of a Sidney or the comments of a watchful Walsingham, change or an unfortunate decay might always be awaiting a commonweal. Obviously, then, continuity was a prime virtue. It might be achieved by art in governing. It might also be achieved more easily in one government than in another. For some writers, if not for Bodin, the mixed state, essentially as described by Aristotle, might be represented as the best type of government. It was seen in Sparta, in Switzerland, and especially in long-established Venice;[50] and Smith sees in English rule comparable features essential for continuance, particularly the mutual restraints on the one, the few, and the many which the English government affords and which diminish the chances of appreciable disruption in the body politic.

Consider, for example, Smith's statement about the three absolute and definite judgments in England: "By order and usage of England there is three wayes and maners, whereby absolute and definite judgement is given, by parliament which is the highest and most absolute, by battle and by the great assise."[51] As it has been noted, Parliament in particular keeps an English king from being "absolute" in peace time; in Parliament there are obviously restraints upon the one, the few, and the many. In other circumstances, the king can dispense with certain laws, has certain prerogatives, and may remedy the fallibility of man, judging in assize, for example. Trial by battle, then, can also balance another process of law. Smith believes it unfortunate that "time and space of yeares" have brought a change so that judgment by battle, never favoured by the Pope and the clergy, is "at this present not much used," though it has never been abrogated, so far as Smith has been able to discover. Any defendant, for example, who has been indicted for murder or manslaughter of a father, son, wife, brother, or "next kinsman" can still appeal from the sentence of outlawry passed, if he has escaped the inquest; and in such circumstances he may put himself either to trial by jury or to trial by battle in person or by champion.[52]

In addition to such balances effected in and between the three absolute judgments, Smith makes it clear that the English ruler, his councilors, and his appointees constantly keep the many and the powerful few in check, just as the few and the many, through Parliament, limit the king's power. To avoid the evil consequences of "the usurping of the rascality," which "quickly bringeth forth a tyrant," a bridle of law is fashioned for them when the king and his council choose every year, or every second year, "certaine articles out of penall lawes alreadie made for to repress the pride and evill rule of the popular." These articles are sent to the justices, who decide how to handle the enforcement of them wisely and circumspectly and who assume the responsibility for executing them. Within a certain time, the justices meet again and certify to the king, or to his Privy Council, how they found their shires "in rule and order" about these laws. This is done, incidentally, "in the beginning of summer or afterwardes (for in the warme time the people for the most part be more unrulie)"; and although such a procedure can be misused, as it has been in France, there "was never in any common wealth divised a more wise, a more dulce and gentle, nor a more certaine way to rule the people." They are "kept alwaies as it were in a bridle of good order, and sooner looked unto that they should not offend, than punished when they have offended." Perhaps one or two are punished, but others needing amendment "take a feare within themselves," and the rest see that their rulers are concerned about their care, "So that it is as a newe forbrushing of the good lawes of the realme, and a continuall repressing of disorders, which doe naturally rest among men." Like the pronouncement of verdict openly in *Corona populi,* such a procedure also shows that the prince considers "his strength, power, and crowne doth stande and consist in the force of his people, and the maintenaunce of them in securitie and peace."[53]

Aside from such a punitive measure, English rulers have encouraged the nature of their subjects, for an Englishman is "free, stout, haulte, prodigall of life and bloud," but "contumelie, beatings, servitude and servile torment and punishment" he "will not abide."[54] Thus, in accordance with a judgment of Cato's, the court Baron has been provided for those who "love their quiet and profit in their husbandrie, more than to be busie in the law," and who have at the same time been accustomed to a justice that gives no more advantage to the rich than to the poor.[55]

The English state, moreover, provides for special restraints on the powerful few, and not simply on the many; and Smith specifies laws that were made because insolent "men of power" began "many fraies, and the stronger by factions and parties" offered "too much injurie to the weaker." No one of the powerful few, consequently, can have more than a certain number of retainers; inquiries about "routs and riots" are made at every session; if any force be assembled, the justices of the peace can also call an assembly and remove the unlawful force; and, finally, the guilty ones can be called to Star Chamber. Because such great insolence is not done by mean men and cannot be dealt with even by "mean" gentlemen, the majesty of the whole realm, except the prince, is utilized in Star Chamber: "For that is the effect of this Court to bridle such stoute noble men, or Gentlemen which would offer wrong by force to any manner men, and cannot be content to demaund or defend the right by order of lawe." By such means in the immediate past, Henry VIII disciplined lawless lords, particularly of the North, until "they began to range themselves in order, and to understand that they had a Prince who would rule his subjects by his lawes and obedience."[56]

Again, however, there is also encouragement for the few as there was for Englishmen in general. Not as a bridle, but as a spur to virtue and honor, if gentility decay—for "such is the nature of all humaine things, and so the world is subject to mutabilitye"—the king and commonweal have the same power as had their ancestors and can, like a husbandman, plant a new noble tree when the old has failed.[57]

That Smith's concern with restraints upon the one, few, and many is characteristic of a process of thought which can be found in political writings regardless of the axe their authors would grind is apparent, for example, in Walsingham's statement that Francis, Duke of Alençon, in contrast with the conquering despot Philip, would rule in the Netherlands as a benevolent monarch. Although the French tend to become absolute if given "once a footing," yet the important burghers of the Dutch, in well fortified towns, are jealous of their liberties and are in the main incorruptible; while the multitude, who cannot be corrupted in secret, would revolt if their rights were abrogated.[58] In such a situation, consequently, a beneficently limited monarchy would naturally result.

Indeed, this recognition of the necessity for a balance between the one, the powerful few, and the many, led Comines to defend the French Estates and to refer in a complimentary manner to English institutions. Similarly, on at least one occasion, the immediate aim of Bodin in the realm of actual politics was to effect a check by classes upon the powerful "few." During the Estates-General of 1576, considerations of indivisible sovereignty, or domain, presumably led him to support the Third Estate against the clergy and, in effect, against the great seigneurs.[59]

In the years of that decade, moreover, as well as later in the century, Huguenot thought and the monarchomachial writings of the Catholics would exalt the ruled—particularly the illustrious few, but also the many—in arguments for a limited monarchy that entailed in varying degrees a germinal contract theory of government.[60] Comparable arguments could be found in the writings of Buchanan, pupil of Major, one-time tutor of Mary Queen of Scots, and tutor also of the future divine-rightist James VI. To Buchanan, in his *De Jure Regni apud Scotos Dialogus,* dedicated to James in 1579, the people had a sort of political existence before a choice of ruler was made, and it was apparently upon such a postulate that Buchanan gave to the people the right to redress wrongs done by hereditary kings through violence, fraud, or even negligence. They were superior to the king, and the assembly of the citizens had the same power over the king as he had over one of the members of the commonweal.[61]

Smith, however, is neither arguing in favor of any "necessary" shift in power to effect an efficient and benevolent rule, nor concerning himself primarily with inculcating such principles as Buchanan apparently thought necessary. He is defending what exists. Thus although his argument when deposition or tyrannicide is concerned will proceed upon grounds vastly different from those just cited in Buchanan's treatise, his defense of English polity rests upon an acceptance of the rights of the Aristotelian "few" and "many," as well as the "one," and consequently upon the means whereby a balanced state is preserved and any serious disjunction or decay is forestalled.

Should, however, an evil state prevail, and should laws be made to maintain it, Smith indicates that the English, presumably like other nations, would have to decide "whether obedience of them be just and the disobedience wrong," "whether a good and upright man, and lover of his countrie ought to maintaine and obey them [that is, the unjust laws perpetuating evil states], or to seeke by all meanes to abolish them." Great and "hautie courages" have often attempted to overthrow evil states "as *Dion* to rise up against *Dionysius, Thrasibulus* against the XXX. tyrantes, *Brutus* and *Cassius* against *Caesar*"; and this "hath bin cause of many commotions in common wealthes." Certainly it is always "a doubtfull and hasardous matter" to "meddle with the chaunging of the lawes and government" and to disobey "the rule or government, which a man doth finde alreadie established." About such matters the common people judge "according to the event and successe." The judgment of the learned, however, will be based upon "the purpose of the doers," and, as one might expect in view of what has been summarized above about mutability, it will also be based upon "the estate of the time then present."[62] To Smith, then, only the wise can decide, on the two grounds indicated, whether the danger of disruption be greater or less than the danger of not resisting and changing the rule of a state.

In this respect, Smith writes both in and to his age. Richard Hooker in entirely different circumstances, and when arguing that something less than perfection should be accepted, was to maintain that the learned were the ones to discuss the variations in ever-present evils and to set the bounds for the execution of principles. Such statements are less aristocratic than they are humanistic, and in the sixteenth and seventeenth centuries, such diverse individuals as Sir Thomas More and Algernon Sidney made similar statements. Smith and his "wise" contemporaries had themselves to make decisions about such "hazardous matter" during the reign of Mary. Later they also encountered the arguments of Catholic monarchomachists and saw the rebellious tendencies of "Geneva-like" writings. Unlike the men of the next century, however, they were not forced by "the estate of the time then present" in Elizabeth's reign to make the difficult decision between obedience and rebellious disobedience.

As it has just been indicated, Smith's process of thought and a corresponding background are elucidated further for England in the late sixteenth century by one who attempted to answer both Catholics and their "radical" opponents. Richard Hooker, consequently, provides examples of a characteristic enlargement of some of Smith's statements. Like the *De Republica Anglorum,* the orthodox *Laws of Ecclesiastical Polity* can be utilized to refer to comparable aspects of contemporary thought, which in this instance were frequently related to the constant problem of church and state. To a modern, it may seem illogical that *The Laws of Ecclesiastical Polity,* a defense of the Anglican church, would embody basic aspects of political thought. As the title of the work indicates, however, Hooker would base his arguments upon accepted ideas about law and the nature of a commonweal. To Hooker the "polity" of the church, as Luke indicated and as reason shows, is a society. Consequently, it must be ruled by laws that pertain to society *qua* society. Furthermore, since there is no member of the Church of England who is not also a member of the English commonwealth—and logically, *vice versa,* if Hooker's theses would prevail—the nature of the polity of England is an additional factor in determining what is ecclesiastical justice for the realm.[63] To Hooker, this last consideration is particularly true, since the form of English polity is supported by those supra-national laws that give force to the positive laws of any realm.

Hooker, consequently, is concerned with the tangle that Smith had no occasion to unravel. Although the definitions of a commonwealth given by both writers are to all intents and purposes identical, Hooker, in accord with his subsequent line of argument, begins with what some in the era might well have considered to be first principles, namely, a consideration of those supra-national laws called the law of God, the law of nature, and the law of reason.[64] The "very Foundation and Root" of his whole treatise is his acceptance of the validity and necessity of all three. Thus, for Hooker, the foundation of legal and rightful power rests not simply upon God's word expressed in the Scriptures and not only upon any action or decree derived explicitly or implicitly from any church mystical or from any church polity, it rests as well upon an enlightened human reason which perceives the nature and function of law and acts in accordance with the law of nature. By this last law, God effects the "manner of working for each created thing." It consequently is applicable to both "Natural Agents" and "Voluntary Agents." Although men may never understand fully the law of nature, just as they, even more certainly, will never understand fully "Law Celestial and Heavenly," as voluntary agents they are subject to the "Law of Reason," which binds all humans and which provides that the reason of man by the light of his natural understanding guide his will to seek good.[65]

Although the effectiveness of the law of reason depends upon man's natural ability and his education, in mundane matters the "decision of reason" may not be between that which is simply good and that which is simply evil. Such a choice is only one of three sorts: "mandatory," involving that which is definitely good or evil; "permissive," involving one of several evils that cannot be avoided; and "admonitory," involving that which of several alternatives is best. Praise or blame for action depends not on the action alone, but on the extent to which man wills the action and the "exigence" of so doing or the difficulty of doing otherwise.[66] Though developed upon entirely different grounds and in a different manner, the conclusion to this process of thought obviously might be used also to confirm Smith's bases upon which the wise judge the question in political history that is most difficult to decide, namely, the relative validity of civil obedience or disobedience, of submitting to evil or of effecting its removal "by all meanes."

In view of his dominant purpose, Hooker will not repeat Smith's conclusion, but, as it will be seen, he does rest heavily upon a definition of Parliament which accords with Smith's. From his basic position, Hooker first argues that the Scriptures do not contain "all sorts of Law." Their primary purpose is to reveal "supernatural law." They do not contain every other sort of knowledge necessary for rule or action but "presuppose" it, just as by means other than the Scriptures one is persuaded there are oracles of God. With Scriptures, as it has just been noted, must be considered the law of nature, which for man involves his adherence to the law of reason; and actually non-Scriptural law is also a "word" of God. It is the wisdom and knowledge of the ages; it is a manifestation of God Himself.[67]

With his emphasis upon man's natural ability and education, Hooker consequently writes in the humanistic tradition of a Pico della Mirandola, which granted wisdom, if not on the tongue, at least in the breast, of the barbarian; thus "there is no kind of knowledge, whereby any part of Truth is seen, but we must justly account it precious." Rational knowledge natural to man can give light to the Scriptures themselves, even to "that Principal Truth, in comparison whereof, all other knowledge is vile"; for systematized bodies of learning handed down by our ancestors undoubtedly can elucidate the Bible "whether it be that *Egyptian* and *Chaldean* wisdom, mathematical, wherewith *Moses* and *Daniel* were furnished; or that Natural, Moral, and Civil wisdom wherewith *Solomon* excelled all men; or that Rational and Oratorical wisdom of the *Grecians,* which the Apostle St. *Paul* brought from *Tarsus;* or that Judaical, which he learned in *Jerusalem,* sitting at the feet of Gamaliel." To detract from the dignity of such learning "were to injure even God himself, who being that Light which none can approach unto, hath sent out these lights whereof we are capable, even as so many sparkles resembling the Bright Fountain from which they rise."[68]

The laws of nature clearly perceptible to reason bind man absolutely. They are perceived in such matters as that dramatized in *Antigone* and presumably they would take precedence over the rule of a tyrant;[69] but, as Hooker will point out, in matters of polity, by their very nature, these laws must be acted upon in accordance with the dictates of past and present wisdom and of exigency; for seldom in such circumstances is a decision of reason other than "permissive."[70]

The laws of nature and reason, however, are effective for understanding what must have been the situation when men who had no "setled Fellowship" would live together. At that time the first of the foundations "which bear up Publick Societies" made itself felt. This was the Aristotelian "Natural Inclination, whereby all men desire sociable life and fellowship" in order to achieve what no man can provide for himself, namely, "a life fit for the dignity of man." Given this first foundation, man then discovers through the law of reason the "Law of a Commonweal," the second foundation that bears up "Publick Societies." He is led to this by perceiving that there must be some agreement about laws "whereby the fellowship or Communion of Independent Society" may stand. Thus the Law of a Commonweal is an order expressly or secretly agreed upon which concerns the manner of men's "Union in living together."[71]

The Law of a Commonweal, then, appears to be the basic principle upon which government is established as a type of polity and as a means whereby positive laws can be effected. It may be "secret" because its express origin is hidden, but it is embodied, nevertheless, in the ancient customs of a nation's polity. Phrased in more detail, Hooker's discussion refers to three principles that a natural human reason could and did perceive. Men knew that, although they might defend themselves when an injury was offered, all should oppose by all good means any injury offered another. They realized also that each man would be so partial to himself that he could not reasonably determine his own right and proceed to maintain it on that basis without increasing trouble and violence. They perceived, finally, that there was no reason for one man to become lord and judge over another without the other's consent. Although from the very nature of the law of reason, there may be "a kind of Natural Right in the Noble, Wise, and Vertuous, to govern them which are of a servile disposition," yet for the manifestation of that right and for a greater mutual contentment, the assent of the governed must have seemed necessary.

Hooker's kinship with Smith, particularly in this conception of a commonweal, is obvious. Although Hooker emphasizes the wise in different circumstances than did Smith, and although he discusses the idea of an initial agreement between governed and governor, there is a basic similarity between the two in the conventional assumption that a polity is a society "united by common accord and covenauntes" for the benefit of its members.[72]

Like Smith, Hooker also discusses a rule other than that effected primarily, or solely, by this Law of a Commonweal. In the *Laws,* however, this involves a consideration not only of rule by conquest but also of a rule by what Hooker calls "mere Divine Right." This last type of rule is given sometimes "extraordinarily from God, unto whom all the World is subject." It is essentially unusual, although it existed at times in the ancient commonweal of Israel. It is "an immediate appointment by God" or "an express Commission immediately and personally received from God" by an "extraordinary Warrant." Thus it can be called rule by "mere [i.e., absolute] Divine Right."[73] Because of its nature and the infrequency of its occurrence, however, Hooker argues that it may be dismissed from consideration in matters of public utility and necessity.

By his phraseology, "mere" or "utter" ("unmixed," "out-and-out") divine right, Hooker's argument, however, might well be considered as striking at the monstrous specter of the Anabaptists and shades of Peter Birchet and his kind, and less directly, perhaps, at the activity of certain Catholics. The matter deserves brief elucidation, particularly since events connected with the consideration just mentioned were undoubtedly impressed on the memories of Hooker's and Shakespeare's contemporaries, and were closely related to the publication in 1593 of the first four books of *The Laws of Ecclesiastical Polity.*

As early as 1577, "radical" Catholics had their English protomartyr in Cuthbert Mayne, whose execution occurred in the wake of the 1570 Bull against Elizabeth; but even before then, in 1573, when Anglican authorities were concerned with suppressing the Puritan *Admonition* to Parliament and ancillary writings, Peter Birchet had attempted to murder Christopher Hatton and had alleged the guidance of the Holy Spirit. In the same year, when Bishop Sandys complained that none of the proscribed tracts had been delivered to him, he said that the people were becoming bold and disobedient; and Matthew Parker then warned Cecil that if the dangerous proceedings manifested in the circulation of the *Admonition* and related works were not suppressed, England would witness a repetition of events that had disturbed Germany nearly fifty years previously.[74]

The events to which Parker referred were well known. In 1525 the Lutheran pastor Münzer had gained control of the Peasant's War and turned its protest against feudal oppression into a protest against all constituted authority. His short-lived commonweal was thought to have been even more viciously intensified in 1532-35 when control of Münster was seized by the Lutheran pastor Rothmann and his associates and the city turned into a "new Zion," where John of Leyden, tailor, might legalize such measures as polygamy under the authority of visions from Heaven. That all things in Münster, including wives, were then "held in common" could, and did, make Anabaptism a byword for vicious disorder; and of this concept Hooker is thoroughly aware.

To him an attack upon bishops is but a step toward the road leading to Münzer and Münster.[75] Indeed, the fear of the Anabaptist in the Puritan was fairly constant. Elizabeth, her councilors, and her divines were troubled at instances of the spread of the "Family of Love," at Robert Brown's *A Treatise of Reformation without Tarrying for Any* (1582), at the activities of a Martin Marprelate or a Henry Barrow, at any sect that seemed to separate itself from the state, like the very Catholics whom the radical Puritans hated. All such signs could be read as possible symptoms of a diseased commonweal, symptoms apparent in an ignorant and zealous extension of the position maintained by those who said they would destroy only the Anglican hierarchy.

Nor were English claims of "extraordinary Warrants" from God lacking in this dangerous tendency. Aside from Birchet, Thomas Asplyn, for example, had acted upon "express Commission," as had Copinger, Arthington, and Hacket. When Asplyn had been once arrested for working in secret on the *Second Admonition* and released, he had been arrested again because of his attempt to kill the printer Day. On "being asked what he meant, he answered 'The Spyrte moved him.'" Even more dangerously, and upon the heels of the Marprelate controversy, Copinger, Arthington, and Hacket, after desiring interviews with the imprisoned Cartwright, had proclaimed Hacket *Messiah redivivus* and had set out to overthrow the government and bring Elizabeth and her counselors to repentance and judgment.[76]

In the early 1590's, soon after Martin Marprelate had been brought upon the stage, Londoners must have been aware of all this, at least in a general way, regardless of their religious convictions. Certainly those aware of potential conflagrations in the commonweal considered even the relatively moderate Cartwright to be maintaining a dangerous position. Although freed of any direct or responsible connection with Marprelate, when he refused to give details about various "Conferences"—for his answers might be dangerous to others—he was reminded that an oath to answer whatever might be asked was substantiated by the law of the land, and his answer was that he was not sure such an oath accorded with God's law.[77] In such circumstances, an appeal to supra-national law might well seem to lead to a position from which the ignorant could claim an "extraordinary Warrant" from God. From Hooker's point of view, such a position as Cartwright's failed to recognize that the Law of Reason was also a Word of God to be found, for example, in the wisdom of previous generations and to be applied in matters "permissive," and, more particularly, in the circumstances of an English society concerned with effecting a life for all that would be fit for the "dignity of man."

Although Cartwright was released, many Puritans of varying degrees of radicalism, including Barrow, Greenwood, and Penry, were in prison when Parliament met in 1593 and considered measures for dealing with seditious and unruly elements in the body politic. Men like Cartwright, it was hoped, might be won over to the Anglican position; but the treatment of those more "radical" than he was difficult to determine. In such circumstances, Edwin Sandys, son of Bishop Sandys, presumably had been struck with the value of what Hooker had written, particularly if the *Laws* from Books V through VIII were revised to answer in detail Cartwright's position and those of his associates. At any rate, Sandys financed the publication of this treatise that Hooker presumably wrote as an aftermath to his controversy with Travers, and the first four books of the *Laws* appeared with a preface that sketched a history of Anabaptism and discussed the dangers of the Puritan position as illustrated by the Barrowists.

On March 13, 1593, the same day on which Hooker sent a complimentary copy of the *Laws* to Burghley, Edwin Sandys spoke in Parliament about a pending bill that originally had been designed to strengthen the penal act of 1581. Although the preamble to this bill spoke only of Catholics, Puritan members like Henry Finch had argued that the clauses of the bill might catch undeservedly some of their co-religionists. As a result, the bill had been committed and so thoroughly altered that Sandys urged it should remain as originally planned, that is, against recusants generally. He thought it just that Barrowists and Brownists be punished. By March 30, however, when Burghley referred to the measure, the initiative had passed to the Upper House, which since February 24 had had a measure pending that was similar to the one in Commons. Revised several times, the two bills finally emerged with one applicable to "sectaries" only, but diverted from Puritans, the other applicable to Catholics.[78]

In the meantime, Barrow and Greenwood were hanged under the act of 1581, with the judges ignoring the qualifying "Popish" phrase of that measure. Penry would be put to death in May under the statute 23 Elizabeth, 2, which was directed against seditious words. Apparently from the point of view of the judges, as well as the Whitgift party, because of the "fourescore severall" ways wherein the radical Puritan "doe resemble the Anabaptist," Barrow and Greenwood became literally, if not legally, advocates of "Puritano-papismus"[79] and should be treated like Papists. Nor was this the first time that such extremes were lumped together. Elizabeth coupled "non-conformity with Catholicism as a menace to the State," while John Aylmer as early as 1577 would turn those extremes against one another by transferring Field and Wilcockes, the authors of the first *Admonition,* to such "barbarous" counties as Lancashire, Staffordshire, and Shropshire, where their zeal might draw the people from Popery.[80] Even the Puritan Henry Finch spoke of his abhorrence for Barrowists and Brownists, though he appreciated their enmity to Catholics.[81]

It is not surprising, then, that Hooker should emphasize the unusual nature of rule by "mere" Divine right. By God's word manifested differently but nonetheless definitely in the Law of a Commonweal, which could be discerned by the Law of Reason, it could be seen that England already had an excellent polity to which her ecclesiastical one was geared, and at the head of such a Christian polity was, quite fittingly, the English monarch.

Even rule by conquest, although it too is from God, who controls all battles, is for Hooker not applicable to Elizabethan England. William I took the name of Conqueror simply because pre-Conquest England had the form of government that limited a king's power in making laws so that it did not rest entirely in the hands of one. Otherwise, William could not have changed the laws of the land by himself.[82] By both previous and subsequent rule, however, by the wisdom of the Elizabethans' ancestors and by the favor of God, the English monarch does not have power in all things. As his inability to change pleas in court indicates, he is restricted not simply by divine or natural law, and the various manifestations of the latter, but also by the positive laws of the realm. Although "through his supreme power" he "may do great things and sundry himself, both appertaining unto peace and war, both at home, by commandemant and by commerce with states abroad," he does so "because so much the law doth permit." On the "other side," "without consent of the lords and commons assembled in parliament," he can not "change the nature of pleas, nor courts." He can not, for example, "restore blood," not because "any law divine or natural" is a "bar unto him" but because "the positive laws of the realm have abridged therein and restrained the kings power."[83]

Although Smith was not concerned with Convocation, the similarity of *The Laws* to the *De Republica Anglorum* becomes even more obvious when Hooker writes that the force and power of the laws of England take their effect from Parliament "with the convocation annexed thereunto"; for Parliament consists of the king "and of all that within the land are subject unto him," that is, the spiritual and temporal nobility and the commoners, either in their own persons or in the persons of their representatives. The ruler is an integral part of Parliament and of Convocation and is naturally the sovereign. In Parliament, however, his sovereignty consists primarily of the right to veto. The Elizabethan Parliament, then, is "that whereupon the very essence of all government within this kingdom doth depend."[84]

Most of the immediately preceding discussion of the English state is drawn from Hooker's unfinished eighth book. Its agreement with Smith's treatise and with other matter noted in this chapter makes it valid here as a further illustration of sixteenth-century ideas about states and about the English state.[85] Book eight, like all of the later books, is based on principles laid down in initial discussions;[86] thus, in his description of England's polity which has just been noted, Hooker proceeds upon a number of those basic assumptions.

One is that where "number is, there must be order, or else of force there will be confusion." This principle obviously explains not only why the institution of bishops is essential but also why among bishops there should be order and degree. "Where many Governours must of necessity concur," one should have "some kind of sway or stroke more than all the residue" if affairs "of what nature soever they be" are to be ordered.[87] This is an obvious natural law.

With it is joined the Law of a Commonweal, the "very Soul" of a politic body. This law, it will be remembered, originated when men had no "settled fellowship." It did not necessarily arise, however, when they first banded together. Then only some general kind of regiment, as of kingship, may well have been established, and everything else left to the discretion of the ruler; but if so, because of man's fallibility, the people in time must have perceived their error. As Cicero and Aristotle indicate, by the force of the whole, men must have ordained laws to restrain the will of one man, to relieve the misery of many, and to publish men's duties and punishments. What had been "devised for a remedy, did indeed but increase the sore which it should have cured"; "to live by one Man's will, became the cause of all Men's misery." "This constrained them to come unto Laws, wherein all men might see their duties beforehand, and know the penalties for transgressing them." Thus the text *Let every Soul be subject to the higher Powers* should be construed as commanding part of a commonweal to submit to the public power of the whole to make laws.[88]

By such a process of thought Hooker obviously produced an effective variation upon some of the most usable of political commonplaces. His conception of the origin of states not only accords with conventional definitions of a commonweal and, as we shall see, with those of the English Parliament as well, but also is joined with a commandment requiring obedience and with the appealing maxim that emphasizes the power of the whole. This last idea, in particular, appears in "radical" English writings, as well as in Huguenot and Catholic treatises written on the Continent, including, for example, the *De Justitia et Jure* (*approbatis,* 1592) by the Spanish Jesuit Molina. Hooker's emphasis varies from Molina's, among other considerations, by the weight Hooker accords to the principles which enlightened human reason perceives when it excludes rule by "mere" divine right and by conquest and examines what must have been the pre-governmental state of society.[89] By its detail and its extension of matter glanced at in the *De Republica Anglorum,* Hooker's emphasis varies from Smith's by moving in the direction of full glosses on portions of Aristotle's *Politics,* although his emphasis on law *qua* law is greater than that provided by Le Roy. To emphasize the power and importance of the whole, however, was thoroughly conventional.

As a consequence, some of Hooker's contemporaries might well have thought of matter mentioned earlier, of ideas about the nature of a mixed state, which fleetingly anticipate the thought of such seventeenth-century classical republicans as Algernon Sidney, or they may have thought of the direction taken by some of the Huguenot writings. In this last instance, both Hotman's *Francogallia* (which advocated a limited French monarchy) and the Huguenot *Vindiciae* emphasized the "stock" and not the "twig" as the basic unit chosen to rule by the governed. Upon such a concept, linked with an emphasis upon the coronation oath, they had defended the right to depose any one ruler.[90]

Hooker, although he shows that he is aware of such current concepts, attempts to block off their radical conclusions. Although he cites *loci classici* for the mixed form of government (Aristotle on Spartan polity and Polybius on the rule of Roman consuls),[91] he does not conclude that great restraint upon regal power is necessarily a sign of good government. He may recognize Sparta as the best ancient example of a beneficent perpetuity, but he does not point out any similarity between Spartan polity and that of the regiment of England. Like Smith and, as a subsequent discussion will indicate, like Philip Sidney, he argues for no one form of government as always being best *per se*. To Hooker, what is desirable is a polity that has resulted from wise and experienced deliberation and that will allow a continuation of this necessary attribute. To him the greatest limitation of regal power does not mean the best limitation; what is more important than restricting the ruler's sovereign action to "fewest things" is to have the ruler's actions "tied unto the soundest, perfectest, and most indifferent rule," and that rule is the law, "not only the law of nature and of God, but very national or municipal law consonant thereunto." Happier is "that people whose law is their king in the greatest things, than that whose king is himself their law." "Where the king doth guide the state, and the law the king, that commonwealth is like an harp or melodious instrument, the strings whereof are tuned and handled all by one, following as laws the rules and canons of musical science."[92]

In such a context, the conventional, and presumably memorable, analogy with musical harmony moves from a world picture to an Elizabethan one. Similarly, Hooker represents the consent and force of the whole—by which their "Union in living together" had been established and from which had resulted the means whereby laws were effected for the common good—as being continued in England, not by successive choices from the stock, and not by any coronation oath, but by parliament.

The contract between ruler and ruled, consequently, is a contract *in perpetuo*[93]—a striking difference from the thought of those who emphasize the Germanic renewal. At the same time, in contrast to Bodin's position, and with a process of thought that also contrasts with the thinking of those who would advocate a mixed government, Hooker considers the supremacy of the prince to be in no way incompatible with a rule that by regiment itself restricts the ruler. In this respect, his closeness to Smith is again noticeable, although his method is quite different. The English king has universal dominion, but that dominion is dependent "upon that whole entire body, over the several parts of which he hath dominion." The axiom in such a case is that the king is *"major singulis, universis minor."*[94]

This particular variation of Hooker's thought can also be illustrated by a number of approaches. Some of his learned contemporaries might have described his position as one that, by utilizing the conventional definition of Parliament, synthesized a concept related to the sinful origin of society with Bracton's concept of regal *jurisdictio,* in contrast to regal *gubernaculum.* The first idea Luther himself had emphasized. Because of the evil in man's will, the state was ordained by God to preserve order, to curb chaos, and to protect the good from the evil. The bearer of office was, in this sense only, a representative of divine order; but all attempts to construct an ideal state were manifestations of a human *hubris*. The ruler's authority was a Christian conscience directly responsible to God, and a state lived only by the conscience of governors, the conscience of subjects, and the conscience of those whose spiritual office it was to admonish both and keep the consciences of both alive.[95] Without such a religious emphasis, Bracton referred to the Germanic renewal and stated that in matters of *jurisdictio,* the king was the fountain of the whole system of his country's courts and laws but was, nevertheless, bound to observe those laws.[96]

Hooker's argument partially accepts both processes of

thought, just as it had accepted the principle of the excellence of perpetuity *per se*.[97] The representative body of the whole in England perpetuates the "soul" of the body politic, and in it, as leaders of the church, appear those who keep consciences alive. From such a body, which constantly renews the original force of the whole, all law had originated and would continue to do so. And in that body also is the ruler who is head of it, as he is head of both church and state.[98] His actions, thereby, in the "greatest things" are "tied unto" the law.

Hooker, of course, accepts the doctrine, found in nearly every political treatise, that the prince is controlled by his Christian conscience. That would be especially true when matters fell under what Bracton called a king's *gubernaculum*. In discussing this aspect of rule—a king's right to govern by his prerogative, to perform his executive duties, to act in matters wherein he alone was sovereign—Bracton had also repeated this commonplace and noted that in such an area, in contrast to that of his *jurisdictio,* the prince was restricted only by higher law, his own conscience, and God's vengeance. Similarly, to the king's Christian conscience and to that of his advisors and appointees, as well as to their wisdom, Hooker leaves the execution of laws;[99] for like Luther and countless others, Hooker accepts man's evil will as a basic and determining factor in all government.

Consequently, when Hooker writes that politic or positive law should be based upon the assumption that the will of man is "inwardly obstinate, rebellious, and averse from all obedience unto the Sacred Laws of Nature" and that the wise lawmaker must proceed upon the assumption that man is little better than a wild beast,[100] he in effect defends the statutes mentioned above that were the concern of the Parliament of 1593. Certainly he repeats an idea congruent, though not identical, with some found in writings that emphasized the sinful origin of society. The idea in its context is not too far removed from basic, hardheaded precepts in *The Prince,* although certainly the total context of the *Laws,* with its emphasis upon a true, not an artificial, religion, is far removed from the spirit of Machiavelli's treatise— which was studied almost as much as it was maligned. In a similar manner, Raleigh would write that it is "hard to say" whether "charity, that divine virtue so necessary in single persons, is dangerous in governors." It is prudent, for rulers at any rate, "to believe all men are bent to mischief, and that good is seldom done but through force or fear, and that most have a wit to put in practice the wickedness of their minds as often as occasion shall serve."[101] Thus, for Hooker, in the making of laws, wisdom proceeds upon such principles, another valid one being that the greater part of mankind prefer their private good, and even things sensual, to things divine or truly good.[102]

In the *Laws,* as a result, Hooker expresses much more forcefully than does Smith ideas related to the fallibility of man, the force of circumstance, and the vicissitude of fortune. Although men are happiest when they fully enjoy God, they are incapable of such perfection in this life; even "in those very actions, whereby we are especially perfected . . . we are not able to persist; forced we are with very weariness, and that often, to interrupt them."[103] In addition, the reason or the will of individual man may not be sufficiently enlightened, for nothing is so good that it may not "have the shew of some difficulty or unpleasant quality annexed to it," nor is there any evil that "hath not some appearance of goodness whereby to insinuate itself."[104] As a consequence, a mean between two extremes is best for all estates, even for kings and princes themselves. In public affairs, however, a mean can not always be expected. In the exercise of any civil or ecclesiastical polity there are, and always will be, evils "which no art of man can cure, breaches and leakes, moe than mans wit hath hands to stop."[105] As with an individual's life, so with the course of any government, the "prosperous and happy" ones can be determined only by "a just survey," and a state is fortunate "which having flourished, doth not afterward feel any tragical alteration, such as might cause them to be a spectacle of misery to others."[106]

For such reasons a constant exercise of wisdom and deliberation is again necessary, and those concerned with matters of polity always must recognize the force of "exigence" and of necessity. Since even natural agents bow to necessity, no censure should be leveled at men who do so, as long as the "Mind is rightly ordered" and nothing is done that is "simply in itself evil," "absolutely evil or wicked." In the first place, when two evils are inevitable, to choose the less is not to do evil. In the second place, "where Council and Advice bear rule," without some extraordinary warrant from God to substantiate an action, men themselves must judge an evil to be inevitable if there is no way of avoiding it. Since there are always evils, variations in evil can not always be judged in relation to general and absolute principles of right or wrong.[107] Considerations of public utility, of the common good, consequently, are at the very least equivalent with "the easier" sort of necessity.[108] In Hooker's English state, necessity is far from being Milton's "Tyrant's plea."

A related characteristic of society Hooker also brings to bear upon questions about "Complements, Rites and Ceremonies of Church Action." Although they are for the most part "such silly things, that very easiness doth make them hard to be disputed of in serious manner," they may be dangerous when the wise "consider not so much how small the spark is that flieth up, as how apt things about it, are to take fire."[109] Such a position is Aristotelian in its implied belief that any government should be able to provide against revolution without trusting to accident. In this instance, however, Hooker's position also appears thoroughly Elizabethan as well, when a concern for apparent trifles is justified by the worn analogy between politic bodies and men's bodies, more of which have been destroyed "through diseases, bred within themselves, than through violence from abroad." An individual is always inclined to watch more carefully that over which he has no control; thus because he believes that he can always master evils within the body more easily than dangers from outside the body, the former are often allowed "to run on forward, till it be too late to recall them." The spirit of contention, "the Gall of Bitterness," is obviously such an evil; for at the best a commonweal will have evils and be by that much unsound, and that relative lack of health will be aggravated "through opposition arising between the unsound parts and the sound, where each endeavoureth to draw evermore contrary ways, till destruction in the end, bring the whole to ruin."

Reformers, however, forget the social nature of the church, the imperfect nature of any body politic, and particularly the imperfect nature of those comprising such a body. They also forget the many difficulties that necessitate a constant, wise rule if order is to be maintained for the public good. The opening sentences of Hooker's first (1593) and fifth (1597) books go straight to the point:

> He that goeth about to persuade a multitude, that they are not so well-governed as they ought to be, shall never want attentive and favorable Hearers; because they know the manifold defects whereunto every kind of Regiment is subject; but the secret lets and difficulties, which in publick proceedings are innumerable and inevitable, they have not ordinarily the judgement to consider.
>
> Few there are of so weak capacity, but publick evils they easily espie; fewer so patient, as not to complain, when the grievous inconveniences thereof, work sensible smart. Howbeit to see wherein the harm which they feel consisteth, the Seeds from which it sprang, and the method of curing it, belongeth to a skill, the study thereof is so full of toyl, and the practise so beset with difficulties; that wary and respective men had rather seek quietly their own, and wish that the World may go well, so it be not long of them, than with pain and hazard, make themselves advisers for the common good.

The idea expressed in the preceding quotations and elsewhere about the difficulties of rule might lead to an emphasis upon the *arcana* of politics. Such a possible consequence will be referred to later; here Hooker's further account of the causes of those difficulties deserves attention. As both quotations given above indicate, those difficulties frequently were considered as arising from constant features of any society. What Raleigh called the "insatiable minds of men" was obviously in Hooker's consciousness as he wrote the beginning of those books which opened the two volumes of *The Laws* as they were published in his lifetime. Their relationship to the constant fear of the Anabaptist and of the multitude is obvious and purposeful. Raleigh's comment, although considerably later and although not applied specifically to any religious controversy, might be an apt gloss to one aspect of the position taken by Hooker and his fellow-Anglicans; for it is those "insatiable minds of men," "impatient under what is present, fond of any alteration," that lead to civil disturbances, especially when such minds are excited "by those that will be under no dominion but that of avarice, ambition, or revenge."[110]

Such expressions of conventional dangers from the many and the few were certainly valid for Hooker. Among the constant ills of church and state, for example, is the evil liable to result from those who incline toward the "gross and bestial conceit of them which want understanding," that is, the belief "that the fullest bellies are happiest." They would have the "riotous" "pour without stint"; the poor sleep and the rich feed them; they would have nothing unpleasant commanded or forbidden that they "have a lust to follow"; to them kings should provide for "the ease of their Subjects, and not be too curious about their manners"; "wantonness, excess, and lewdness of life" "should be free" and no fault should be "capital, besides dislike of things setled in so good terms." Such individuals do not realize that overabundance may produce as much evil as a scarcity, which sinks men in beggary, dejection, or baseness, and which makes them irrational. Constantly dangers appear also from the "over-high exalted either in honour, or in power, or in nobility, or in wealth." Although the many may perform "petty mischiefs" by themselves, the few, as Smith also noted conventionally, are "exceeding apt unto outrages"; and neither group easily gives ear to reason.[111]

Also among those persons whose presence makes a commonweal apt "to take fire" are the "turbulent wits," whom Hooker discusses when he considers volition. Because all men sometimes act through a certain natural *virtù*, through a desire for action itself, this end may be so perverted that disturbance itself is desired. Such individuals think "the very disturbance of things established, an hire sufficient to set them on work."[112] When some of Hooker's opponents had erected a complete form of public service, they utilized some of the preceding principles valid in any society, for they knew they could not put their discipline into effect without "the strong hand of the people." This meant that they represented their cause as embodying the people's "own interest, right, and title." Then they pretended that the people were "necessary Actors in those things," although the people's ability in such matters is "as slender, as their title and challenge unjust." Whether the originators of the idea of lay-elders were sincere or not, they gained by it the advantage that the people were drawn to it as something favoring their interests. Since Hooker's opponents also allowed for "special illumination" when they attacked the established order under cover of divine authority, the people mistook that claim for the true "Grace and Countenaunce of that Power."[113] Instead of utilizing the rational, though slow and wearisome, "help of proceeding by publick Authority," the precisians took what lay closest at hand and what seemed likely to appeal to the many.[114] When such "turbulent wits"[115] resist public authority, they resist the power of the whole, and by that resistance they weaken the power of wisdom, deliberation, and the basis of all law in England.

If the power of the whole be allowed to work, although proceeding by public authority may be slow, both that same power and authority are so constituted in England that it is very difficult to see how any serious disjunction could occur between the one, the few, and the many.[116] Once more, if not in specific purpose and details, Smith and Hooker agree essentially—in Parliament, the ruler and the estates are one. The agreement between Smith and Hooker arises, in part at least, from the fact that the Tudors, however strong their absolutist ambitions, found it convenient to identify their actions as closely as possible with the will of Parliament.[117] To do so, at the very least, was a safeguard against relying upon the doctrine that "the Crowne once possessed, cleaneth and purifies all manner of defaults or imperfections." Even Mary and Philip, particularly in matters of religion, had attempted to work within the framework of English institutions.[118]

Other conventional ideas related to the complex of rule also appear in Hooker's defense of the Anglican church, and a few of them should be indicated, although the total argument of his work is quite inadequately represented here. As might be expected, they are closely related to matter already noted. Consider the idea that the few have a vice of their own that can corrupt the many and lead to disturbances. Just as any kingdom is upheld by wisdom and valor, and just as those who excel in either are justly ennobled for their service, so every kingdom—even one ruled by the best of kings—is, conversely, in danger from the very fact of nobility. For high position may cause some to run into malice, crime, and disorder. Witness Achitophel and Joab under David. By the existence of spiritual lords, however, an eccclesiastical hierarchy matches the secular hierarchy and thus helps, both to control those who might become "exorbitant," and to correct the abuses to which the "Courage, State, and Dignity" of the nobility makes them prone: ". . . what help could there ever have been invented more Divine, than the sorting of the Clergy into such Degrees, that the chiefest of the Prelacy being matched in a kind of equal yoke, as it were, with the higher, the next with the lower degree of Nobility, the reverend Authority of the one, might be to the other as a courteous bridle, a mean to keep them lovingly in awe that are exorbitant, and to correct such excesses in them, as whereunto Courage, State, and Dignity maketh them over-prone?"[119]

By performing such a function in the body politic, the spiritual nobility aid the ruler, but what "establisheth and maketh" laws is "power, even power of dominion," and that rests chiefly in "the person of the king." By him the law that takes its force from the power of the whole can be put into effect throughout a realm, and thereby the king's power, corresponding to the law, is military, judicial, and religious:

The axioms of our regal government are then: "Lex facit regem": the king's grant of any favor made contrary to the law is void; "Rex nihil potest nisi quod jure potest." Our kings, therefore, when they take possession of the room they are called unto, have it painted out before their eyes, even by the very solemnities and rites of their inauguration, to what affairs by the said law their supreme authority and power reacheth. Crowned we see they are, and enthronized, and anointed: the crown a sign of military; the throne, of sedentary or judiciall; the oil, of religion or sacred power.[120]

Thus in contrast to those who relied upon the Germanic theory, but in accord with his concept of a contract *in perpetuo*, Hooker gives weight to the coronation ceremony as a representation of a public judgment, in this instance one which granted chief dominion and sovereign power within the law to the English ruler. Only by such sovereign authority are kings able to preserve a balance among the estates of the ruled; only by such authority are they able "when need serves to do as virtuous kings have done" and suppress both turbulent wits and those overly exalted. By that means they control especially the usurpers of authority who have no right to what they have seized or who have used "more authority than they ever did receive."[121]

A prince's sovereign power, as it applies to an entire realm, also demands that the ruler and his counselors exercise their *virtù* in the art of governing, an art that throughout *The Laws of Ecclesiastical Polity* is represented as a difficult one. Such an idea has been touched on before, as it might lead to an emphasis on the mysteries of politics. Earlier in the Tudor period, William Thomas had frankly expressed this last emphasis and even advocated a necessary duplicity.[122] This might accord with statements about the irrational, insatiable, even bestial nature of men; and individuals like Morison, thoroughly steeped in *The Prince*, would sometimes express these and kindred ideas in advocating an absolutism comparable to that in Machiavelli's treatise.[123] Certainly, the practicality of *The Prince* could not be denied. Hooker, however, always within his major premises, quite logically avoids any position that might advocate duplicity, however secret it be. Nor is it one demanded by an emphasis on the difficulties of rule. To many, as to Louis Le Roy, the art of governing was sovereign in its excellence. If its difficulties were great, the fame it afforded was likewise above that of other endeavors.[124]

Obviously, upon Le Roy's grounds, this art was meant to be most laudable, and equally obviously, to a churchman, it should emanate from a truly Christian person, for only a Christian prince could effect a Christian rule. For Hooker, as for Bodin and others, religion supports a ruler's exercise of his art.[125] By its dictates, as well as by the dictates of wisdom and necessity, a sovereign strength and vigor attempts to control a mutable, or even a viciously inclined, body. Part of the Christian art of governing, therefore, is a merciful but preventative application of laws framed severely. If it can effect nothing else, Christianity can give governors fortitude in adversity, as well as in the troublesome twists of society that are always present.[126] A basic precept for Hooker and the majority of contemporary writers, indeed, was that, other things being equal, no rule will exist long unless it be Christian. In the *Laws,* this does not simply mean that Christianity restrains a king from becoming a tyrant; it also means that nothing approaching perpetuity can be achieved unless it be based on true religion. Although Hooker allows for the force of necessity, he shows only contempt for those who extol the "wisdom of Paganism" and, like Machiavelli, counsel a prince as if they were able to "create God in man by art."

In which respect, there are of these wise malignants, some who have vouchsafed it their marvellous favourable countenance and speech, very gravely affirming, That Religion honoured, addeth greatness; and contemned, bringeth ruine unto Commonweals: That Princes and States which will continue, are above all things to uphold the reverend regard of Religion, and to provide for the same, by all means, in the making of their Laws. But when they should define what means are best for that purpose, behold, they extol the wisdom of Paganism, they give it out as a mystical precept of great importance, that Princes, and such as are under them in most authority or credit with the people, should take all occasions of rare events, and from what cause soever the same do proceed, yet wrest them to the strengthning of their Religion, and not make it nice for so good a purpose to use, if need be, plain forgeries. Thus while they study to bring to pass, that Religion may seem but a matter made, they lose themselves in the very maze of their own discourses, as if Reason did even purposely forsake them, who of purpose forsake God, the Author thereof: For surely, a strange kind of madness it is, that those men, who though they be void of Piety, yet, because they have wit, cannot chuse but know, that treachery, guile, and deceit, are things which may for a while, but do not use long to go unespied, should teach, that the greatest honour to a State, is perpetuity; and grant, that alterations in the Service of God, for that they impair the credit of Religion, are therefore perilous in Commonweals, which have no continuance longer than Religion hath all reverence done unto it, and withal acknowledge (for so they do) than when people began to espie the falshood of Oracles, whereupon all Gentilism was built, their hearts were utterly averted from it; and notwithstanding counsel Princes, in sober earnest, for the strengthning of their States, to maintain Religion, and for the maintenance of Religion, not to make choice of that which is true, but to authorize that they make choice of, by those false and fraudulent means, which in the end, must needs overthrow it. Such are the counsels of men godless, when they would show themselves politick devisers, able to create God in Man by art.[127]

When one considers the fact that even in pagan rule the guilt of tyranny punished such a ruler as Tiberius, let alone his subjects,[128] a "just survey" of England's recent history shows that true religion in a body politic constitutes, in any ultimate analysis, true fortune. Hooker's conclusion to the first volume of the *Laws,* consequently, constitutes in effect an answer to both Catholics and sectarians.

When the ruines of the House of God . . . were become not in his sight alone, but in the eyes of the whole World so exceeding great, that very Superstition began even to feel it self too far grown; the first that with us made way to repair the decays thereof, by beheading Superstition, was King *Henry* the Eighth; the Son and Successor of which famous King, as we know, was *Edward* the Saint: In whom (for so, by the event we may gather) it pleased God Righteous and Just to let *England* see, what a blessing sin and iniquity would not suffer it to enjoy. . . . But what ensued? That work, which the one in such sort had begun, and the other so far proceeded in, was in short space so overthrown, as if almost it had never been: Till such time as that God, whose property is to shew his mercies then greatest when they are nearest to be utterly despaired of, caused in the depth of discomfort and darkness a most glorious Star to arise, and on her head setled the Crown, whom himself had kept as a Lamb from the slaughter of those bloody times, that the experience of his goodness in her own deliverance, might cause her merciful disposition, to take so much the more delight, in saving others, whom the like necessity should press. . . . That which especially concerneth our selves in the present matter we treat of, is, the state of Reformed Religion, a thing at her coming to the Crown, even raised, as it were, by miracle from the dead; a thing which we so little hoped to see, that even they which beheld it done, scarcely believed their own senses at the first beholding. Yet being then brought to pass, thus many years it hath continued standing by no other worldly mean, but that one only hand which erected it, that hand, which as no kind of imminent danger could cause at the first to withhold it self; so neither have the practises, so many so bloody, following since, been ever able to make weary. Nor can we say in this case so justly, that *Aaron* and *Hur,* the Ecclesiastical and Civil States, have sustained the hand which did lift it self to Heaven, for them; as that Heaven it self hath by this hand sustained them, no aid or help having thereunto been ministred for performance of the Work of Reformation, other than such kind of help or aid as the Angel in the Prophet *Zachariah* speaketh of, saying, *Neither by an army, nor strength, but by my Spirit, saith the Lord of Hosts.* Which Grace and Favor of Divine Assistance, having not in one thing or two, shewed it self, nor for some few days or years appeared, but in such sort so long continued, our manifold sins and transgressions striving to the contrary; What can we less thereupon conclude, than that God would at leastwise by tract of time teach the World, that the thing which he blesseth, defendeth, keepeth so strangely, cannot chuse but be of him? Wherefore, if any refuse to believe us disputing for the Verity of Religion established, let them believe God himself thus miraculously working for it; and wish life, even for ever and ever, unto that Glorious and Sacred Instrument whereby he worketh.

To sum up briefly: although Hooker believed the preceding *peroratio* to Book IV to be true, equally true is his belief in the necessity for other remedies against fortune that involve wisdom and the law of reason and that are one manifestation of God's Word. He also recognizes man's fallibility and the force of necessity, as well as the fact that the great majority of politic judgments are "permissive," involving one of several evils that cannot be avoided. Thoroughly consistent with this process of thought, as it involves the law of reason, is his emphasis upon the Law of a Commonweal and the perpetuity of the contract that embodied the force of the whole and that was apparent still in the law and the ancient custom of Parliament—in the public authority that embraced both ruler and ruled, both lay and ecclesiastical. Thoroughly conventional is his process of thought that focuses attention upon the natural vices of the one, the few, and the many (in his discussions, for example, of governmental origins and of the actions of his opponents). The Elizabethan method of government, including a prince's exercise of sovereign power within the law, is thus essentially and indubitably, in its main and important features, a Christian art, both as regards its derivation from the Word of God, manifested in the custom established by wise ancestors, and as regards its constant exercise, in which wisdom and force and the greatest skill, working within the custom of ages, is necessary. When a government is not separated from "Verity of Religion," God himself, even when all else fails and at last "by tract of time," sustains the nation and its "Ecclesiastical and Civil States."

# III

# Sedition and Pageantry

THAT HOOKER should emphasize the exercise of power based on wisdom and true religion is not surprising. All propagandists utilized that basic approach. At the beginning of the seventeenth century Essex raised the cry in the streets that he meant to rescue Elizabeth from bad counselors. During the preceding decade, that is, after the proclamation against the Jesuits, "radical" Catholics proceeded from a concern with true religion to attack the new nobility of Elizabeth—those atheistic upstarts who surrounded an atheistic ruler and who effected, or aided her in effecting, a false wisdom and valor.[1] Cecil, "the old Atheist," "the malignant and wrangeling worme," was plotting to marry his grandson to Arabella Stuart. Certainly Elizabeth should leave "the bloudy humour of this old ambitious serpent." The painful deaths of Walsingham and Leicester were just retributions, and an epitaph by a friend of Leicester should be recognized as true.

> Heere lies the woorthy warrier
> That neuer bloodied swoord:
> Heere lies the loyall courtier,
> That neuer kept his woord.
> Heere lies his noble excellence,
> That ruled all the states.
> Heere lies the Earle of Leicester,
> Whome earth, and heaven hates.

Thirty-three years of Elizabeth's peace had led thousands of Englishmen to ignominious deaths, not for the good of the commonweal, but for the private gain of Leicester and Raleigh, who with Cecil had corrupted the administration of justice. Bacon, as well as Cecil, was thoroughly vicious, as were the "suavissimos Adonides" about Elizabeth, among whom was Raleigh once more—that common soldier raised on high merely by the Queen's favor. Like Sir Francis Drake, he was such a knight "as other countries spoke shame of." As with Essex explaining his revolt (although afterward he would be likened to Wat Tyler and Jack Cade), so it was with the radical Catholics. The doctrine they would utilize was a commonplace one, apparent not simply in the form of its particular variation in Hooker's *Laws* but apparent also in the works of Castiglione and Elyot, and, for that matter, in all treatises *de regimine principum*: great evils result if a ruler is not surrounded by good nobles and especially by good counselors, whether they be lay or ecclesiastic.

It may verge upon the naïve and even upon the risible so to gloss the necessity for good advice, but the constant use of the maxim indicates that its force was great. It appears with a different emphasis in the pageantic displays of the era, and the validity for both Catholic and Puritan propagandists of such concepts as those emphasized or qualified in the works of Smith and Hooker can be shown by considering briefly a tract that appeared in the year after the publication of Hooker's first four books.

It was in 1594 that a group of people were represented as meeting in Antwerp and discussing the question of the English succession. They argued that succession was determined by the positive laws of a realm, which were subject to change. They maintained that although monarchy may be the best form of government, in England the authority of the king was limited by councilors and by Parliament, particularly Commons, and that a king must be accepted by the people. They provided examples from English history to substantiate the validity of the precept that rulers may be deposed for good cause. All of this, as it has been pointed out above, might be conventional, in part, to one process of thought; but when these fictitious individuals discussed the claims of possible successors to Elizabeth, they argued by implication that if birth were placed alongside of election Parliament could take away the Protestant James's right. The Infanta of Spain, as well as the King of Spain and his son, held hereditary rights to the English throne from John of Gaunt, Duke of Lancaster.

These conclusions appear over the name of Doleman and were published as *A Conference about the Next Succession to the Crown of England*.[2] Actually they were the work of the English Jesuit Robert Parsons, and, like the attacks on Elizabeth written by the Catholic Allen, they were definitely meant to be "seditious," for men like Parsons, even though Mary Queen of Scots was now dead, would stir up any trouble that they might with precepts calculated to appeal to advocates of both an incipient divine right and an incipient contract theory of government. They might indicate that not simply the Infanta of Spain but even the Earl of Essex—to whom the tract was dedicated and whose ancestral line could be derived from Thomas of Woodstock—had an unquestionable claim to the throne. Essex's cool reception at court and Burghley's notes out of Parson's tract show that Elizabeth and her counselors still recognized their liability to attack on one of the basic propositions in a political theory that emphasized descent and might be calculated to appeal to "those gazing with longing at the old order."

Nor did Peter Wentworth's refutation of Parsons please the court.[3] Sure of James's Protestantism, this fiery advocate of parliamentary rights placed himself, ironically, in the position of attacking the Jesuit propagandist for over-exalting Parliament. Parliament to Wentworth is still "the court of most pure and exquisite judgment," but it can not transgress right. Hereditary right is a fundamental principle and is, moreover, conditional upon maintaining God's truth and observing the laws of England. These considerations and not parliamentary election "were the conditions that would validate James of Scotland's succession." The situation is a neat example of the fact that one is concerned with political thought, not political theory, for Wentworth "would have been as pragmatical as Parsons and would have found a way to exclude James" had he not been sure of James's religion.

Wentworth was egregiously guilty of handling vigorously the characteristic but touchy policy of Elizabeth that would dangle the rich prize of England in front of James. In 1594 Wentworth was also in prison for having attempted to stir up the question of succession during the period 1589 to 1593 by a number of projects aimed at moving Elizabeth to read and act upon the good advice of his *Pithie Exhortation,* in which it is interesting to note that he retold the tragic story of Gorboduc.

In this respect, too, it is pertinent to note that Puritans, like the exiled Fenner in 1585, had already marshalled some of the arguments to be found in Parsons' tract but placed them in a context calculated to appeal to those who might become intoxicated by "the divine authority of the Sanhedrin or God's favors to the chosen people." Such a line of thought would lead to premises of popular sovereignty, while emphasizing the essentially official nature of kingship and the congruent right of resistance when the "truth" was not followed.[4]

Consequently upon a lower level than that of the *De Republica Anglorum* and *The Laws of Ecclesiastical Polity* appear precepts that seem to have had a constant valid appeal for any propagandist and that were general enough to be used for a great variety of purposes. Even more revealing of this fact, perhaps, is the process of thought in a "dangerous" treatise that Bancroft and other Anglican divines were anxious to attack in 1593. Bancroft calls it *Obedience* and declares its conclusions "very seditious and rebellious."[5] Although he is speaking the truth, it had been written and published earlier by a Marian exile who was an associate of Burghley's, Smith's, Haddon's, and the elder Sandys'. The author was Bishop Ponet, writer of the Edwardian catechism and former protegé of Cranmer. With Protestants in and Catholics out, with Catholics in and Protestants out, and with Protestants in again, general ideas of the age applicable to rule were grist for any propagandist's mill. In this instance, in direct contrast to their use by Hooker and Smith, they had been used, as they would be used by Catholic polemicists, to stir up dissatisfaction and, it was hoped, rebellion. For that matter, one account of Ponet's activities reports that he had taken part in Wyatt's revolt and had started for the Continent only after he had been unable to persuade Sir Thomas to abandon a gun with a broken carriage in order to continue his advance upon London, where friends were scheduled to meet him at dawn.[6] From a writer of a catechism inculcating obedience to an active rebel might seem a startling move. To Ponet, however, as to Foxe, England in 1554 seemed to be dancing to Philip's, or the Devil's, pipes;[7] and thus it was his voice that in 1556 called upon Englishmen to revolt.

Well-educated, and apparently well-read in political thought, Ponet nevertheless attempted, pretty clearly, to be intelligible and meaningful to those who might be much less well-educated than himself. Both he and those whom he meant to address would be familiar, presumably, with the orthodox tracts calculated to allay seditious thoughts in 1547, one of which was the famous sermon ordained for reading in all parishes, the *Exhortation concerning good Ordre and Obedience to Rulers and Magistrates*. Both he, and his readers perhaps, probably knew Cheke's tract of 1549, directed against the Norfolk rebels lead by Kett. At any rate, Ponet's *A Shorte Treatise of politike pouuer, and of the true Obedience which subiectes owe to kynges and other ciuile Gouernours* (1556) turns back upon the ruler those conventional analogies that treatises on obedience inculcated; and in a similar manner it utilizes the concept that there are three basic and unified laws superior to mundane laws and more binding upon men than any one positive law can possibly be.

Ponet, consequently, emphasizes the idea that members of the English body politic should perform their functions as physical members do when man's body is sound. Thus the head and the body should function as a whole for the good of the whole, but under Mary, the direction of the head, and even the proportion between head and body, is awry. Capitalizing upon the vulgar interest in monstrosities, Ponet accordingly illustrates this last statement by referring to a monstrous birth at Fulham that had a head bigger than it should be. Similarly, he argues that just as the body of man is kept in good order by the sinews, so the body politic is "kept and maintened in good ordre by

Obedience"; but just as the sinews cause great pain to the body when they are shrunk or racked and stretched, so obedience ill used can cause much evil and disorder in the politic body. Too little obedience breeds "a licencious libertie, and maketh the people to forget their duetie," but too much obedience makes rulers forget *their* duty and "usurp vpon their subiectes."[8]

In elucidating his points, Ponet uses examples that are specific and understandable, and he also appeals constantly, like Hooker's "turbulent wits," to any people's desire for prosperity. When, for instance, he writes about supra-national law, he illustrates his point by instancing both the legality and the illegality of a positive law that might prohibit the sale of pins, except for those made in one's own country. If this law kept the people busy, it would be a good law. If the people were well occupied otherwise, however, and if inhabitants of another country lived by pin-making, it would be a wicked and unjust law, for it would be designed to create famine. In the latter instance, both the commandment "Thou shalt not kill" and the Golden Rule would be broken.[9] Consistently, when he discusses or refers to the law of nature and the law of reason, Ponet circumscribes his argument so that he can assert that both of the above laws are summed up in the Golden Rule of the law of God. It is the touchstone to determine whether any positive law be valid and "to trye euery mannes doinges (be he king or beggar) whether they be good or evil."[10] Hooker would emphasize the fallaciousness of such oversimplification, especially when it was used to appeal to the people's interest, but such an appeal is what the educated Ponet, like any propagandist, wants, and his experience with the Edwardian catechism may well have helped him.

As a result, he would have rulers judged by the Golden Rule in matters that constantly tend to become questions of private property, and in the course of such discussions, he may attempt to turn against the "wicked king" the abhorrence with which Anabaptism was usually regarded. Since private property had been established after the Fall by God's express word that man live by the sweat of his brow, as well as by God's commandment not to steal and not to covet—whereby the distinction of things "mine" and "thine" was also established—any community of goods arises after such a distinction and is derived only from the liberality of the giver. When wicked rulers forget this fact, they err more grievously than the Anabaptists. The latter, although they consider other men's goods to be theirs, also consider their goods to be other men's, whereas "euil gouernors and rulers will haue all that their subiectes haue, common to them selues," but to their subjects they "will departe with nothing, but wher they ought not."[10a]

Wicked rulers despoil the people under pretense of doing good, as when they place a great tax and imposition on drink, or they may despoil them by a subtlety like debasing the coinage. They may take the people's property by promising payment or by using "the name of loanes, beneuolences, contribucions, and such like gay paynted wordes." A ruler of this sort may even cite Scripture for his actions, but the citations are false. When he has his subjects' property, moreover, he does not use it ". . . to the benefite and profit of the common wealthe, but on hoores, hooremongers, dyceing, carding, banketting, vniust warres, and such like euilles and mischieues, wherein he delyteth."[11] The conventional basis for this last thought, as it involves the definition of a commonweal, has already been pointed out.

Ponet goes on to say that people may be forced to lend their property through fear of worse consequences, and then the ruler will assemble a Parliament made up of those who loaned nothing, or who are afraid to displease the king. By such a Parliament the debt will be remitted. Because both king and Parliament do not "as they wolde be done vnto," a great number of people are ruined.[12] Such actions are one with other features of tyranny—extreme suspicion that leads to imprisonment, cruelty that tends to racking and burning, ungodliness that leads to swearing and forswearing. Such rulers should be deposed or killed, whether they have come to power by succession, by election, or by usurpation; for their actions show that they completely neglect "the cause why kinges, princes, and other gouernors in common wealthes be made," namely, for "the wealthe of the people."[13] In brief, Ponet obviously hoped to make his tract appeal constantly to what contemporary thought considered a characteristic of the many who were relatively prosperous, namely, their love of plenty and of their purses and their fear of beggary, dejection, and baseness.

The argument in *A Shorte Treatise* returns constantly to what Ponet has represented as the basic reason for all rule, that is, the welfare and wealth of those for whom the ruler assumed responsibility. Thus states originated from God's command given to Noah after the Flood: "He that Sheadeth the bloud of man, his bloud Shal be Shed by man. For man is made after the ymage of God." States exist as the result of a command against a grievous sin hurtful to others; and in accordance with such an origin they make and enforce more laws, although the number and nature of magistrates is left "to the descrecion of the people." From this "descrecion," monarchies, aristocracies, and mixed states came into being; but only for the purpose of a "common wealth" did kings, for example, receive authority from God.[14]

Of course the people should obey rather than disobey and should hold magistrates "in honour and reuerence, according to his [God's] ordinaunce."[15] Similarly, the ruler should be like the sun, and the "princes watch" should be like that planet's movement about the world, beneficent and continual. The resulting passage, by the very force of its conventional nature, reminds one of Elizabeth's speech to the seven score delegates, which will be mentioned below: "The princes watche ought to defende the poore mannes house, his labour the subiectes ease, his diligence the subiectes pleasure, his trouble the subiecttes quietness. And as the sunne never standeth still but continually goeth about the worlde, doing his office: with his heate refreshing and comforting all naturall thinges in the worlde: so ought a good prince to be continually occupied in his ministrie, not seking his owne profit, but the wealthe of those that be committed to his charge."[16]

Ponet also cites Antiochus and Scipio on the heavy duty of pagan rulers and asks how much heavier must be the duty of a Christian ruler, who should demonstrate a heavenly love.[17] Instead of emphasizing the difficult nature of the art of government or the force of any necessity, however, he returns to his definition of the purpose of rule and to his basic intent, arguing that a ruler, when he consistently fails to show an awareness of the Golden Rule, may be deposed.

As Ponet represents it, the nature of a ruler's political power corresponds essentially to that derived from any trust. Just as those who have appointed a proxy or given someone a letter of attorney may revoke the office when it pleases them, so may the body politic revoke the office of a ruler.[18] For proof, one need only to notice that in some states the power of a ruler is greater than in others and that states exist wherein "the people haue not geuen this autoritie to any other" but retain and exercise it themselves. The Israelites changed from a rule by judges to a rule by kings because of the iniquity of the children of Samuel. The Romans changed from kings to consuls because of the tyranny of Tarquin. They also changed from consuls to decemviri and to triumviri, and finally to an imperial state. Yet in these changes the people always preserved and maintained their authority "albeit they altred and chaunged the kinde of gouernement."[19] They realized "by the lawe of nature and their owne reason" that without this basic authority over their governors, the rich and strong would oppress the poor and weak. Just as no ruler of free men (as opposed to servants and bondsmen) can himself be free of all restrictions, so the ruler, however absolute may have been the power delegated to him, is ordained to do good and can not make or dispense with laws that affect the profitableness, let alone the godliness, of the commonweal.

In indifferent matters that effect "a decent ordre" the absolute prince may act as he pleases; but, as Antigonus and Antiochus indicated, without the consent of the people he may have nothing to do with that which might injure the ruled.[20] Country and commonweal are always a degree above any king. Thus Ponet defends the castigation of any ruler by an analogy between the whole and the part. To rid oneself of an incurable member of the body which would otherwise injure and destroy the whole body is a law of nature.[21] It is "no priuate lawe to a fewe or certain people, but common to all." It is "not written in bokes, but graffed in the heartes of men: not made by man, but ordained of God; which we haue not learned, receaued, or redde, but haue taken, sucked, and drawne it out of nature: whereunto we are not taught, but made: not instructed, but reasoned: and (as S. Paul saieth) mannes conscience bearing witnesse of it."[22]

The pagans, endowed with the law of nature and reason only, considered tyrannicide such a worthy action that they gave to its perpetrator great rewards and honored him in song and monument. Even though the tyrant may have been the father of the assassin, the deed was pardoned. From such action "came the name of Nobilitie," and of "this kinde of nobilitie was Hercules, Theseus and suche like."[23] Even the Church of Rome has demonstrated the appropriateness of punishing a ruler by deposing not only emperors but popes as well. Against such a background appear many examples drawn from the Old Testament, particularly "the boke of Iudges," examples that accord with the word, "Let euil be taken out of the middes of the congregacion, that the rest whiche heate of it, maie be afraide, and not entreprise to doo the like." Moses was commanded to hang the princes of the people against the sun. Athaliah was deposed and killed by "the nobilitie and commones" and Jehoash made king. Jehu killed Jezebel and Joram, the "right enheritour of the crowne of Israel." Ahud killed the foreign prince Eglon. Jael killed Sisera. Mattathias killed the Jew that sacrificed as Antiochus commanded and killed the king's officer as well. And so on.[24]

The examples, as the one from *I Maccabees* indicates, are obviously contrived to point as directly as possible to the situation in England. To Ponet, Eglon is Philip, and the fact that both were foreign princes is developed and underlined for readers of *A Shorte Treatise* as a warning of Philip's intentions:

This Eglon vsed the matter so with bribing those Israelites, that for preferrement wold be traitours to their natural countrey, and specially in bringing in a great power of Ammonites and Amalekites (two kinds of people in beggerly pride and filthinesse of life muche like to the common nature of Italianes and Spaniardes) as well to garde his person, as to fortifie the strong holdes and municiones: that by and by seing him self strong ynough with his straungers and Inborne traitours, he brought the countrey and people vnder his subiection by fine force, so that he continued their ordinary Prince and chief ruler xviij. years long.[25]

All ages, in fact, have seen natural and divine law put into effect by this deposition of evil rulers and killing of tyrants. In England, Cardinal Pole—to Ponet, "Carnal Phoole"—had himself cited the depositions of Edward II and Richard II. In Switzerland, Petrus Aloysius, "Pope Paule the thriddes sonne, and duke of Placenza," was killed by his own people because of his evil government and his tyranny. To Ponet, there is, in brief, no need to wonder that no positive law sanctions deposition and tyrannicide; the particular offenses that should be punished are enumerated in the commandments of God.[26]

Ponet considers anyone irrational who says, by analogy with the martyrs, that all should obey a king even though he causes the death of "true ministers and confessoures of Christ." Such a statement amounts to saying that to do good is to resist the ordinance of God. Just as Major before him, Ponet argues that the words of Peter, which such persons may cite, "Seruauntes obeie your masters, although they be froward and churlishe," are applicable only to bondsmen, not to the free men who make up a commonwealth. A statement such as that by John of Salisbury to the effect that tyrants are God's ministers to punish the wicked and chasten the good is to Ponet "great blasphemie," for it makes God the author of evil. Unless justice is executed upon heads of government, a most corrupt and vicious state will result. In other words, Ponet shifts the responsibility for a tyrant from God to the people. It is their failure to act by God's law and resist such a one that results in tyranny, the greatest of evils.[27]

Even more specifically does Ponet apply such principles to England, for sometimes "the state of the policies and common wealthes haue ben disposed and ordained bi God, that the headdes could not (if they wolde) oppresse the other membres." The Spartan state had Ephors to guard the people against the kings. The Romans had tribunes. The Germans, a diet or council between Emperor and people. In France and England, Parliaments were instituted wherein people of all degrees ("all sortes of people") were meant to assemble, and "nothing could be done without the knowladge and consent of all."[28] England, moreover, at one time had a high constable "vnto whose autoritie it perteined" to summon the king before Parliament and other courts "to answer and receaue according to iustice."[29]

Ponet may have taken this last detail from Thomas Starkey's *Dialogue between Cardinal Pole and Thomas Lupset*,[30] but whether or not he utilized that Henrican treatise, the conclusion Ponet is again working toward is obvious. Not simply from the general nature of rule or from the laws of reason and nature, but also from the distinguishing characteristics of the state involved —in England, for example, even more than in some other states —is it lawful to depose an evil ruler and to kill a tyrant. If the absolute prince cannot break godly and natural and positive law, "how muche lesse maie suche gouernours, kinges, and princes to whom the people haue not geuen their autoritie (but they with the people, and the people with them make the lawes) breake them or dispense with them?"[31]

In addition, Ponet plays upon the dangers liable to result from the "policie" of kings, the "arte of subtiltie of princes." A realm must be continually on the watch for this "policie."[32] Particularly must all members of councils and parliaments not neglect their duty or "decaue the people of the trust and confidence, that was put in them." They should consider how one man is punished in this world and the next because he has deceived another poor man about a trivial matter. How much greater punishment will there be for those who have deceived many people on the most important matters and who, moreover, have solicited their office by all possible means.[33]

Both councilors and members of Parliament are reminded of their duty, which the Duke of Norfolk and Lord Windsor forgot, though not so completely as others. When Mary's marriage with Philip was considered in Privy Council, the first doubted that the great promises then made would be performed. When the matter was discussed in Parliament, the other asked "who would be suertie for the perfourmaunce." Long experience in princes' practices had given Norfolk the foresight and wisdom to see "that vnder painted papir, muche mischief was hidde," and nature "suffred not" Lord Windsor "to be vtterly voide" of wisdom. But both lacked courage, magnanimity, and fortitude —again, conventional remedies against Fortune appear. The one hoped to recover what he had lost; the other feared to lose what he had. Obviously those who are "alwayes or ofte at princes platters, or in practicers Palaces" cannot be true protectors of the people for long, and membership in Parliament is too often sought for vainglory or profit.[34] The English Council and Parliament are not like those in Venice, where long experience has taught the Venetians to suspect princes' promises and resist "practicers doinges." There the Senate and officers "dare [not] talke pryuily with an other, nor take rewardes or fees of any forayn Prince."[35]

At any rate, since none can escape responsibility, all Englishmen should beware of this "policie" of kings. England suffered greatly under William the Conqueror, who "spoiled the nobilitie of their goodes and possessiones, made them slaues, and his owne slaues Lordes: and vpon the Commons he put wonderfull taxes and imposiciones." He took from the people their weapons and armor and made a law requiring all to stay within doors after curfew.[36] England will suffer the same under the foreign Philip, the modern Eglon:

Your winges must be dubbed, your fethers must be pulled, your combes must be cut, you must be cleane piked, your substaunce shalbe gotten by littel and littell out of your handes, by taxes and subsidies, by beneuolences and loanes, and so from a litell to more, and from more to more: and at leynght all the marchauntes goodes to be confiscate in Flaunders by an inquistion, and others in England by an open excommunication. And whan ye be ones cleane stripped of your stoare, and thus weakened out of courage, and your harte in your hose, as they saie: than shall your king returne to his welbeloued wife, England, with great pompe and power, and shall compell you (in despight of your hartes) to rendre and deliuer her holly in to his handes.

"Easterlings" will aid Philip, an invasion will take place, and if nothing worse happens, shiploads of Englishmen will be transplanted to slavery in New Spain.[37] Wicked rulers must be disobeyed in any evil thing "be it neuer so litell," or they will at length, like the Turk, be obeyed in all things: "What letteth but that they maie not only sende for mennes goodes, but for their headdes also, as the Turke dothe to his best Bassa, and all his subiectes whan it pleaseth him?"[38]

As it can be seen, like the later Parsons writing about Elizabeth's reign, Ponet would focus hostility upon those around the Tudor ruler. Philip is singled out, but there are others also who can not be excused by Eve's or Adam's or Aaron's excuse and who, unless they repent, are "sure of hell fyre."[39] Ponet constantly plays, however, not upon the "newness" of these individuals' importance but upon English hostility to foreigners.

Finally, he sets up an order of revolt based on England's regiment. Those about Mary are corrupt and vicious. Therefore one should turn to other councilors and to members of Parliament. If they do not defend a realm, then one should complain to some minister of the word of God, who has the power of excommunication.

Such a minister, however, can not be a churchman who disturbs the necessary love between nobles and commons and thereby causes a mutual distrust; so if the remedy of complaining to the clergy is not possible, there are certain examples in the Bible, as Ahud's killing Eglon, to which one may turn. Although it probably can not be maintained out of God's word that any private man may kill a tyrant unless he has some "special inward commaundement," Ponet lists his examples, cited earlier here, of the cutting off of the tyrannical and diseased members in the body politic, in order that they may be the subject of "further debating and iugement" by his readers' "owne conscience, through the holy goost"; for the Holy Ghost had "enrolled" such examples "for our learning." Finally, there is, of course, always penance and prayer, which when invoked by Luther at last took effect on George, Duke of Saxony.[40]

Only by the fact that Ponet adheres to a principle of order in revolt does he avoid a simple advocacy of those "extraordinary warrants" that disturbed Elizabethan England. Certainly he opens the door wide to their being alleged, but the fact that the vast majority of the other maxims from which he develops his arguments were accepted as valid is attested by their appearance and their qualification elsewhere.

Ponet did not live to see a beneficent truth manifested in England as Hooker spoke of it. If we can judge by his official actions under Edward he might well have been amenable to the doctrine of Elizabethan necessity[41] and might not have turned even in a Cartwrightian direction, although his activities in Marian exile would have had to be received by Elizabeth as John Hales advocated in the speech that he wrote for delivery at her coronation.

Although he did not live long enough to see Elizabeth placed upon the throne, some of the basic precepts of a regal English Christianity that Ponet and nearly all propagandists used in advocating the greatest variety of immediate positions were also embodied in the display that greeted Elizabeth as she went through London on the way to her coronation.[42] At that time, from Christmas week of 1558 until January 14, the city of London was "at very great charge" preparing music, speeches, and verses, painting conduits, and erecting "magnificent scaffolds and pageants." The account of that event has been repeated often, but parts of it will bear retelling; for contemporary descriptions show that by those speeches and verses, by the scaffolds and pageants, there were being spelled out in the streets of the metropolis for all to see certain precepts of government directed primarily, not at the body, but at the head of the realm of England.

As Elizabeth proceeded through the streets of her city, the five principal spectacles were so contrived that their devices might build one upon the other. Although interpreters were provided to elucidate the moral of the individual pageants, and although the traditional giants of the city, "Gotmagot the Albione" and "Corineus the Briton," summed up in Latin verses "theffect of all the Pageantes," the chronicler of this royal entry pauses when describing the fourth pageant to comment upon the fact that this one "dependeth of them that went before." The first had shown that Elizabeth came out "of the house of unitie." The second, that she was placed in "a seat of Governement," upheld "with Vertue, to the suppression of Vice." The third, that the eight blessings of Almighty God might well be "applyed unto" her. And now the fourth, by putting "her Grace in remembrance of the state of the Commonweale," expressly indicated that she "cannot but be mercifull and careful for the good government thereof."

This fourth pageant, erected at the Little Conduit, represented two hills, or mountains. The one on the north side was "cragged, barreyn, and stonye"; on it was one tree "all withered and deadde," and under the tree sat "one in homely and rude apparell, crokedlye, and in mourning maner." Over his head was a placard on which were written the words "Ruinosa Respublica" and "A decayed Commonweale." Upon the tree were similar placards detailing the cause of the decay. The first cause was "Want of the feare of God." From it, the rest presumably developed. Not all, however, were represented as arising from the actions of the body politic. Disobedience to rulers, rebellion and unthankfulness in subjects, and civil disagreement are listed as contributing to a decayed commonweal, but so are "Blindnes of Guides," "Briberie of Magistrats," "Flattering of Princes," and "Unmercifulness in Rulers." As it might be expected, the hill on the south side of this pageant, "fayre, freshe, grene, and beawtifull," was in every respect the direct opposite, with placards indicating fear of God, obedient subjects, lovers of the commonweal, a wise prince, learned rulers, virtue rewarded, and vice punished. The moral, revealed by Time and Truth, repeats in a different form the precepts of the second pageant: wherein the "Seate of worthie Governance" was represented as being upheld by Pure Religion, treading upon Superstition and Ignorance; Love of Subjects, treading upon Rebellion and Insolence; Wisdom, treading upon Folly and Vainglory; and Justice, treading upon Adulation and Bribery. In other words, just as Elizabeth had been established in the seat of government by virtue, so she would "sette fast in the same" as long as she embraced it and "helde Vice under foote"; for "if Vice once gotte up the head, it would put the seate of Government in peryle of falling."

The first and third spectacles need not detain us now, for it was in the fifth and last that Elizabeth was told more specifically how those vices of governing could, and should, be suppressed in England. There from the conduit to the north side of Fleet Street was a pageant developed on the theme that Elizabeth was another Deborah, "the judge and restorer of the house of Israel," who was seated on a chair at the top of the pageant. With a meaningful anachronism Deborah was "richlie apparelled in

Parliament robes," and upon either side of her were six persons, "two representing the Nobilitie, two the Clergie, and two the Comminaltye." Thus to achieve a rule both wise and just and thereby gain a loving obedience, to avoid folly, vainglory, bribery, and—twice is it mentioned—adulation and flattery, the Queen was reminded to consult her estates in Parliament; for even though a woman, she might rule as well as Deborah "whych governed Israell in peas the space of xl yeares." Indeed, "it behoved both men and women so ruling to use advice of good counsell."

Spectacles incorporating precepts concerning the conduct of rulers were not an innovation in 1558-59, nor did they stop with the royal entry of Elizabeth; but among other important features of Renaissance pageantry, such oblique advice has frequently been overlooked. Elizabeth herself, nevertheless, understood the purpose of the city of London quite well, as did the people—or at least those who devised the spectacles. For that matter, it is hard to see how the veriest lout on the streets of London from Christmas week to Saturday, January 14, could have missed the point completely. Without a running commentary, however, such as that supplied by the chronicler of the entry, some, if not all, of the pageants might at first sight look very much like the flattery that the ruler was told to avoid.

Consider the third one. It seems to be egregious adulation, applying to "our Soveraigne Lady Quene Elizabeth" the "eight Beatitudes expressed in the v chapter of the Gospel of St. Matthew." When viewing this pageant, however, the Queen, "geving most attentive care, and requiring that the Peoples noyse might be stayde," heard encomium slip into advice—a relationship which Aristotle, for example, had specified.[43]

> Thou hast been viii times blest, O Quene of worthy fame,
> > By mekenes of thy spirite, when care did thee besette,
> By mourning in thy griefe, by mildnes in thy blame,
> > By hunger and by thyrst, and justice couldst none gette.
> By mercy shewed, not felt, by cleanes of thyne harte,
> > By seking peace alwayes, by percecucion wrong.
> Therefore trust thou in God, since he hath helpt thy smart,
> > That as his promis is, so he will make thee strong.

The advice is the barest of generalities, but "the People therby put her Grace in mind" that if she continued in her goodness, she might "hope for the fruit of these promises due unto them that doe exercise themselves in the blessinges."[44] When one considers Hooker's reminder about God's hand supporting Elizabeth and considers also the difficulties she had encountered before ascending the throne, the verses make sense; and when they are placed in their context between the second and the fourth pageants, the advice is somewhat more concrete. If the seat of government is preserved by virtue, the eight blessings "might well by applyed" to Elizabeth, who, it is hoped, will remain strong and will remember the causes for any flourishing commonweal and (by the fifth pageant) avail herself of the "Parliament robes" given this Deborah, that is, of the Nobility, Clergy, and Commons, who would surround her in Parliament and offer the good counsel and the legislative support that the English commonwealth makes available to an English ruler.

For that matter, teaching by praise was recognized in the Renaissance as one of the ways to advise a prince. At the beginning of the next century when Ben Jonson was preparing his courtly entertainments for Elizabeth's successor, he states that all public spectacles either have been, or ought to be, mirrors inculcating doctrine particularly fitting for their audience. In his Entertainments, Masques, and Barriers, he constantly repeated to James or Henry or Charles precepts on the conduct of rulers, but he repeated those precepts in a manner suitable for royalty, and elsewhere he writes that by praising most people he hoped "to have made 'em such." The idea is not original with Jonson; the humanist Vives, for example, says that toward a prince one should act with modesty and respect, in a manner as free from flattery as it is free from insolence, speaking as though "the *Prince* were already furnish'd with the parts hee should have, especially in affairs of State." Erasmus expresses the same idea, as does Guazzo in *La Civil conversatione* and as does Bacon when he says, "Some praises come of good wishes and respects, which is a form due in civility to kings and great persons, *laudando praecipere,* when by telling men what they are, they represent to them what they should be." By "words of silke not iron," as Sir Charles Cornwallis phrased it, should a prince be reminded of his duty.[45] The tradition of advice through praise was a strong one, and can be found in much English pageantry since at least the days of Lydgate, in the many welcomes to rulers, for example, and, later, in the lord mayors' shows.[46]

That there is a history of allegorical instruction *laudando praecipere* need not detain us. Elizabeth was thoroughly aware of it and in 1572, at least, had the precept publicly called to her attention. In that year at Warwick when she was welcomed to the city, a certain Mr. Aglionby, the recorder, was to address her. After pointing out the etymology of the word *panegyric,* he passed on to the reason for such praise in formal orations. Although the commendations so set forth pleased evil princes who heard their "undeservid praises," good princes were made better by such a rehearsal, "being put in mynde of their office and government." When he had ended, Elizabeth accepted a purse with twenty pounds from the bailiff, although she remarked to the bailiff, recorder, and burgesses that such a present was unnecessary, since "a myte of their haunds is as much as a thowsand pounds of some others." She then gave her hand to the bailiff to kiss and called Mr. Aglionby to her. Then, offering her hand to him, she said smiling, "Come hither, little Recorder. It was told me that youe wold be afraid to look upon me, or to speak boldly; but you were not so fraid of me as I was of you; and now I thank you for putting me in mynd of my duety, and that should be in me."[47]

Thirteen years earlier on the way to her coronation, she had exhibited the same perception. The first pageant of Elizabeth's royal entry had represented "the uniting of the two Howses of Lancastre and Yorke." On the lowest level sat Henry VII, enclosed in a red rose, and his queen, Elizabeth of York, enclosed in a white rose. From the two roses sprang two branches "gathered into one," which extended to the second level, where Henry VIII and Anne sat. From them extended one branch to the third level, where "sette one representyng the Queenes most excellent Majestie Elizabeth nowe our moste dradde Soveraigne Ladie, crowned and apparalled as thother Pryncves were." The noise of the people, however, was such that Elizabeth could hardly hear the child "whiche did interprete the said Pageant," and her chariot had come so close to the spectacle that she "coulde not well view the personages"; so she asked to have the matter explained and she moved backward, but even then she saw with difficulty. "But after that her Grace had understode the meaning thereof, she thanked the Citie, praysed the fairenesse of the work, and *promised that she would doe her whole endevour for the continuall preservation of concorde, as the Pageant did emport.*"

After viewing all five pageants, she answered the people as appropriately as she was to answer Mr. Aglionby. While a child richly attired was saying farewell to her and in that farewell repeating "certeine wishes" for the "maintenaunce of Trueth and rooting out of Error," Elizabeth "now and then helde up her handes to heavenwarde, and willed the people to say, Amen. When the childe had ended, she said, 'Be ye well assured I will stande your good Quene.' " Thus she promised the people at large what earlier in the procession she had promised the lord mayor, the recorder, and the aldermen—the representatives of the "Comminalitie of the Citie": "And whereas your request is that I should continue your good Ladie and Quene, be ye ensured, that I will be as good unto you as ever Quene was to her People. No wille in me can lacke, neither doe I trust shall ther lacke any power. And perswade your selves, that for the safetie and quietnes of you all, I will not spare, if need be, to spend my blood. God thanke you all."

Throughout the procession, Elizabeth appeared as the good ruler should appear, "secure in the midst of secure citizens." The people were "wonderfully rauished with the louing answers and gestures of theyr Princesse"; and the Queen was marvellously pleased to see that "which all good Princes have ever desyred," the "so earnest love of subjectes, so evidently declared even to her Grace's owne person, being carried in the middest of them." By "holding up her handes, and merie countenaunce to such as stode farre of, and most tender and gentle language to those that stode nigh," the Queen expressed her thankfulness for the people's good will. "To all that wyshed her Grace well, she gave heartie thankes, and to such as bade God save her Grace, she sayde agayne God save them all, and thanked them with all her heart. . . ."

As a consequence, the religious themes of the royal entry and the emphasis throughout on the "maintenaunce of Trueth and rooting out of Error" certainly seem to reflect something more than the Protestantism of the city; and although the advice given Elizabeth was phrased for the most part in generalities, it is singularly interesting, largely because of the way it had been, and would be, utilized by political writers. The good prince should act justly; the good prince should reward virtue. But to be just and to be able to distinguish between virtue and vice, the prince must avail himself of good counsel; for the peculiar force of flattery is to confuse virtue with vice, particularly as it plays upon vainglory. Through flatterers "the very principle and fountain-head of living" is perverted "inasmuch as they are investing vice with the name of virtue." They are especially dangerous since they have "a good base of operations against us in our self-love," thus he "who is condemned as a lover of the flatterer is very much a self-lover." These precepts of Plutarch were widely known in the Renaissance, and similar sentiments were echoed by moralists like Clichtoveus and Egidio;[48] they were repeated, echoed, and enlarged upon by all concerned with the conduct of princes, by Erasmus, Comines, Castiglione, Machiavelli, Sidney, and by such early Tudor writers as Skelton and Lyndesay. It is not surprising, therefore, that in two of the elaborate pageants, adulation or flattery appears as a major vice of a poor governor. With flattery, how might wisdom result, which, as the second pageant represented it, should trample on folly and vainglory? How might virtue be rewarded and vice punished, as in a flourishing commonweal? Without wisdom, actually and Platonically, there could be no justice; and, of course, to avoid such a calamity the state of England also provided parliamentary robes for her new Deborah. Such a title for Elizabeth was only natural, for running like a major theme through the whole occasion was the assumption that in the Word of God is set out the duty of the monarch to her subjects.

Some public spectacles, although they may reflect precepts in works *de regimine principum,* were pretty clearly contrived by those about a monarch to explain and popularize his policy—as Henry VIII underscored his break with Rome by pageantry in London and upon the Thames.[49] Elizabeth undoubtedly knew what was in store for her at this as at other public appearances. Upon being offered the purse at Warwick in 1572, for example, she turned to Leicester and said, "My Lord, this is contrary to your promise."[50] That remark in itself, however, was extremely adroit, especially when it was followed with words to the effect that many a one could spare a thousand pounds better than the commons could this twenty. There is no need to comment upon Elizabeth's art, but simply because of that, there is no need to question her sincerity. In governing she may well have striven for a major ideal that, among other things, contributed to a religious tolerance which the modern approves but which her contemporaries at times found irritating, especially those "stalworth" but "radical" members of her Commons.[51]

Yet even if the pageantry of 1559, as well as contemporary accounts of it, be viewed as a calculated attempt at queenly popularity, it should indicate what Elizabeth's propagandists realized. The English body politic apparently expected its ruler, like all good rulers, to extend a vigorous and unenvious love downward. It apparently felt strongly that its prince should not act as an absolute monarch, that Elizabeth should not simply demonstrate Erasmus' reciprocal affection but also submit to good advice and recognize the position of Parliament, and that only by such actions could the reign be stable. Viewed as an attempt *laudando praecipere* or as an attempt at popularizing the person of the ruler, for our purposes, such pageantry amounts to much the same thing. It, too, indicates the commonplaces that had a basic appeal and that run through the political thought of the later sixteenth century, whether that thought be developed by the learned and read by the educated or seen and heard by those who derived an education not simply from liturgy and its ancillary matter but also from the streets, the sights, and the news of London.

Of this, Elizabeth herself seems to have been as thoroughly aware at the close of her reign as she was at its beginning. Although her last Parliament was not as troublesome as others, it gained its point, particularly about the abuse of monopolies and privileges. At the final session of December 19, 1601, when the ceremony of the royal assent had taken place and all were ready to leave, Elizabeth rose, and in an extempore speech, letting Parliament know "the grounds and nature of the war" to which it contributed, she revealed incidents in her relations with Spain and the Low Countries, and she expressed her affection for her subjects and her appreciation of their reciprocal love. At the same time, one realizes that, as it has been noted earlier, at least the Londoners who were alert to the winds that blew knew something of what went on in Parliament.

Before your going down at the end of the Parliament, I thought good to deliver unto you certain notes for your observation, that serve aptly for the present time, *to be imparted afterward where you shall come abroad—to this end, that you by me, and other by you, may understand to what prince, and how affected to the good of this estate, you have declared yourselves so loving subjects, and so fully and effectually devoted your unchangeable affection.* For by looking into the course which *I have ever holden, since I began to reign, in governing, both concerning civil and foreign causes, you may more easily discern in what kind of sympathy my care to benefit hath corresponded with your inclination to obey, and my caution with your merit.* . . . My care was ever by *proceeding justly and uprightly to conserve my people's love, which I account a gift of God,* not to be marshalled in the lowest part of my mind, but written in the deepest of my heart, by cause without that alone all other favours were of little price with me, though they were infinite.[52]

Undoubtedly "warmed by the emotion of those about her," Elizabeth continued to a *peroratio,* "written in the calm of her study": "This testimony I would have you carry hence for the world to know: that your Sovereign is more careful of your conservation than of herself, and will daily crave of God that they that wish you best may never wish in vain."[53]

The dedicated devotion of that *peroratio* expressed the sentiment of her Golden Speech, delivered on November 30 to seven or eight score gentlemen who had come from a House of Commons that was grateful for the Queen's actions to do away with the abuses about which they were concerned. For example,

And as I am that person that still yet under God hath delivered you, so I trust, by the almighty power of God, that I shall be His instrument to preserve you from every peril, dishonour, shame, tyranny and oppression; partly by means of your intended helps which we take very acceptably, because it manifesteth the largeness of your good loves and loyalties unto your sovereign.

Of myself I must say this: I never was any greedy, scraping grasper, nor a straight, fast-holding Prince, nor yet a waster. My heart was never set on any worldly goods, but only for my subjects' good. What you bestow on me, I will not hoard it up, but receive it to bestow on you again. Yea, mine own properties I account yours, to be expended for your good. . . . Therefore, render unto them, I beseech you, Mr. Speaker, such thanks as you imagine my heart yieldeth, but my tongue cannot express.

Or witness this passage, unadorned by the rhetorical artifice in which the Queen later clothed her speech:

I do assure you that there is no prince that loves his subjects better, or whose love can countervail our love. There is no jewel, be it of never so rich a price, which I set before this jewel, I mean your love. For I do esteem it more than any treasure or riches. . . . And, though God hath raised me high, yet this I count the glory of my crown, that I have reigned with your loves. This makes me that I do not so much rejoice that God hath made me to be a Queen, as to be a Queen over so thankful a people. Therefore, I have cause to wish nothing more than to content the subject; and that is a duty which I owe. Neither do I desire to live longer days than I may see your prosperity, and that is my only desire.[54]

Throughout her reign, Elizabeth had exhibited the happy ability to say and do the right thing at the right time. Certainly the modern critic is privileged to believe in the sincerity of her art of government and in her desire to show the nation an unenvious love. Although Parliament may not be dramatized, the emotional reaction to concepts that might otherwise be connected with rule for the benefit of the ruled, that were constantly referred to by England's own ruler, and that were specifically connected with discussions of England's institutions and of effective English rule, could certainly be utilized in the theater. Nor need they be used there simply to emphasize only one aspect of the idea that government originated in sin. They might also be used to effect in part a moving play-world showing the actions of rulers who lacked political art, whose love could be "countervailed," who could not, or did not, perform the duty that they owed—who, in brief, had not daily craved of God that they who wished their subjects best would never wish in vain.

# IV

# Sir Philip Sidney

FROM THE PRECEDING discussions emerges a process of thought conventional to the era when men spoke or wrote about states and the problem of rule. Essentially it might be called a Christian Aristotelianism, merged with a relatively few ideas that had been valid throughout the Middle Ages. Although basically simple, it was capable of relatively complex ramifications and capable also of being made applicable to all sorts of immediate events and existing institutions.

Not simply in arguments and pageantry about England's current rule, but also in some of the public but ordinary events of Elizabethan life, might such a process of thought seem valid; for the function in England's polity of her governors did not lead, necessarily, to an emphasis only upon an intellectualized standpattism. England's rulers at times might resolve a catechistical Christianity into the theory that men should trust Providence and recognize the neat equilibrium of goods whereby the poor were blessed with a better chance of heaven and the rich ran a greater risk of hell. But even very minor rulers of England had to do more than control the "rascality" or the many-headed by carrying out such measures as that described by Smith when he speaks of "a newe forbrushing" of the good laws of the realm each summer. As representatives in England's government, they might well be concerned with effecting workable measures that would provide for the poor, from whom might be drawn support of any "hurlyburly innovation"; and an interest in economic and social problems is shown not simply by the vagabond and rogue literature of the age but also by the legislative provisions that culminated in the acts of 1597 and 1601, acts that were not substantially altered until 1824.

In this respect, too, it is interesting to note that as the 1597 legislation was being considered, an anonymous speaker in Commons referred to the eyes of the poor which were upon them as he and his fellow members stood in this place which was "an epitome of the whole realm." Although he might be an advocate of the welfare state and his opponent, Henry Jackman, a disciple of Adam Smith, yet the description of Parliament is an Elizabethan commonplace, and the motive is that of a superior acting with an "unenvious love."[1]

At the same time, as an increasingly commercial and industrial society continued to develop under a money economy, although what would now be called corruption was omnipresent, the rulers of England attempted to foster industries thought beneficial to the country as a whole, though perhaps detrimental to an individual. By such means, at any rate, there might well be developed "citizens" of substance, work for the many, as well as gentlemen and noblemen grateful for benefits bestowed through the court's control of commerce and industry.[2]

In a number of ways, England's rulers seem to have been animated by a desire to effect balances comparable to those apparent in Smith's treatise. Even though citizens might generally be referred to as caring unduly for their purses, this class of the many could effect a balance with the "yeoman artificers" and "labourers." Because of this last group in particular, there existed a fear of the multitude and of anything leading to the instability they might effect through their thoughtless strength—a strength that would make "fat and greasy citizens" with Hooker's "fullest bellies" also anxious to see the many-headed controlled.

Such a fear was considered a wise fear, to be sure, not so much because the many were dangerous when they were left to their own devices (then they could be controlled by a virtuosity in rhetoric or arms), but because they might be led by Hooker's "overly exalted" or "perverse wits," or by ambitious, unsatisfied noblemen. Under a wise and able ruler, however, this potential danger could be controlled, sometimes by a wise bestowal of benefits, sometimes in the manner that Smith mentions when he discusses Star Chamber and cites Henry VIII's effective action, sometimes, perhaps, by that interweaving of ecclesiastical and secular lords which Hooker defended. At any rate, the noble few, theoretically, could also be balanced against one another; and, like gentlemen commoners, they should be watched by a ruler anxious for good servants, but also alert to stamp out any flame before it might become a conflagration.

In such an environment, a gentleman-commoner like Sidney would be expected to show his capabilities in order to get ahead, and even when position and favour were won, he would be expected to persevere in his duty. Elizabeth's Commons certainly gave counsel and advice. So did other writers and speakers, even though they used the vein *laudando praecipere.* Privy councilors, when the occasion warranted, might have to give advice boldly. By the efforts of Parliament and Privy Council, Mary Queen of Scots was finally executed; and in other circumstances, men like Hatton would risk retirement for the sake of outspoken counsel or, like Sidney, accept the fact that a "sweet stream of Sovereign humors" might run against them if they objected to such a proposal as the French match.[3]

In this last circumstance, Sidney's counsel shows concepts and a process of thought already discussed, and comparable matter is elaborated in the *Arcadia* in a manner revealing for our present purpose. As a summary of preceding matter, both Sidney's reasoning about the French match and his *Arcadia* can serve to illustrate doctrine common to the variety of treatises and speeches so far cited and common also to some of the pageantry of the era.

Furthermore, the Ponsonby Quarto of 1590, which presents Sidney's revisions of his *Arcadia* as far as part of the third book, and the 1593 Folio, which gives the rest of the story from the "Old Arcadia," undoubtedly were read by writers and by many literate, if not necessarily learned, Elizabethans.[4] Since some of the stories in that romance built upon familiar political concepts, they might well have caused as many of Shakespeare's contemporaries to meditate or discuss questions of justice and rule as did Smith's short political tract. The *Arcadia* is also valuable here in that, of all Elizabethans, Sidney seemed, and seems, most thoroughly imbued with the private and public virtues that a Renaissance education was meant to inculcate. Quite naturally, his romance both delights and teaches, morally, religiously, and, as his revisions show, politically.[5]

Before instances of Sidney's political thought are examined, however, his Puritanism and his "radical" background need brief attention, for too great an emphasis upon certain features of his life may lead to some confusion about the nature of his thought and about his purpose. Although Sidney's attitude toward rule may seem confusing at times, it is essentially orthodox, just as his Puritanism, like Spenser's, is essentially Anglican and, like Walsingham's, protectively militant.[6] Neither his religious nor his political ideas, for example, lead to any defense of the mixed state, although his emphasis upon the merits of an existing limited monarchy may involve related concepts;[7] and even when it is obvious that Sidney is aware of "radical" Continental developments, his thought seems to be grounded in the English scene.

The immediate point can, perhaps, be represented briefly as follows. Sidney admired William of Orange and he was aware of Huguenot publications. He knew Languet, whose name has been associated with the *Vindiciae contra Tyrannos;* he was a friend of Hotman and a close friend of Du Plessis-Mornay. He also knew Thomas Wilson and Daniel Rogers, who, like Sidney, corresponded with Buchanan when the *De Jure Regni* was published. He married into the Walsingham circle, and like most of Elizabeth's counselors, he knew personally individuals who were unquestionably "radical" and may have been friendly with them. One of Walsingham's brothers-in-law, Robert Beale—possibly the "R. B." who recommended Smith's treatise—was outspoken against the bishops in 1585.[8] Another brother-in-law of Walsingham's was even more notable, or notorious. This was Peter Wentworth, the member of Parliament who built upon the thought of his brother Paul, of Yelverton, and of others concerned with parliamentary freedom of speech and who followed his "questions fearlessly through to the simplicity and clarity" of his great oration in 1576.

Undoubtedly, part of Sidney's environment can be considered

"radical," but English "radicalism" was not the necessary result of an awareness of maxims and doctrine associated usually with Puritans because of developments yet to come in the seventeenth century. It is more than possible that Sidney sometimes parallels the thought of Huguenot writers or of Buchanan because he was an educated Englishman, aware of his country's "ancient customs and usages" and aware also of the Aristotelian process of thought found in the *De Republica Anglorum* and elsewhere. Undoubtedly he also knew such kindred precepts *de regimine principum* as are found in the 1559 spectacle. This is not to deny that radical French treatises or Buchanan's tract may have italicized similar elements in Sidney's own thinking. It simply means that, like Smith and Hooker, Sidney was thoroughly alive to political ideas embodied in the heritage of the late sixteenth century—ideas expressed by militant commoners in Parliament and by all sorts of religious and political propagandists—and that he had been schooled, and was schooling himself, in working with them.

In such a light, rather than simply in the light of French monarchomachial writings, or Sidney's opposition to the French match, or Leicester's concern to support the Netherlands, the *Arcadia* and other political remarks of Sidney should be read. Their background need not exclude such specific considerations; but it should be large enough to allow for what seems to be a conventional approach to analyses of a state—an approach based on potential variations in rule as determined both by the nature of the Aristotelian one, few, and many and by the particular nature or history of the state in question. Certainly part of the corollary to this, whereby relative permanence in any variety of rule may be achieved through disciplined restraint, mutual duties, and, particularly, good counsel, is amplified fully in the *Arcadia*.[9]

In this last respect, another preliminary consideration arises, for Sidney's romance develops a particular aspect of an idea in back of Renaissance education much more fully than anything so far noted here. Constantly it supports the belief that sound discipline upon good parts acquired by gentle blood, when put into action, can solve difficulties and effect progress as successfully as the imperfections of man and the world will allow. Sidney may accept the reality that nothing is more certain than uncertainty, as well as the possibility that at any one time nothing may be more obvious than a lack of virtue; but he also emphasizes, as a valid reality, "vertue" itself, in a sense of the word that includes both goodness and an amoral forceful accomplishment.[10] Such an emphasis, moving from the "humanistic" toward the "aristocratic," makes the political aspects of the *Arcadia* focus upon rule by the one; and in this respect, the romance accords with the characteristic tone of English theories about kingship between the years after Henry's break with Rome and before 1588. In other words, by a glorification of the ruler and the discipline that makes a ruler, its emphasis may seem to move in the direction of Continental thought that affirmed the ruler's absoluteness. But just as such a tendency in England, even during the years of its fullest expression, never was divorced irrevocably from the concepts of natural law, of a ruler's religious discipline, or of the king as an integral part of Parliament,[11] so in Sidney's revised form of the *Arcadia,* the tendency resulting from the central narrative—from Sidney's emphasis upon gentle blood and upon rule by one—is interwoven with ideas that qualify the concept of a ruler's absoluteness; and as Sidney develops those ideas, though they are subordinate to his romantic emphasis, he repeats a process of thought already discussed here and enunciated also in his reasoning about the Anjou match.

An interpretation of Sidney's letter to Elizabeth about the French marriage as being written "because he was ordered to do so, presumably by Leicester," has been dismissed long since. As will be pointed out, basic features of Sidney's thought about the marriage accord with what one finds in the *Arcadia*. In addition, it is very probable that Sidney's concepts were "not easily misunderstood nor easily forgotten by so intelligent a man and so reverential a friend as Greville,"[12] by whom the details of Sidney's reasoning were published.

Similarly, as it has just been noted, one can easily overemphasize the fact that Sidney's view of French history is substantially the one taken by Hotman in the *Francogallia*. It is also substantially the same as that found in Smith's treatise or

Walsingham's notes.¹³ Witness Sidney's censure of the French government as one that has been weakened through "absolutism" and tyranny. Surprising Calais or Rochelle would be beneficial to the French, not only in that it would show "to their hot spirits, and young Councels, that undertaking is not all," but also in that it would demonstrate clearly ". . . how that *once wel-formed Monarchy had by little, and little, let fal her ancient, and reverend pillars, (I mean Parliaments, Lawes, and Customs) into the narrowness of Proclamations or Imperiall Mandates*: by which like bastard children of *tyranny* she hath transformed her Gentry into Peasants, her Peasants into slaves, Magistracy into Sale works, Crown-revenues into Impositions." Such an action would thereby publish "the differences between Monarchs, and Tyrants so clearly to the world, as hereafter all Estates, that would take upon their necks the yoke of Tyranny, must justly be reputed voluntary slaves in the choise of that passive Bondage"; "unlimited *French Grandees*" have "grown up *per saltum* with their *Kings above Laws, Parliaments, and Peoples freedom.*"¹⁴

Eminently suitable as a background for such a statement would be Smith's comments on Louis XI's tyrannical administration, which wrested France from a "lawful and regulate raigne" to an "absolute and tyrannical power and government," as would Smith's constant tendency to equate absolute rule with tyranny. Equally appropriate are Hooker's or Wentworth's definitions of the relationship between law and king and—for Sidney's further argument—Smith's, Hooker's, or Mildmay's definition of the English Parliament.

In contrast with the French government, to Sidney the government of England is "our moderate form of Monarchie," which, if the French prevail, will be metamorphosed "into a precipitate absoluteness." England's rule still exists in "ancient legall Circles," in her "pleas, pulpits, and Parliaments," which are not molded by "Royal Proclamations."¹⁵

Although the immediately preceding phrases are taken from the eighth, seventh, and fifth steps in the disintegration that Sidney believed the French marriage would start, their meaning has not been wrested from that supplied by their context. For

Sidney reasoned that if the match were effected, measures would be taken to undermine religion (the first four steps) and to bring in Catholicism (the eighth step). As a corollary of what precedes and in preparation for the last action, there would be attempts to rule by proclamation, attempts that would stir up almost as much confusion as the confusion of tongues and that would involve decrying England's "ancient Customes and Statutes" (the fifth step). In such an attempt "to secure the old age of Tyranny," the French prince would arouse what all try to avoid, the "danger of popular inundations," a danger "which is never old." This would be particularly likely to succeed inasmuch as there probably would be used "no instruments among the people, but such as devise to sheer them with taxes, ransome them with fines, draw [them] in bondage under colour of obedience" (the sixth step). Without "free spirits, and faithful Patriots," England's monarchy would be taken out of "ancient legall Circles"; for in accordance with the nature of French rulers, the French prince would be forcing the issue, hoping to banish all free and faithful individuals "with a kinde of shaddowed Ostracisme, till the *Ideas* of native freedom should be utterly forgotten." He would become "the head of all discontentedness" and stir the people "up to depose their natural annointed Soveraign" (the seventh step). Should the French marriage take place, then, instead of her "moderate form of Monarchie," England could envisage a Catholic and "precipitate absoluteness" (the eighth step).[16]

The process of Sidney's thought is obviously a familiar one. Although there is no incitation to revolt, steps five through seven are strikingly similar to a basic aspect of Ponet's attack upon Philip. In addition to those comments by Smith, Hooker, Mildmay, or Wentworth which accord with Sidney's references to the English commonweal and current French rule, the precepts about good counsel and true religion devised for the pageantry of Elizabeth's coronation are also congruous. Although the references to France's tyrannical state, as opposed to her former "welformed Monarchy" with its "Parliaments, Lawes, and Customs," undoubtedly parallel current Huguenot thought that would turn definitions of a "lawful and regulate raigne" into polemical weapons, yet the appearance of such ideas, in other and in English contexts, seems to indicate that, as always, a propagandist is here utilizing what is conventional, accepted, and capable of emotional appeal for the immediate purpose of influencing events.

The point can be illustrated further when the name of Languet, one of the Huguenot leaders, appears in the "Old" *Arcadia;* for his song, which is sung by Philisides (Sir Philip Sidney), can also be paralleled in English thought expressed by both radical and orthodox writers.[17] It is concerned with the establishment of rule—with the theoretical origin of government and perhaps with the "old age of Tyranny" in Sidney's sixth step noted above. When the beasts of the field had speech, they requested a king from Jove so that they might avoid faction, but Jove warned them of a possible, unfortunate consequence:

> O beasts, take heed what you of me desire.
> Rulers will think all things made them to please,
> And soone forget the swincke due to their hire.

Although there can be no doubt that Sidney sang such a Languet-like, anti-French verse in his opposition to Anjou, the thought of Jove is also that of Ponet and that of Hooker on the Law of a Commonweal, and the song continues along such lines. To establish the rule that the beasts wish, Jove agrees to grant a part of his celestial fire. What else is necessary must come from the beasts themselves:

> . . . the rest your selves must give,
> That it both seene and felte may with you live.[18]

With such a turn of thought, one cannot fail to be reminded of the doctrine of election with which the bitter enemies Parsons and Wentworth would attempt to stir up the succession question.

As the story continues, the beasts grant their ruler that for eternity none shall speak but he. The results for them are calamitous; for certainly under such an absolutism, whereby proclamations and laws can emanate only from the prince, a commonweal would not be likely to exist for long, as Smith and countless others defined it. In such circumstances, something much worse than faction develops. Man first gets rid of "the nobler beastes," who go to the deserts, where they are forced to prey upon other animals through hunger.

> That craftily he forst them to do ill,
> Which being done he afterwards would kill.

In such a manner, the ruler allied himself with the weaker but more numerous beasts to destroy the powerful few. Although "the common cattell of the fielde" were at first "blith" to see "their foen of greatnes kilde," they suffered in time, for man was no longer content with what his subjects might spare even with pain. He plucked their "plumage" first and then their very flesh.[19] One is reminded not simply of Sidney's letter or of French monarchomachial writing, both Protestant and Catholic, but also of the antecedents of such treatises in earlier centuries, of Ponet's words about the excommunication of righteous ministers of God, or, even more apt, his words about the purposeful malice a ruler may stir up between the few and the many, with the consequent signs of a diseased commonweal: "Yea and that (that is worst of all, and to be lamented of all englishe men) ther is inward grudge, and secret malice betwene the membres, that is, the Nobilitie and Commones. The one hateth and contemneth the other, which is the work of the deuil, and his ministers the popish Prelates and priestes . . . for they knowe, onles such diuision and dissension be fostred and nourished, their kingdome wolde sone lie in the dirte."[20]

As has been indicated, even more appropriate to the English roots of the *Arcadia,* if not necessarily to Sidney's opposition to the Anjou match, would be a gloss to Languet's song drawn from Hooker's discussion of the way in which the "Law of a Commonweal" was discovered. Hooker grants, it will be remembered, that this law may not have appeared immediately, but only after some sort of regiment, as of kingship, had been established and everything else left to the discretion of the ruler. Then, however, "the thing which they [the governed] had devised for a remedy, did indeed but increase the sore which it should have cured"; "to live by one Mans will, became the cause of all Mens misery."[21] The point, it is hoped, needs little elaboration.

In Sidney's song a conventional process of thought again seems to be at work.

As far as the French match is concerned, Sidney's concepts were akin to a conventional attitude about the English state and about French rule that was made applicable to a current political proposal. In his romance, aside from its topicality, Sidney's concepts should probably be related also to ideas frequently enunciated when a commonweal was defined, even in its hypothetical, in what Hooker would call its "secret," beginnings; and such an interpretation of the song agrees with what Sidney writes elsewhere in the *Arcadia* when he speaks of the "sacred name" of a Prince.

References to the nature of princely rule appear in the *Arcadia* in a variety of instances, but most striking perhaps is Sidney's treatment of the question of whether Pyrocles and Musidorus can be judged legally: "For how can any lawes, which are the bonds of all humane societie be observed if the lawe givers, and lawe rulers, bee not helde in an untouched admiration?"[22]

The thesis of the argument is a conventional crux; Sidney resolves it with no reference to the institutions of a particular state, although his conclusions are comparable to Hooker's and comparable also to Wentworth's axiom that the prince is under no man but "under God and under the law because the law maketh him a king." The ruler acts as "God's vicegerant" in executing His will "which is law and justice."[23] Thus Sidney's Euarchus, as his name implies, is more concerned with justice, which to Spenser was a sign of divinity and the remedy against mutability, than he is with the bonds of family:

Bee it so, bee it so, let my graye heares bee layde in the dust with sorrow, let the small remnant of my life, bee to me an inward and outward desolation, and to the world a gazing stock of wretched missery: But never, never, let *sacred rightfulnes* fall. *It is immortal and immortally ought to be preserved.* If rightly I have judged, then rightly I have judged myne own children. Unlesse the name of a child, should have force to change the *never changing justice.* No no *Pyrocles* and *Musidorus* I prefer you much before my life, but I prefer Justice . . . before you. . . .[24]

Justice is the reason for all rule and judgment. As was noted in the first chapter here, it is the special virtue that rulers must effect; its sacredness is directly related to the sacredness of rule and overrides such an aspect of natural law as the bond between father and son.

Romanticizing and elucidating, not rebelling, Sidney also handles the problem with an eye fixed, perhaps, upon arguments concerning the treatment of Mary Queen of Scots; for when the princes refer to their "sacred" name, they also claim immunity by the law of chivalry and by the fact that they are not Arcadians. Although the Scottish Queen was not to be executed until February 8 of the year following Sidney's death, Sidney's answers to these last two points would be partially appropriate to her refuge in England and to the plots against Elizabeth which were centered about Mary since 1568. As regards the law of chivalry, the conduct of the individual determines his treatment: if, for example, he breaks his oath, if he performs acts of hostility without declaring them, courtesy is the "best custom he can claim." Concerning the fact that they are foreigners, if the princes have offended against laws peculiar to Arcadia, they are to be tried by Arcadian laws; for they have no claim on the region by "magistry" or by "alliance to the princely bloud."[25] This last point, of course, would not be applicable to Mary, but since all can know the customs of a country before entering it, if they voluntarily enter and offend by law, they are to be tried by law. Thus the reasons for punishing those of "a sacred name"[26] are drawn from a superior law and from the laws of chivalry and of a nation.

Complementing this treatment of the sacredness of princes, but certainly more difficult to resolve, would be the identical crux applied, not to a foreign prince, but to a native one in his own kingdom. Although Sidney avoids a complete representation of this problem, he does enlarge upon such a situation with matter that is applicable to Arcadia and that could represent some of the premises upon which the judgment of an Arcadian ruler in his native land might have proceeded.

The premises are indicated by one of Philanax' statements and by the second of two questions by Musidorus. Taken together, they point to at least a partial resolution of the crux in other portions of the romance. In the first place, Philanax argues that "the laws of *Arcadia* would not allowe any judgement" of Pamela, "although she her selfe, were to determine nothing, till age or marriage enabled her."[27] By Arcadian law she is, temporarily at least, above the law. Speaking from a more general point of view, which approaches that of the "sacred" position the princes would maintain, Musidorus appeals to the Arcadians by referring to Pamela as the very life of their laws: "Where is that justice, the *Arcadians* were wont to flourish in, whose nature is to render to every one his owne? Will you now keepe the right from your Prince, who is the only gever of judgement, the keye of justice, and life of your lawes?" His next question, nevertheless, implicitly grants to the governed at least the ability to establish the line of their rulers, although Musidorus argues that in the present instance to do so would be not only unjust but also impractical: "Do you hope in a fewe yeares, to set up such another race, which nothing but length of time can establish?"[28]

The force of positive law, here Arcadian, and the derivation of civil power from the ruled, in part at least, are certainly implied, and one is reminded of at least six other situations connected with the institution of a government. In all instances an agreement of some sort exists, or derivation of power from the people is apparent, or the nature of a prince's rule is circumscribed in some way, either with or without specific mention of justice. Taken together, they illustrate one aspect of the way in which Sidney would qualify the sacredness upon which some of the princes' arguments rest.

The Jove of Languet's song, it will be remembered, granted rule to man only in part. The remainder of the right to sovereign power, he said, must emanate from the speaking beasts themselves. It is also granted that the people could prescribe limits of rule when, for example, they appear in a popular government as assembled members of a state; and so Sidney writes when, in arguing for the existence of a Supreme Power, he develops, in passing, a conventional analogy between the macrocosm and society. In answer to Cecropia's "atheism"—that things follow only the course of their own nature—Pamela answers vigorously:

But you will say it is so by nature, as much as if you said it is so, because it is so: if you meane of *many natures conspiring together, as in a popular governement to establish this fayre estate; as if the Elementish and ethereall partes should in their towne-house set downe the boundes of each ones office;* then consider what followes: that there must needes have bene a wisedome which made them concurre: for their natures beying absolute contrarie, in nature rather would have sought each others ruine, then have served as well consorted partes to such an unexpressable harmonie.[29]

Both the context of the passage and the specification of "a popular government" forbid placing too much emphasis upon this argument, but the casual nature of the analogy within the analogy certainly speaks for Sidney's granting validity to a rule that is not monarchial and for the possibility of his granting validity also to the power of assembled estates within a monarchy. This we know to be true from other considerations.[30]

In the *Arcadia* alone, assembled estates establish a government not simply in the circumstances of Languet's song. The procedure there described is validated, for example, by the account of Musidorus' fortunes in Phrygia. At the same time, Sidney also recognizes the fact that allowable "cautions" may be placed upon monarchial rule to keep it from degenerating into tyranny. In that country Musidorus was chosen king by the natives, by both the wise few and the many, who, when their tyrannical ruler had been slain in battle, wished to live under the prince. From this, develops a second situation. Because of his magnanimity and because of his respect for "the bloud Roiall," Musidorus then gave his regal power to "an aged Gentleman" who, though related to the tyrant, was a person "of approved goodnes." In this second transfer of government, although the governed are not mentioned as taking part, Sidney's prince granted rule to the aged relative only under conditions that would deter Phrygian rule from becoming tyrannical. He resigned "all to the noble-man: but with such conditions, and cautions of the conditions, as might assure the people (with asmuch assurance as worldly matters beare) that *not onely that governour, of whom indeed they looked for al good, but the nature of government, should be no way apt to decline to Tyranny.*"[31] The relationship between this second incident, Smith's defense of English rule, and Sidney's objection to the French match are obvious, particularly since the nature of government would be kept by conditions and cautions within lawful and "regulate" bounds.

Possibly because of his familiarity with the *Cyropoedia*, Sidney repeated this Phrygian pattern, and thereby emphasized it. In Pontus, Pyrocles turned the crown over to a sister of the late tyrannical king, for rule had been granted him under the same general circumstances as it had been granted Musidorus in Phrygia.[32]

In the light of these five instances, notice how Euarchus and the Arcadians, when the princes and Pamela are to be tried, enter into a mutual agreement. Euarchus assumes rule "which by free election" has been bestowed upon him. In return for obedience, he will execute justice, but only as protector. He "will not leave any possible culloure, to any of my naturall successors, to make claime to this" kingdom.[33]

In view of these situations, one of Philanax' statements to Philoclea, as well as Sidney's description of the Arcadian estates, seems especially revealing. Although the description may seem to contradict the statement, both may be related to the possible conditions and cautions upon monarchial rule mentioned above. Speaking when the ruler in a monarchy is apparently dead, Philanax tells the Princess that nothing can be done "without all the states of Arcadia"—without apparently an approximation of what Hooker would later consider to be the force of the whole.[34] Yet nothing effective is done by the Arcadians themselves when they do assemble. When they have no king, they are subject to all sorts of fears—of foreign invasion, of civil dissension, of the cruelty of a new prince. They listen to all rumours and are "Altogether like a falling steeple, the partes whereof, as windowes, stones, and pinnacles, were well, but the whole masse ruinous."[35] The "sacred" force of the "gever of judgement, the keye of justice," and the life of the laws is gone.[36]

In this instance, however, Sidney makes it clear that the

consequences just enumerated result not simply from the absence of Basilius but also from the fact that in Arcadia "Publicke matters had ever bene privately governed" and the Arcadians "had no lively taste what was good for themselves." They "had not experience to rule, and had not whome to obeye."[37] In other words, the situation seems to indicate that the instability of the Arcadians, before the force of Euarchus makes itself felt, would have been less had Arcadian rule provided for a greater number of public subaltern rulers.

The point is of more than passing interest. It is inherent, in Sidney's conception and development of the figure of Philanax, and consequently in his entire conception of the actions of Basilius. It accords with a constant element in contemporary political thought, with Smith's, and especially with Hooker's, emphasis upon public authority other than that of the prince alone. It accords with the importance that not simply Mildmay and Wentworth, but also Wentworth's examiners, would give to the distinction between a private person and one who was "a public, and a counsellor to the whole State," that is, a member of the House of Commons. It is not incongruent with a principle adhered to in some revolutionary tracts: with the statement in the *Vindiciae*, for example, that only properly qualified persons should resist a tyrant or with the order of revolt that Ponet would preserve (except *in extremis*). In this last respect, it is particularly interesting to note that the preceding point accords also with some of the "true commonplaces" enunciated by the rebellious Amphialus, though not with his "false application" of them.

Amphialus, quite incorrectly to be sure, had attempted to represent himself as the principal subaltern and to demonstrate that Arcadian rule was approaching tyranny. The reasons for the falseness of his claims and the occasion of his advancing them need not detain us now; the point is that, for Sidney, Amphialus enunciated valid maxims for a false conclusion. His arguments proceed on the following grounds: (1) duty to country is beyond all other duties since it contains all duties; (2) the commonwealth is above any person or magistrate; (3) the "good estate" of thousands did "kindly appertaine to those, who being subalterne magistrates and officers of the crowne, were to be employed as from the Prince, so for the people"; (4) of these persons, Amphialus by blood and by "continuall carefulnes" was especially important; (5) if his proposals seemed strange, "new necessities required new remedies"; (6) the true heirs should be delivered from the danger of Philanax and a "generall assembly of the estates" should determine how best to "match" them; (7) if the Prince opposed this, he should be opposed as he would be if he should "call for poison to hurt himself withall."[38] Thus "with some glosses of probabilitie," Amphialus would "hide indeede the foulenes of his treason; and from true commonplaces, fetch downe most false applications."[39]

Especially the third, the second, and the "generall assembly" in the sixth of these commonplaces, in conjunction with what Sidney writes elsewhere and particularly in the light of his statement about the reason for the Arcadians' great fears and ineffectual actions, seem to indicate that Sidney considered subalterns established publicly in government to be a necessary feature of a commonweal that would weather successfully any great vicissitude. Considering Sidney's own position in life and considering also the positive emphasis of the *Arcadia,* one would expect Sidney to conceive of public subalterns as stable points in effecting a continuously beneficent rule.[40] That Sidney also demonstrates how equivocality, irony, and hypocrisy might arise from their existence, or from arguments about their existence, does not negate such a consideration; it accords with Hooker's attitude, when he indicates how false leaders can always gather a following and have done so in their attack upon the Elizabethan church settlement.

The need for public subalterns, then, seems to explain in part the ineffectiveness of the Arcadians, but to a very appreciable degree the blame for this fact of disorder rests upon Basilius himself. Although no society, not even the Helots in rebellion against the Lacedemonians, can dispense with a prince if there is to be any hope for stability,[41] for a period of time Basilius had not been exercising the forceful virtue of which he was capable, a virtue that had accorded formerly with "the sacred titles of good, just, mercifull, the father of the people, the life of his Countrie."[42] Such a description in the shepherds' eulogy of their apparently dead ruler should have been applicable to Basilius' actions throughout his life, and so Philanax reminded his monarch in the conclusion of his exhortation not to remove the siege: "In sum, you are a Prince, and a father of people, who ought with the eye of wisdom, the hand of fortitude, and the hart of justice to set downe all private conceits, in comparison of what for the publike is profitable."[43]

When what has just been surveyed is considered together, it seems fairly clear that to Sidney the singular wisdom of God provides for a prince's power and titles. They are of the greatest importance because they are concerned with effecting a beneficent virtue, especially justice. They also derive in part from the ruled, who need a regal virtue constantly at work in commonwealth affairs and from whom should be drawn public subalterns as a check upon disorder. That disorder can result not simply from the actions of the many and the few but also from the actions of the one. Sometimes a wise lawgiver will embody in the constitution of a government the safeguards against tyranny. But whether or not that be true, if a ruler does not in his public actions effect as much justice and stability as possible, he is culpable. The resulting disorder may have to be corrected or judged by a publicly recognized and disciplined force devoted to the overriding purpose of all rule. To Sidney the "sacred name" of a prince can not be equated with the sacredness upon which Pyrocles and Musidorus would base one of their arguments. To Sidney, such a name is essentially a merited one. It is not, for example, Bacon's "sacred word" in the *Post-Nati* case.[44]

Obviously such a process of thought might have provided premises for judging an Arcadian ruler in his native land, had that been necessary; and such a process of thought, as the preceding chapters have indicated, is thoroughly conventional. As will be seen, it also agrees with Sidney's portrayals of tyranny and with his entire portrayal of Basilius. So far it has appeared where one might expect it: when Sidney represents the institution of rule (Languet's song; the democratic analogy; the princes in Phrygia and in Pontus, including the second transfer of government in Phrygia) and when he portrays a perilous time in a monarchy under the rule of one who does not exercise his regal force as he should (the supposed death of Basilius, the revolt of Amphialas). In this last situation, political precepts are falsely applied, as they might also be falsely applied in those "seditious" tracts noted in the previous chapter. Yet, in either instance, as maxims, they are "true commonplaces."

In addition to what has just been noted one must realize that as Pyrocles and Musidorus are being judged, the Arcadian state, although in peril and although disintegrating, is in the process of being controlled by Philanax and Euarchus. The present discussion, consequently, must move to Sidney's major emphasis. For throughout the *Arcadia,* Sidney constantly portrays a disciplined and forceful gentility that produces a Christian *virtù* and virtue, the efficacy of which is undoubted, regardless of the circumstances. Even among the Helots, it effected what stability that unfortunate country witnessed, and there the agreement between subjects and "king" had been so violated that even the name of king was hated. From other considerations also, this major emphasis is apparent. In the *Arcadia,* only the "discoursing" rather than the "active" sort of men prefer, from "imagination" rather than from "practise," the Athenian form of government "where the peoples voyce helde the chiefe aucthoritye." In the same context of Arcadian ineffectiveness, Sidney also remarks that some preferred to a monarchy the "Lacedemonian Government of a fewe chosen Senatours."[45] Such a description of Spartan rule may reflect, of course, Sidney's knowledge of Bodin's argument against the existence of mixed states, while the context of both references emphasizes the fact just referred to—that it is the activity of single, disciplined individuals that effects stability. Granted that a monarchy has perilous times and that Arcadia feels "the pangs of uttermost perill (such convulsions never comming, but that the life of government drawes neere his necessary periode),"[46] and granted that any assurance of beneficence and permanence is only "as-much assurance as worldly matters beare,"[47] yet in the optimistic world of the *Arcadia,* Sidney's main portrayals of virtue are triumphant. His overriding political emphasis is upon the lawgiver, upon his approximate representation of those outstanding persons whom Le Roy and others praised when surveying the history of politics and commonweals.[48]

Similarly, Sidney's dominant romantic emphasis is upon the *virtù* and virtue of a Renaissance nobility. To illustrations of its political force, the romance constantly returns; for to Sidney, as well as to his age, such a force might be a constant, determining factor in the affairs of commonweals. Without it, all varieties of rule in the *Arcadia* become ineffective, if not worse. Without it, even members of the estates are ineffective when they assemble as components of the "people" in Jean Boucher's sense of that word.[49] Without it, the many show the most prominent of their conventional attributes, that of a dangerous disorder "which like a violent floud' carries them they knew not whither.

As the immediately preceding quotation indicates, the conventional vices and virtues of the components of a state appear constantly in the *Arcadia*. To consider first those of the many: in circumstances other than the supposed death of Basilius, for example, they are stirred up by the cowardly Clinias, an agent of Cecropia's, and their attitude thereby changes from preserving Basilius' life, to reforming him, to murdering him: "O weak trust of the manyheaded multitude, whom inconstancie onely doth guide to well doing: who can set confidence there, where company takes away shame, and ech man lay the fault of his fellow?"[50]

Hooker and countless of his contemporaries had also pointed out that the danger from a turbulent wit is great, and for Sidney that turbulence results, in this instance again, from an inadequate discipline. Clinias has been a "scholler" "so farre, as to learne rather wordes then maners, and of words rather plentie then order." Having been a tragedian also, he is acquainted with "a slidingnesse of language" and with many passions. He is consequently able "to frame his face to beare the figure" of appropriate emotions, and long used to the eyes and ears of men, he considers "shamefastnesse" alone to be a fault.[51]

At the same time, from even an "unruly set of clowns"—who would be comic in their burlesque of force and wisdom were they not dangerous—there may appear a yeoman-like sturdiness and sententiousness, which can control the many-headed until the force of a Zelmane's rhetoric can operate. Witness the young farmer who aids in silencing the "rascality": "Fie fellowes, fie, (said he) what will all the maides in our towne say, if so many tall men shall be afraide to heare a faire wench? I swear unto you by no little ones, I had rather give my teeme of oxen, then we should shewe our selves so uncivill wights. Besides, I tell you true, I have heard it of old men counted wisdome, to heare much, and say little. His sententious speech so prevailed, that the most parte began to listen."[52]

The saving grace of the many, in other words, is that they can be swayed by a true and not simply by a feigned or a rustic orator; nor is their potentiality for good represented simply in the circumstances of one particular occasion that was ultimately controlled by a sound rhetoric or by the better wisdom of some of the many. The Helots, who had been "freeman and possessioners" before being subjected to misrule and its bestial consequences, once more gain under Pyrocles the status of freemen. They are also to assume some duties in government and some voice in the election of magistrates; their children are to be raised in a Spartan discipline; in brief, they can be expected to take care of their estate since it now is theirs. Although they had been moved by Pyrocles' martial ability and by his authority, rather than by his reason, this prince's rule had "brought up their ignorance, and brought down their furie, to suche a meane of good government" that the successful and honorable terms just enumerated could emerge from warfare.[53] The multitude benefits greatly from a wise "virtue" that would train them in any of their public cares, and like the giants of Phrygia, they can be useful to a wise prince, but when misused by a vicious ruler, a vicious subaltern, or an undisciplined speaker, their danger is made greater through their ignorance.

Although to Sidney the multitude needs control by a manifestation of practical and forceful virtue, so also do the powerful few. In view of what has been indicated already, the conventional nature of such an attitude needs little elaboration, yet Sidney develops it interestingly. If the few gain ascendancy in rule, with theoretical authority residing elsewhere, they have "the power of kinges but not the nature of kings," and thus they may use their "authority as men do their farms" which are held only temporarily. When Euarchus came of age, such a situation had developed in his country. The name of king had become odious by great ones' abuse of regal power; faction and favoritism had developed; the people had no knowledge of where rule resided; in brief, the worst kind of oligarchy existed.[54] Once more, Sidney thereby develops a principle that was conventional well before the days of *Gorboduc,* namely, that the exercise of authority should correspond with its public origin and, ultimately, with its theoretical one as well.

The specific ills that result from this rule by a few Sidney describes as "grievous taxations to serve vaine purposes," laws "made rather to finde faults, then to prevent" them, and a licentious court. The great become increasingly "factious" "by the nature of ambition never satisfied." The underlings become glad to take service under those they hate least, in order to preserve themselves from those they hate most. Men of virtue are suppressed "lest their shining should discover the others filthines." Finally, virtue itself is so forgotten that old men are scornful of reforms and young men are entranced with faultfinding and newfangledness. Change *qua* change is welcome; "marchandise" is abused, towns decayed, offices sold, public defenses neglected; "and in summe, (lest too long I trouble you) all awrie; and (which wried it to the most wrie course of all) witte abused, rather to faine reason why it shoulde be amisse, then how it should be amended."

As both author and audience of the coronation pageant knew, these are signs of a commonweal progressing toward ruin. In such a direction Arcadia also is declining; but there, virtuous subalterns, like Philanax, Kalandar, and Sympathus, still make their force felt. The first two are described specifically as being of the blood royal. Other great men in Arcadia, however, are "looking to make themselves strong by factions." Since "mutuall diffidence" makes them fearful "of their utter destruction," they give ear easily to anything new; for "as they had most to lose," they were "most jealous of their owne case."[55] An extremely ambitious person like Timantus, however, to whom it made little difference how his power was acquired, actually effects his own downfall. The rest turn against him when the chance for quiet occurs, for in Arcadia no such severe measures were needed as when Euarchus made some notable few an example to the rest and thereby established his estate.[56]

In the Arcadian milieu, as has been noticed, Amphialus also appears. He is no Timantus; he is certainly no Philanax. As Basilius is unduly influenced by women, so Amphialus is incited, and even more evilly advised, by his ambitious mother Cecropia. But as his unjust effectiveness could appear only under weak monarchial rule, so his aspiring nobility, linked by blood to the ruling house, is attractive and lamentably sympathetic even in its course of revolt. In many respects, Sidney represents him as admirable, in spite of his calculated appeal to the important, dissatisfied elements of a state.

Other ideas utilized by Sidney in depicting Amphialus' *virtù* and his qualified virtue—which is imperfectly disciplined but disciplined enough to be partially effective—can be illustrated by noticing how Sidney represents Amphialus' valiancy and blood as being effective and admirable in themselves. His vigor, both on seeing a particular enemy and in inaugurating revolt, breeds in many "a coolenesse, to deale violently against him, and a false-minded neutralitie to expect the issue." He is "such a right manlike man, as Nature often erring, yet shewes she would faine make." He is "well beloved" of the people, who "when they sawe him not vanquished, they esteemed him as victorious, his youth setting a flourishing shew upon his worthinesse, and his great nobilitie ennobling his dangers."

Like the commonplaces of Amphialus' letter, however, such worthy attributes are misapplied, although they are less culpable than they might be. His reliance upon the fortress and the "Arte of man" shows a knowing discipline, but an obviously incomplete one; for even though he is "commonly called the courteous *Amphialus*," he is unable to conquer Anaxius, that is, insupportable pride. Of "a melancholie (though I must needes saye courteous and noble) mind," Amphialus retires to be alone with his melancholy after he has killed Parthenia, "labouring onely his wittes to pearce farther and farther into his owne wretchednes."

In other circumstances, he recognizes the evil of his and his mother's actions, and when he is represented at death's door, one of the reasons for the "astonishment" of the beholders is his "person full of worthines."[57] Sidney obviously meant him to be a figure capable of producing admiration and pathos, a youthful figure standing to Musidorus and Pyrocles as the older Basilius stands to Euarchus, a valiant portrait much more virtuous, in the sense of goodness, than the figure of Timantus or Plexirtus, but unable to conquer Anaxius and unfortunate in being linked with an atheistical Cecropia and with weak kingly rule.

A forceful king might have realized, as did Leonatus with Plexirtus, that if wickedness stems from violence of ambition, then one can try to satisfy that ambition by giving it a difficult but honorable task.[58] That Sidney planned a virtuous end for Amphialus after the death of Cecropia is fairly obvious; at any rate, if Fulke Greville is right, he was to marry Helena and leave a worthy line.[59] To the rule of a youthful *virtù*, Amphialus, in brief, appears as Tydeus and Telenos appear to friendship: ". . . men of such prowesse, as not to know feare in themselves, and yet to teach it others that should deale with them: for they had often made their lives triumph over most terrible daungers . . . and truely no more setled in their valure, then disposed to goodnesse and justice, if either they had lighted on a better friend, or could have learned to make friendship a child and not the father of Vertue."[60]

The developing portrait of Amphialus is a notable feature in Sidney's portrayal of a youthful "Heroicall virtue," best illustrated, of course, by Pyrocles and Musidorus. Such a virtue is progressing toward a Platonic ideal that will result from education and discipline in the widest sense of those words and result also from the "good parts" of noble or royal ancestors. To Sidney and to his age, this ideal was as essential as the more experienced, and hence more settled, attributes of good rule.

Just as the relationship between Amphialus and Cecropia and that between Amphialus and Anaxius show the tenuous line between private vices and public ones,[61] so in Sidney's portrayal of rulers, a private vice, and even a natural disposition, may lead to public vice. The Phrygian king's melancholy disposition, his musing of horrible matters, and his suspicion lead to a "tode-like retyrednesse, and closenesse of minde," which, when played upon by sycophants and incited by the fear of a prophecy, results in his letting "nothing passe which might beare the colour of a fault, without sharpe punishment." Having lost the way of nobleness, the king strives "to clime to the height of terriblenes." But by the slight wounding of a soldier, the tyrant's men fight one another and a chain of events is started that leads to revolt, the king's death, and an end of tyrannical rule.[62] Similarly, the inconstant, insensible King of Pontus, in conjunction with a counselor who is the most envious of men, himself causes a successful invasion of his country that results in the revolt of many of his people to Pyrocles and leads to the ruler's death.[63] A third example is provided by the King of Iberia. He is a man "of no wicked nature"; but he has become so subject to his wife, her thwarted lust, and her vicious machinations—whereby she also controls the Parliament of the realm—that his son and true heir escapes death only through the aid of a band of friends and followers.[64]

Also appropriate here is Sidney's portrayal of Antiphilus, who, when he exercises rule, appears in many respects to be similar to the King of Pontus. But in contrast with the description of this last monarch, Sidney makes it clear that Antiphilus' actions result from inability to acquire the necessary requisites of a gentleman. "Obscurely borne," but loved by a Princess, he is "in Nature not able to conceyve the bonds of great matters (suddenly borne into an unknowne Ocean of absolute power)." Swayed "(he knewe not howe) as everie winde of passions puffed him," he is especially subject to "that poysonous sugar of flatterie." Some used that "sugar," "out of the innate basenesse of their hart"; others "secretely hating him, and disdayning his great rising so suddenly, so undeservedly (finding his humour) bent their exalting him only to his overthrow." This innate baseness of a "little mind" is emphasized when he and Eron are captured. She so bears herself that she wins the love of the noble Plangus, while Antiphilus "was readie to fall faster then calamitie could thrust him; with fruitlesse begging (where reason might well assure him his death was resolved) and weake bemoaning his fortune, to give his enemies a most pleasing musique, with manie promises, and protestations, to as little purpose, as from a little mind."[65] The relationship between such a description and Sidney's and his age's emphasis on gentility and blood is obvious; and quite understandably, therefore, it is gentlemen whom Philanax collects to aid Basilius against the rebellious multitude.[66]

With delineations of tyranny hovering about the central situation of Basilius in retirement, Sidney pictures Arcadian rule as being one that leads to revolt, but yet one against which armed opposition is unjust. Such a course of events, as it has already been noticed, results from this king's failure to continue exercising his disciplined rule of the past; and a constant feature in Sidney's delineation of vicious rule is the dangerous conduct most strongly warned against in Elizabeth's coronation pageantry —a heedlessness to good advice and a reliance upon ignorant, flattering, and vicious counselors. In a revealing manner, instead of listening to Philanax, Basilius has the loutish flatterer Dametus at hand, a person guilty of cupidity and himself liable to flattery, but in contrast with the advisor of the King of Pontus, a ridiculous, rather than a vicious, figure.[67] The sum total of Basilius' retirement is that Euarchus pities the Arcadians "who were in worse case then if death had taken away their Prince." Had that happened "their necessitie would have placed some one to the helme: now, a Prince being, and not doing like a Prince, keeping and not exercising the place, they were in so much more evill case, as they coulde not provide for their evill." In other words, a *roi fainéant* is worse than no king at all.[68]

Basilius, in brief, has abjured the art of government. Hence Philanax's question: why has Basilius deprived himself of government for fear of losing government, "for who wil stick to him that abandones himselfe?" In a literal, rather than a figurative sense, Basilius has made himself "another thing from the people." In other words, although the Machiavellian precept might be true in some instances that, for "great persons," "the higher they be, the lesse they should show," yet a ruler should be seen by his subjects and particularly should let them see the benefits of his justice. Basilius by "his retiring back did encourage injuries." When perplexed, "he tooke the common course of men, to flie only then to devotion, when they want resolution."[69] For Basilius such a flying to devotion had been reinforced by his dotage for Zelmane and his being overly affected by his wife Gynecia. In Arcadia the failure to exercise a royal force and goodness corresponds, to a lesser degree, to what occurred in Iberia, when Plangus' father became subject to the sensual mutability of his wife—a thing that happens sometimes when a prince is matched, as Sidney ironically remarks, to "some Heroicall minded Ladie."[70] Sidney has Cecropia, another such lady, enunciate a principle of action that Basilius has neglected: "But I (remembring that in all miseries weeping becomes fooles, and practize wise folks) have tried divers meanes to pull us out of the mire of subjection. And though many times Fortune failed me, yet did I never fail my selfe."[71]

In contrast to Basilius, Euarchus always exercised his power forcefully. Although circumstances at first demanded that he use "some even extreme severitie" to produce a fear of his justice, once this was done, he won his subjects' love by appearing "unto his people, such as he wold have them be." He cared for them "as he woulde for his owne limmes." He never restrained their liberty unless they had "it stretched to licenciousnes." Nor did he take their goods from them without their perceiving that what he had received was "imployed to the purchase of a greater good." All his actions, which showed "a delight to their welfare, broght that to passe, that while by force he tooke nothing, by their love he had all." One might as easily "sette downe the whole Arte of governement" as to depict his proceedings. Like Elizabeth herself, the age recognized such attributes as signs of a good ruler, and their emotional validity is attested even by the reception of Elizabeth's speeches. As far as Euarchus goes, the result is described once in a manner strikingly similar to Smith's description of Parliament or to Hooker's argument about the lawful source of English lawmaking. Euarchus "with his people made all but one politike bodie, whereof himself was the head."[72]

At the same time, with such an emphasis on vigor, Sidney shows that he recognizes the truth of other maxims. Time is "the mother of many mutations,"[73] and to gain time is, consequently, of the greatest value. He is also aware that even the most lasting monarchy may be subject to an end, for in mundane affairs nothing is so sure as a continual instability.[74] Politic matters, in brief, "receave not geometricall certainties."[75] As a result, a related precept was apparently as true for Sidney as it was for Hooker and Smith—that the greatest caution must be exercised in advising "any thing, directly opposite to the forme of . . . present governement," particularly if done "singly without publike alowaunce."[76] Finally, in more than one instance, he bows briefly to the compatible doctrine of "ever-pardonable necessitie,"[77] which can cause actions even by a Euarchus that might appear "a trifle rough."

Throughout the *Arcadia,* Sidney shows great faith in the "Arte of man," for men are "the weapon of weapons, & masterspring (as it were) which makes all the rest to stir." In such an art, stands "the quintessence, & ruling skill of all prosperous governement, either peaceable, or military."[78] But to Sidney, as to Bodin, Hooker, and most writers, such an art must be based on true precepts; and although, in accordance with its milieu, such an art in the *Arcadia* can not be drawn from the law of God or from the models of later governments, it can be drawn from the kindred laws of nature and of reason. In the world of the *Arcadia* certain absolute values hold true, and when the art of government is neglected or used tyrannically, rule tends to destroy itself, the extent of the destruction varying inversely with the probity of the ruler. Musidorus, for example, is to vicious Phrygian rule as Amphialus is to weak Arcadian rule. Thus a fictional optimism results, which Machiavelli would remind his readers did not always agree with the facts of history; but in this instance, the facts are those of literary romance.

Sidney's political thought is strikingly similar to what has been noted in the previous chapters. Although, in accordance with his purpose, his emphases may vary from those of the other writers here considered, such a variation is one of degree rather than of kind. It gives importance to public subaltern rulers rather than to the actual English Parliament, but its basic process of thought is similar to that which in other circumstances seems to underlie even a scale of revolt. As details in both his thinking about the French match and his romance accord with the commonplaces of Smith, Hooker, Ponet, and others, so this general process of Sidney's thought is the same as theirs, especially when he touches upon the nature and the reason for rule, the origins of governments, the "cautions" upon monarchial rule, the conduct of the many and the few, the necessary and animating force of a ruler, the conduct of princes, and the uncertainties, natural vicissitudes, and unavoidable necessities existing in any state. When all of the material so far sketched is considered together, a treatment of political commonplaces emerges which is more complicated, more realistic, more conducive to ironies than that represented by any Elizabethan world-picture of a musically simple order and degree. In the *Arcadia,* for example, as in Elizabethan life, "true" commonplaces could cut both ways, even though Amphialus was unsuccessful. Such a view of the state and of its problems was developed by the learned, read by the educated, and used by propagandists of all sorts. Although aspects of this thought might be developed into such a complex ramification as a Pythagorean theory of cycles, its basic assumptions seem to have been deeply entangled in the emotions of the age; and thus propagandists would utilize them when they dealt with a particular body of facts and argued for conclusions both orthodox and rebellious.

Part Two

Censorship and a Dramatist's Capabilities

# V

# Clinias or Dramatist?

IN VIEW of the nature of what has been sketched in the preceding chapters, it would be surprising if the commonplaces and the process of thought there indicated were not used by some Elizabethan dramatists. They, of course, need not have been concerned with reformation, or with political ventures, or with disputing points of law and custom; but if they wished to make a play-world of high degree convincing and compelling, one would expect them to utilize ideas about the body politic, especially those deeply rooted in the emotions of the age. The nature of a commonweal, the nature of the many and the few, the requirements for kingship, the necessity for good advice, signs of a prosperous or of a ruined commonweal, a movement toward an un-English tyranny that violates the laws of nature, reason, and God could all be grist for a dramatist's mill.

In writing his early history plays, such a complex of ideas seems to have provided Shakespeare, at first or at second hand, with some useful ready-made concepts.[1] Similar ones were used by Marlowe, by the authors of *Woodstock, James IV, Edward III;* and as the reign of James I succeeded that of Elizabeth, Shakespeare would refer to some of the commonplaces noted in previous chapters and also utilize a process of thought that might arise understandably and conventionally in any censurable state.

In *Measure for Measure,* Duke Vincentio neatly enumerates qualifications for a ruler when he speaks to Escalus:

> The nature of our people,
> Our city's institutions, and the terms

> For common justice, you're as pregnant in
> As art and practice hath enriched any
> That we remember.
>
> (I, i, 10-14)[2]

The nature of the ruled, the nature of the government, the propositions to effect justice, the necessity for knowing the art of governing and for having practice therein have appeared constantly in a wide variety of circumstances.

Ruling action should exist, of course, within the framework of mutual duties and a mutual love. Thus it is interesting to note that Angelo's "scope" is as the Duke's:

> So to enforce or qualify the laws
> As to your soul seems good.
>
> (ll. 66-67)

The phrase is applicable not to Sidney's lawgiver but to a ruler who is working, as Hooker's must, within the scope of existing laws framed severely. But severity of action was suited, conventionally, only to unusual situations; and thus the wonder of Claudio moves, also conventionally, in a radical direction when he suffers from the fact that justice is being equated with authority (I, ii, 124-27). Angelo's tyranny may emanate from his person or from the nature of his "place," which is that of an absolute ruler (I, iii, 13):

> And the new deputy now for the Duke—
> Whether it be the fault and glimpse of newness,
> Or whether that the body public be
> A horse whereon the governor doth ride,
> Who, newly in the seat, that it may know
> He can command, lets it straight feel the spur;
> *Whether the tyranny be in his place,*
> *Or in his eminence that fills it up,*
> I stagger in. . . .
>
> (I, ii, 161-69)

Of greater interest than any characteristic of the dramas just noted is the way in which Shakespeare grasps firmly and boldly an unresolved crux in orthodox political thought when he dramatizes the deposition of Richard II. When the one, the few, and the representatives of the many seemed corrupt, Ponet turned to the Golden Rule and a scale of revolt. But in the Elizabethan milieu of the coronation pageant, and with a perpetual contract between ruler and ruled, Hooker apparently could envisage no lasting breach between the English king and his estates, although to the defender of orthodoxy, no less than to the seditious bishop, the name of "king" was essentially a merited one, as it was to Sidney, Smith, and others. Sidney's fiction avoided representing the final judgment of a native ruler. Smith refused to enunciate any dogmatic rule of thumb about the justness of disobedience or changing the rule of a state. The *De Republica Anglorum* referred instead to the judgment of the vulgar and the judgment of the wise, the former considering only the success of resistance, the latter considering the nature of the times and the motives of the doers. All agreed that such action carried with it the greatest of dangers. As a result, since Shakespeare exploits with striking effectiveness the unresolved nature of this crux when circumstances were not as they seemed to Ponet, the treatment of Richard's deposition provides a fitting conclusion to this study.

As the introduction has indicated, by the very fact that Shakespeare was representing a most perilous situation, he ran a different sort of danger. The difference between a treatise by a principal subaltern of England or a romance by a noted gentleman-commoner and a drama by a practicing playwright was great. The treatise or romance would be read in relative privacy; the drama was to be performed before the many-headed. A representation of the vices to which the components of a state were liable might show a conventional process of thought, but in the public theater one might well consider, in Hooker's words, "not so much how small the spark is that flieth up, as how apt things about it, are to take fire." Without censorship, the authorities might argue, one simply could not control either a willful or an unwitting Clinias turned playwright.

Aside from the official censors who perused Elizabethan literature, any audience might include a "politique *Picklocke* of the *Scene*," one whose tribe in the next century was said to infect the theater even when a comedy was being performed.³ Such a one took delight, apparently, in finding veiled references to great persons, and he may have been ready to see and speak about "sedition" in a drama. As *Woodstock* made ridiculously clear, if one wished he could find treason in whistling. Because of delators and censors, then, an Elizabethan dramatist might well have been wary about what he wrote, even though an established acting company under the patronage of an important official probably found censorship by a licenser, or censure by a delator, less fearsome than did some printers and booksellers.

Furthermore, concepts of the nature of history might also seem to make censorship necessary. To Dionysius of Halicarnassus, history was "philosophy teaching by example," and similar ideas must have been familiar to educated Englishmen of the late sixteenth century. Witness comparable remarks in Aristotle's *Politics* or in Cicero's *Epistles*, works firmly embedded in the academic tradition.⁴ The idea that the past might guide the present gave substance to such a title as *Mirror for Magistrates*, and when relatively objectivized and subject to speculative scrutiny, the history of a nation might be conceived of as providing the present with power. Such an idea underlies Bodin's *Method for the Easy Comprehension of History* and reminds one of the concept embodied in Bacon's later definition of "civil history": the study which results when "the utility of historical narratives" is increased by "penetrating political and psychological analyses" and one can formulate inductively principles of civil philosophy. Less ambitious were those historical accounts that Bacon was to call "ruminated"—selected narratives from which might be drawn political reflections.⁵ In brief, the purposefulness of any history was something for which an educated person might search, and thus the purpose of such partially ruminated narratives as those embodied in *The Mirror for Magistrates* might well have seemed to be different from the purpose underlying the performance of a historical drama. As the previous reference to Clinias has indicated, the latter instance might seem very close to those perversions of ruminated history that propagandists would use in their desire to influence events, and such a process of thought might also seem to make censorship necessary or cause the censor to push to the limit the concepts that history might teach and rhetorical teaching might move.

That a theatrical occurrence might fan into new flames a recent fire, that it might cause the reappearance of an objectionable event which would have to be suppressed, has been suggested as an explanation for the trouble of the playwrights with *Sir Thomas More.* That a stage performance might be part of an attempt to set the commonweal on fire seems to underlie the appearance of members of the Lord Chamberlain's Company before the Privy Council to explain a performance of *Richard II* on the eve of Essex' revolt (Feb. 7, 1601). The constant fear of the mob underlies both occurrences, and the additional wise fear that the mob, if aroused, would be controlled by an ambitious nobleman certainly underlies the second. Furthermore, because Elizabeth referred to herself as Richard II, it has sometimes been tempting to give to Shakespeare's play a topical significance.

A further examination of this second occurrence, however, leads one to resist such a temptation. In the first place, Elizabeth's remark undoubtedly arose from the immediate circumstances of Essex' revolt. In the second place, the authorities seem to have been interested primarily in immediate events, as one might expect. And even when they were so interested, as a further consideration will indicate, they may have been willing to grant that an apparent topicality could result simply from the use of political commonplaces conceived to be universally valid.

The nature of the workable commonplaces outlined in the preceding chapters was such that Essex himself could fit easily into a conventional picture of perilous ambition. Thus William Barlow's sermon at Paul's Cross in March, 1601, elaborates the idea that Essex' treason was "the compound of all famous rebellions." In the course of the sermon, an Elizabethan would hear that its "pretence original" was that of Tyler's revolt, but its "pretence final" was that of Lancaster's rising against Richard.

Both Lancaster and Essex pretended to be concerned with "removing certain which misled the king."[6] Certainly it is tempting to relate this "final pretence" to *Richard II,* in view of the performance mentioned above.

Barlow's point of emphasis, however, is not Bolingbroke, but Essex, and Essex' misuse of the accepted idea that a ruler must be surrounded by good counselors. The preacher's discourse arose purposefully from immediate currents set in motion by the particular form of Essex' revolt,[7] and it is those currents which are probably apparent also in Elizabeth's well-known comment to W. Lambarde (August, 1601).[8] That remark she made as she read from "the beginning of King John" through Lambarde's Pandecta of the "rolls, bundells, membranes, and parcells" that were in her Tower. Occasionally asking the meaning of a word, "her Majestie fell upon the reign of King Richard II saying 'I am Richard II. know ye not that?'":

W. L. 'Such a wicked imagination was determined and attempted by a most unkind Gent. the most adorned creature that ever your Majestie made.'

*Her Majestie.* 'He that will forget God, will also forget his benefactors; this tragedy was played 40tie times in open streets and houses.'

So they passed on to the meaning of *praestita,* to a comment about Henry VII, and to the incident of Lord Lumley's giving Elizabeth a picture of Richard II, now kept in the gallery at Westminster.

Lambarde's answer to the Queen's question may reflect Barlow's sermon or the publication of Hayward's history, to be considered below. Barlow's reference may also reflect the publication of this history or simply the cry Essex raised in the streets. It is just possible that the "tragedy"—in this instance a tragic event—which was referred to by the Queen was a general one, illustrating the precept that those who forget God forget all duty, including that due their benefactors. Like Barlow's "final pretence," Elizabeth's answer to Lambarde, as well as her initial question, may also reflect, though with an exaggerated "40tie times," a particular performance of *Richard II.* According to the actor Phillips' testimony, this had been arranged by Sir Gelly Meyrick, a follower of Essex, in consideration of forty shillings more than "ordynary for yt"; and the performance did occur on the eve of the revolt.

Regardless of the possibilities, a point worth making is that comments like those just noted can easily be overemphasized when taken out of their actual context and placed into one essentially literary. Like the commonplaces of polity currently conceived to be valid, such illustrative examples from history as those used by Barlow were utilized constantly for a polemical purpose. About this, there can be little argument. What is sometimes forgotten is that historical examples usually were employed to illustrate commonplaces, which in turn were used to bolster the particular argument of a propagandist, be he orthodox or unorthodox. The situation is quite different from that wherein historical events and current ideas might be used to create a believable play-world. In the first instance, instead of being controlled by any factualness, the events of history usually were referred to as illustrations of simple, and hence flexible, precepts that were being utilized to give force to the argument of the moment. In the Elizabethan House of Commons, for example, the wildest of historical precedents were sometimes alleged for a "custom" that gave form to the application of a "natural" precept.[9] During the months of the Essex trouble, the force of pulpit and officialdom was being used to slow a possibly fearsome rush of events. In such instances, history was of tertiary importance; the precept illustrated took precedence; and current situations, whether they were to be changed or to be preserved, were primary.

In connection with the Essex affair, aside from the actors of *Richard II,* Sir John Hayward was also examined, for he was the author of *The First Part of the Life and Raign of King Henrie the IIII,* a prose treatise that had been entered in the Stationers' Register as far back as January 9, 1599. In contrast with Shakespeare's company, who were acting within ten days of their examination, Hayward was imprisoned and tried twice. The dedication to Essex was cut out of unsold copies of the first edition of his work. The entire second edition was seized and burned. John Wolfe, Hayward's printer, was sharply interrogated and briefly imprisoned; and Samuel Harsnett, who had licensed the work, had a harrowing experience with the authorities.[10]

Although one of the questions the examiners asked Hayward was whether or not he thought his book might be dangerous if it came among the common people,[11] the history itself does not seem to have aroused the suspicions of the examiners as much as its dedication to Essex, even though that preface was in Latin. Apparently the players' testimony about Sir Gelly Meyrick satisfied the authorities as to their innocence. They apparently were not the ones who would know anything about the use of history for an ulterior purpose. But the same, pretty clearly, might not be said for an author whose dedication might seem to indicate his complicity in a rebellious event well before it broke out; further information about an ambitious nobleman's attempt to arouse support might be gained from him. Renaissance censorship in this situation seems to have existed in the area, not of Hayward's history *per se* (from which nothing treasonable could be made),[12] but in the area of Hayward's history, its prefatory matter, and a related event; just as for *Richard II*, it existed not in the area of the practicability of history, or the practicability of precepts in the complex of rule, but in the area of its performance at a particular time. The authorities were interested obviously in immediate events.

To what has been written might well be added some considerations that do not lead necessarily to an emphasis upon the deterring effect of possible censorship or upon the possibility that when a dramatist uses history that was also used by propagandists he was writing with an eye on current events or writing in an admonitory manner directed at individuals of high, or even of the highest, degree. As the preceding chapters have indicated, in the late sixteenth century certain ideas appeared fairly constantly in a process of thought that seemed valid for describing the nature of states and their vicissitudes. Such a complex of ideas resulted from political speculation, or existed for such a purpose, and might or might not draw examples from history. As a result of the way in which such concepts were used, but in accordance with them, or to rectify and qualify some of them,

Bodin wrote his *Methodus;* Smith, his *De Republica Anglorum;* and Hooker, his *Laws of Ecclesiastical Polity.* Any historian, on the other hand, would presumably believe in the practicality of his subject. In still another direction, both precept and history would be used to agitate the contemporary scene. However, there is no necessary, and certainly no intricate, relationship between any one of the preceding emphases and drama.

If there exists a body of doctrine believed by the age to be valid and hence utilized by political agitators like Ponet, Parsons, and Wentworth in an attempt to direct their audience's speculations or arouse their audience's emotions, thus promoting the agitator's concern with manipulating reality, and if such a body of doctrine is also utilized by literary men, it is only sensible to assume that the appearance of common or related matter in both propaganda and drama does not necessarily mean that drama has a point of reference in the contemporary scene similar to that of the agitator's or that it is derived from his propaganda. Any similarity may well be the natural result of the use in drama of a process of thought that the age considered valid and that was developed from an initial conception and for a purpose completely alien to those of the non-dramatic propagandist. That A can exist in conjunction with B for the purpose of influencing C, and that A can exist in conjunction with D, does not mean that A plus D exists for the purpose of influencing C, or because of A plus B. It is certainly conceivable that this A plus D results simply because some playwrights wished to represent as theatrically and convincingly as possible a sequence of events and that, to them, such a theatrical appeal seemed likely to arise when a relationship between incidents and participants was established which would draw upon all sorts of accepted ideas and accepted processes of thought, including political ones.

Still other dramatists might wish to emphasize ideas rather than events and characters, but yet not have a point of view that in any way approached that of the political agitator. To insist upon such a consideration is to do little more than to insist that any work of art has an integrity of its own. The major portion of the following pages elucidates such a point of view in the circumstances of Renaissance censorship.[13]

As is consistently true in all such matters related to Shakespeare, a relatively safe beginning can be made by turning to a non-Shakespearian consideration and to a drama that, in this instance, is of a different sort than Shakespeare's play. Although it was first performed early in the seventeenth century, Samuel Daniel's *Philotas* seems especially apt for our immediate purpose, for its author was called before the Privy Council because of some real or fancied relationship between the play and Essex' revolt. Inasmuch as "the maister of the Revells had p*er*vsed" the drama, Daniel's troubles, like that of the actors of *Richard II*, probably resulted from delation. His examination, at any rate, occurred soon after January 3, 1605, when the Children of the Queen's Revels, presumably, had performed the play.[14]

In his defense, Daniel clearly states his purpose in dramatizing a classical legend that he had found in Plutarch and Quintus Curtius Rufus. Thus, when defense and drama are considered together, one may find some relatively firm ground upon which to proceed in turning to Shakespeare's play. If that ground, in the morass of conjecture about dramatic composition, censorship, and delation, be not as firm as one would wish, it is, nevertheless, broader than anything that can be derived from Phillips' testimony in 1601 (which concerned only a particular performance of *Richard II*), clearer than anything that can be made out of Jonson's comment about his trouble with *Sejanus ca.* 1604, and more extensive than anything connected with the incidental satire on knighthood and the Scots that caused trouble for Jonson, Chapman, and Marston in 1605.[15]

A fair beginning, then, would be to turn to *Philotas*. When that is done, it is immediately noticeable that, although criticism of the play is generally unfavorable, such an opinion usually results from centering one's attention upon Daniel's interlocking portrayals of Philotas and Alexander. If one is to relate the play "seditiously" to the Essex conspiracy, such a focus seems necessary. Certainly Daniel manipulates his sources in at least three major incidents to place Philotas in a relatively favorable light. But he also, especially during the first three acts, portrays Alexander more favorably than do some current traditions concerning that conqueror.[16] The result is a short play wherein

Philotas is represented in a comparatively unsympathetic fashion and Alexander, relatively sympathetically, until the climax of the fourth act. Then the ending of the drama reverses that situation. Philotas is treated with relative sympathy, while Alexander appears in his most unsympathetic light. Even when one allows for the force of the tradition that predicated pathos of a fall, this drama, judged by its characterization, seems unconvincing.

Whether such a view of the play accurately represents Daniel's purpose is debatable. Constantly, details that may seem connected with characterization involve doctrine about conduct in high places, and constantly that doctrine is applicable to both Philotas and others. Although different in kind, the fears of Philotas regarding Alexander's "easie nature" are also the fears of Alexander's counselors.[17] Consider also Philotas' words: illustrious people like himself "roule the stone" of their "owne toyle" and men suppose their "hell, a heauen the while" (II, ii, 642-43). Such a maxim is applicable also to Alexander, as it can be illustrated by his "feare" and sorrow resulting from Philotas' actions (III, i, 952-61). Those words, moreover, anticipate the thought at the end of the drama:

*The which may teach vs to obserue this straine,*
*To admire high hills, but liue within the plaine.*
(V, ii, 2131-32)

Similarly, the end of the fourth act, in conjunction with the fifth, makes it apparent that results tragic for any state occur when any one (be he Alexander or Philotas) extends too far, actually or figuratively, either his rule or his concern for remaining in a ruling position.[18]

In addition, it is quite noticeable that the purpose of speakers other than Philotas is never revealed by soliloquies, only two of which appear in the drama. In the first, Philotas rejects the advice of Chalisthenes as being the unappreciative, "discoursiue" talk of "Book-men" (I, i, 156-69). In the second, although he is talking in "true" maxims, Philotas neglects the conspiracy against the head of the state in his concern over his own "wise" fear of those who would "displace" *his* fortunes (II, ii, 608-43). Even these soliloquies concern immediate situations only, not any underlying ambition Philotas may have had, not any belief he may have entertained about the conspiracy, nor any loyalty he may have felt for Alexander. Otherwise there are no other soliloquies. In general, the sympathetic or unsympathetic nature of a character—impressions that might have been developed by soliloquies—does not seem as important to Daniel as does the doctrinal picture of the difficulties inherent in high place when illustrious persons must act upon valid precepts that can be interpreted equivocally both when a course of action is contemplated and when it is judged.

Certainly, for the purpose of literature appreciable to non-regal and non-aristocratic ages and generations, Daniel has represented neither Philotas nor Alexander with sufficient sympathy or fullness; but one cannot assume that the audience Daniel had in mind was uninterested in ruling conduct *per se*—in the fact, for example, that the bestowal of benefits could be an equivocal good. Elizabeth and Lambarde were not the only ones aware of this aspect of a doctrine connected with the idea of magnificence. With varying emphases, it continually recurred in treatises *de regimine principum,* as well as being apparent in everyday life.[19] The constant use elsewhere of ideas appearing in this drama seems to indicate their validity for Daniel's contemporaries; and equally valid seems to have been the conception that the complexity of true commonplaces was not universally recognized, as Hooker had argued most eloquently. Thus a case can be made out for a serious acceptance of the consideration that Daniel in his *Philotas,* like Greville in his monarchial tragedies, was interested primarily in ideas conventionally related to the complexities of rule. When the play is so read, it can be seen that just as it develops in accordance with academic precepts about structure, so it represents, in a variety of lights, ideas about conduct in high place. That those ideas in their execution are ambiguous, and that the result can be equivocally interpreted, especially by a chorus of the vulgar, seems to be an important aspect of Daniel's purpose. *Philotas* seems to be poor artistry, indeed, only when one assumes that the events and the characters were to the author of primary importance.

In the first place, two of the statements made by Daniel in his defense seem to confirm such a suggestion. He insisted that he chose to dramatize the Philotas story because "it hath a generall alliance to the frailty of greatnesse, and the vsuall workings of ambition, the perpetuall subiects of books and Tragedies."[20] He also pointed out that the first three acts were written "before the Shrouetide" of Essex's revolt and were written with the idea that the play would be presented "in Bath by certaine Gentlemens sonnes, as a priuate recreation for the Christmas."[21] Should one wish, he can, of course, doubt everything in Daniel's defense; but if the modern critic and historian is to consider the play as at least some of Daniel's judges did, such statements point to a thematic, academic purpose. The second statement, especially, is given substance by the Elizabethan "habit of mind fostered by the debate" and nourished on occasions of "priuate recreation" for gentlemen.[22]

A third statement in the defense is undoubtedly true—that Daniel chose the story because of "the aptnesse" he saw "it had to fall easily into act." Although this may seem to be unconnected with the purpose of the drama, a consideration of the narrative structure of *Philotas* leads to conclusions that support what has just been written. Other things being equal, one would expect crucial speeches to occur at points of structural significance and to accord with one another. Thus when one examines the play in some detail, it becomes apparent that although it shows the influence of Garnier and of French Senecanism—as do other plays of the Wilton circle—*Philotas* also shows a development which reflects precepts that during the late sixteenth and throughout the seventeenth century were being progressively disseminated and finding a place even in the grammar-school curriculum. An outline of the drama from such a point of view not only provides a useful résumé of the action but also leads directly into a consideration of Daniel's artistry.

The first two acts introduce the characters and give a handsome "promise" of what is to happen when the complexity of the play will be developed. The choruses of the vulgar will be considered later in a discussion of the way in which Daniel develops contrasting aspects of related ideas.

Act I, scene i: The warning counsel of Chalisthenes is not heeded by Philotas, even though it reinforces advice to Philotas in a letter from his father, Parmenio. Cebalinus reveals the conspiracy against Alexander and is briefly dismissed by Philotas.

Scene ii: Antigona tells the jealous Thais of Philotas' words spoken in heat which refer to Alexander as a "yong-man," words that Thais plans to report to Craterus.

Act II, scene i: Alexander relates to his counselors the ingratitude of Philotas. He has fostered a "home-bent cowardize"; and he has protested Alexander's assuming the title "sonne of *Iupiter*," although he neither knows, nor has he considered, the reason for such a title, which in no way makes Alexander insensible of his human frailty. Ephestion suggests that a withdrawal of Alexander's favor would cause Philotas to "be safe brought in." Alexander and Craterus doubt it; and the latter, having just been told of Philotas' contemptuous words, suggests a close watch upon Philotas' actions and a use of Antigona so that any incipient revolt may be caught in time and hence with safety. Alexander approves, but in view of Parmenio's power and his rule of Media, he insists that it be done carefully.

Scene ii: Cebalinus comes to Philotas a second time to hear what has been done about the conspiracy and complains about Philotas' light treatment of such weighty news. Philotas, however, is concerned with giving a Captain the sum he had promised him, even though Philotas' coffers are empty at the moment. He then speaks in soliloquy about his fear of having lost Alexander's favor and of his refusal to act as basely as his adversaries in order to regain it; but he is confident of being in Alexander's graces simply by his "presence and accesse," whatever his foes may do behind his back.

Scene iii: By threats, Craterus gets from Antigona a promise to confirm Thais' account of Philotas' contemptuous words.

The conventional function of the protasis, that is, an elucidation of the grounds for the argument (Philotas' position and that of Alexander's) and the beginning of the action (wherein II, ii, builds on the last incident of I, i; and II, iii, on that of I, ii), has been effected. In addition, the situation and speeches in II, i, neatly balance those of I, i, and enunciate ideas that had already appeared in the different circumstances of that earlier scene.[23] The focal point of the action that involves the conspiracy proper is represented here by Philotas' lack of interest in the matter, by his concern with attentions to the unnamed Captain who had just visited him, and by his reflections in soliloquy about Alexander's "easie nature."

The play then continues as follows:

Act III, scene i: Alexander receives news of the conspiracy from Metron, and Cebalinus is about to be led to punishment for having delayed three days in telling Alexander of this plot when the delay is explained as having been caused by Philotas. Alexander marvels at such ingratitude but is unable to question Dymnus, for the conspirator stabs himself and dies. When Philotas appears, Alexander tells him of the punishment Cebalinus would have had if he had been guilty of concealing the conspiracy for such a length of time, an offense "which had beene lesse foule in him than thee." Philotas defends himself by explaining that the news seemed to him to be "the brabble of two wanton youthes," which he smothered until some proof might be forthcoming, and asks that he be judged not by this one "ouersight" but by his "actions past." Alexander forgives him and alone with his counselors wonders about the action, but he argues that a guilty conscience cannot "Put on so sure a brow." Craterus argues that clemency should not have been shown so quickly in a matter of such great importance, particularly since Parmenio, ashamed to confess such a great error on Philotas' part, may actually consider the benefit of pardon to be an injury. Perdiccas thinks it unlikely that Philotas would have suppressed the news unless he were a party to the conspiracy, for it cannot be denied that while Philotas has spent "thousands" to advance his own fame, he has failed to say a word to the ruler about this matter of the greatest importance to the state. Craterus points out that although Philotas said he considered the news worthless, he nevertheless did not dismiss Cebalinus; thus he caused the news to be concealed for two days. The scene closes with lines that concern the fears, not of private men, but of kings.

Scene ii: Dialogue between the cynical Thais and Antigona occurs, wherein the latter refuses to become the mistress of Philotas' unspecified "greatest enemy" and vows to remain faithful. The scene closes with her singing "heauy notes of mone."

Scene iii: A council of lords led by Craterus fears the effect on Alexander of Philotas' "cunning straines/Of sweet insinuation" during the forthcoming banquet. They argue that every day lost allows the conspirators an advantage; thus one of those named by Cebalinus must be tortured, and Craterus argues with Clitus that it should be Philotas. The conclusion by Ephestion is that "some course" must be taken at once before Alexander retires.

For convenience of reference, the speeches of the third act have been summarized in more detail than would be necessary for a structural résumé; but it is quite obvious that the epitasis, the "most busie part" of a play, has begun. Equally apparent is the fact that it is to be followed by "the desperate state of the epitasis."

Act IV, scene i: Attaras and Sostratus marvel at the sudden turn in Philotas' fortunes, for he is to be tried before Alexander, who according to "the Macedonian vse," is himself judge in "cases capitall." Attaras recounts the seizure of Philotas at the "blackest houre of darknesse," and Sostratus marvels that the reported deep sleep and composure of Philotas could go with a guilty conscience.

Scene ii: The trial takes place before Alexander, all of his council, Dymnus' body, the revealers of the conspiracy, and the assembled soldiers. Alexander, Nichomachus and Cebalinus speak, with Alexander arguing the case against Philotas but leaving without hearing Philotas' defense. His defense is a stout one, despite the arguments and accusations of Craterus and Ephestion and the vituperation of Belon and Caenus. The soldiers' desire to tear Philotas to pieces is quieted by Alexander's return, who dismisses the court until morning.

In this last scene, obviously, the process of debate, apparent in all of the counsel scenes (II, i; III, i; III, iii), has taken over. The catastrophe then follows. A chorus of Greeks and Persians appears for Act V, scene i; and the first 89 lines of Act V, scene ii, are an account by Polidamas of Alexander's command that he kill Parmenio; thus he who killed Attilus for Alexander must now be killed. These speeches precede the long account by the Nuntius of *"the sad Catastrophe,"* when Philotas, after repeated torture,

> ... *so forgot*
> *Himselfe that now he was more forward to*
> *Confesse, than they to vrge him thereunto,*
> *Whether affliction had his spirits vndone,*
> *Or seeing, to hide or vtter, were all one;*
> *Both wayes lay death: and therefore he would vie*
> *Now to be sure to say enough to die.*
>
> (ll. 2036-42)

The detailed account of the conspiracy then follows as it is given by Quintus Curtius Rufus (with a marginal gloss that gives a reading of the text which is adverse to Philotas).

This obvious structural movement of the play, arising from conventional precepts about the parts of a drama, needs little elaboration. Particularly revealing of Daniel's major emphasis is the debate form of his conclusion to the epitasis, and the constant repetition of ideas, apparent even in the preceding résumé, seems to be thoroughly congruent.

This last point can be illustrated easily. It has been noted already that an idea, expressed as far back as the ending of the protasis, appears at the end of the play. In his worried soliloquy, Philotas spoke of how great ones "roule the stone" of their "owne toyle," "And men suppose our hell, a heauen the while." Quite appropriately, such an anticipation of the complication of the action is given an explicit, but more general and more positive, form in the terse maxim that ends the drama.[24] It is interesting to note, consequently, that another facet of this general maxim had appeared in Philotas' defense during the close of the epitasis, and had been made applicable to the immediate situation being dramatized:

> For oft, by an vntimely diligence,
> A busie faith may giue a Prince offence.
> So that, what shall we do? If we reueale
> We are despis'd; suspected if conceale.
> (IV, ii, 1519-22)

Such a dilemma of high place, from Philotas' point of view, is specified later in the scene and leads to his censure of the "wrath of kings":

> If I must needs be made the sacrifice
> Of enuy, and that no oblation will
> The wrath of Kings, but only blood, suffice,
> Yet let me haue some thing left that is not ill.
> . . . .
> And this is that high grace of Kings we seeke,
> Whose fauour and whose wrath consumes alike.
> (IV, ii, 1683-1720)

This last turn of thought anticipates the more general and more forceful reference to the wrath of kings in the final speeches (V, ii, 2113-24). Not content, however, with the interlocking and purposeful development of such ideas, Daniel reversed the situation in the fourth act by Ephestion's speech. Thereby the specific difficulty of high place that has just been mentioned is represented from the ruler's point of view:

> Lo here the misery of Kings, whose cause
> How euer iust it be, how euer strong,
> Yet in respect they may, their greatnesse drawes
> The world to thinke they couer do the wrong.
>
> (IV, ii, 1721-24)

Here in the *summa epitasis* of the play, and as we shall see in the choruses especially, the author places in juxtaposition different —indeed, antithetical—aspects of one situation and one idea connected with the conduct of rulers.

Such a procedure seems natural for the dramatic representation of accusation and defense, but as in the first scenes of the two acts of the protasis (with discussions of the title "sonne of Iupiter"), the procedure is characteristic of Daniel's artistry throughout. Witness other appearances of the thought of the general maxim that closes the play; just as that maxim is represented by the entire course of the drama, so it is expressed in variously worded "sentences" as different ideas or situations appear that are applicable to rulers and to their immediate and principal subalterns. The difficult relationship between a wise fear and a magnanimous and an "easie nature" appears in Philotas' final scene during the protasis (II, ii); it had appeared in Alexander's scene (II, i), and it is developed fully in the first part of the epitasis (III, i). At the same time, the chorus that bridges protasis and epitasis ends with the sententious statement:

> *It is that height of fortune doth vndoo*
> *Both her owne quietnesse and others too.*
>
> (ll. 750-51)

In this chorus, *"Restlesse ambition"* is specified as the cause of such unquietness (ll. 712-13), but as the speech is developed it is made almost synonymous with high place:

> *For when thou has attaind vnto the top*
> *Of thy desires, thou hast not yet got vp.*
> *That height of fortune either is controld*

*By some more pow'rfull ouerlooking eye,*
*(That doth the fulnesse of thy grace withold)*
*Or counter-checkt with some concurrency.*
*As it doth cost farre more ado to hold*
*The height attain'd, than was to get so hie,*
*Where stand thou canst not, but with carefull toile,*
*Nor loose thy hold without thy vtter spoile.*

(ll. 718-27)

"*Iealousies*" that "*counterplot*" against "*vnder-working pride*" are then spoken of; and although this specific development, as well as the position of the chorus, makes the speech just quoted applicable to Philotas, the idea at the end of the chorus about the height of fortune undoing her own quietness could also be applied, with but very slight change, to Alexander, sorrowing from wise fears, in the first part of the epitasis. Such an idea is also applicable to the Alexander of the first chorus after the epitasis. There he is referred to as the ruler of "*a Campe of Kings*" that "*inter-shocke / Each others greatnesse*" as conquest is extended (V, i).

In the meantime, just as a "*Restless ambition*" was applicable to Philotas in the chorus between protasis and epitasis, so "*ieolousies*" that "*counterplot*" against "*vnder-working pride*" will be applied to the rivals of Philotas during the chorus between the two parts of the epitasis (i.e., between Acts III and IV). This later chorus, which had followed immediately after the council scene dominated by Craterus (III, iii), spoke of "*great men*" who clothe their "*priuate hate*" in the "*faire colours of the publike good*" (ll. 1110-11), and as a result, Philotas' argument in his subsequent defense had been developed briefly:

*. . . no one action shall seeme innocent;*
*Yea, valour, honour, bounty shall be made*
*As accessaries vnto ends vniust. . . .*

(ll. 1117-19)

By the end of this chorus, however, Daniel had effected a partial turn of the idea toward the direction Ephestion is to take when he speaks of "the misery," not the "wrath," of kings. In the chorus, Philotas' kind, and not the preceding *"great men"* with a *"priuate hate,"* had again appeared censurable: *"spirits of worth,"* rather than those of *"meaner skill,"* cause unrest in a state; they are *"aboue"* rather than *"equall to imployment,"* and their *"selfe-opinion"* seems to them wiser than *"present counsels, customes, orders, lawes."* In order to effect a change, such a one

> *The Common-wealth into combustion drawes,*
> *As if ordained t'embroile the world with wit,*
> *As well as grosnesse, to dishonour it.*
>
> (ll. 1145-47)

Such a shifting of the chorus' views here and elsewhere makes one wonder whether Daniel also meant the actual chorus of the vulgar, divided or together, to walk upon the stage in accordance with the direction of the thought expressed in their speeches.

Be that as it may, without opening a window into men's hearts, no sure decision can be made about the censurable and the uncensurable, and such mysteries certainly are not in the possession of a chorus of the vulgar. Thus the portrayal of Craterus can also serve as an example of Daniel's technique, which is indicative, perhaps, of his purpose; for no "window" by soliloquy reveals Craterus' heart, any more than it reveals Alexander's heart or attitudes crucial to the interpretation of the role of Philotas. Only in "The Apology" does one read that Craterus pursued the matter "wisely," that he "is deemed to haue beene one of the most honest men that euer followed *Alexander.*" The apology, however, was not spoken at the performance of the play. Craterus' nature, consequently, is revealed in three ways only. There is a derogatory speech of the cynical Thais that may refer to him (III, ii, 1018-23). There is also the characterization that Alexander gives both him and Ephestion at their first appearance, a characterization that, at the very least, balances directly Thais' words:

> *Ephestion*, thou doest *Alexander* loue
> And *Craterus*, thou the King; yet both you meet
> In one selfe point of loyalty and loue,
> And both I find like careful, like discreet.

Therefore my faithfull'st Counsellors, to you
I must a weighty accident impart. . . .

(II, i, 433-38)

Finally, there are Craterus' words and the words of the chorus. When one turns to Craterus' lines, one encounters once more a repetition of ideas capable of an equivocal interpretation. If his counsel is taken at its face value,[25] it proceeds from a wise fear based upon the assumption that Philotas' greatness has transformed his heart (a possibility first expressed by Chalisthenes to Philotas in Act I, scene i). If so interpreted, his counsel is also based upon the maxim that the body politic suffers usually from *"spirits"* who are *"aboue,"* rather than *"equall,"* to employment (an idea that concludes the chorus within the epitasis, that is, the chorus between Acts III and IV, which follows directly the scene of the counselors). Yet Craterus, apparently, is the chief person referred to by this same chorus when they begin with lines about great men who clothe their private hate in *"faire colours of the publicke good."* Thus Craterus' portrayal remains equivocal, and the chorus, in accord with the attributes of the many, fluctuates strikingly.[26]

At any rate, not as ephemeral literature but as virtuous verse, as honest learning and pleasant counsel, the entire five acts of *Philotas* were addressed in 1605 to Prince Henry; and in view of the present argument, the lines deserve attention. In his play, Daniel says, the young prince

> . . . *may beholde*
> *With what encounters greatest fortunes close,*
> *What dangers, what attempts, what manifolde*
> *Incumbrances ambition vndergoes:*
> *How hardly men digest felicitie;*
> *How to th'intemprate, to the prodigall,*
> *To wantonnesse, and vnto luxurie,*
> *Many things want, but to ambition all.*
> *And you shall finde the greatest enemie*
> *That man can haue, is his prosperitie.*

(ll. 5-14)

Here can be seen how men *"disguise their ends"* and how the vulgar cannot judge. Instead,

> *. . . th'easie multitude*
> *Transported, take the partie of distresse;*
> *And onely out of passion doe conclude,*
> *Not out of iudgement of mens practises, . . .*
>
> (ll. 19-22)

Here too will be seen,

> *How pow'rs are thought to wrong, that wrongs debar,*
> *And Kings not held in danger, though they are.*
>
> (ll. 23-24)

And here will it become apparent that these *"ancient representments of times past"* show how *"men haue, doe, and alwayes runne / The selfe same line of action"* (ll. 25-30).

To the *"most hopefull Prince,"* not as he is, but as he *"may be,"* does Daniel *"giue these lines"* (ll. 1-2). Daniel is making the point made also at the beginning of his play:[27] tragedies of state may be deterred by close attention to words of "Bookmen," other learned counselors, and such poets as Daniel himself, whose purposeful art virtuously arose from such a virtuous age as the *"late Eliza's raigne."*[28]

In view of what has been written, it seems amply clear that if a number of years elapsed between the writing of the first three acts and the last two, Daniel at least carefully knit together his entire play. From late dedication, through protasis, epitasis, and catastrophe, it is of a piece. Actually the play can be interpreted as referring to the Essex conspiracy only if one emphasizes material in the fourth and fifth acts to the exclusion of lines and situations in earlier scenes, and even to the exclusion of doctrine in the latter part of the play. Certainly it is only fair to assume that Daniel's drama should be read in the light of its basic structural movement and the ideas expressed therein, both by the characters and by the chorus. Furthermore, Daniel did defend his play successfully against the information of at least one *"politique Picklocke* of the *Scene,"* and in all probability he defended it upon the grounds that its purpose and artistry were essentially what has been indicated by even such a cursory analysis of the play as the one given here—a purpose and artistry explicitly but briefly expressed in the "Apology," in the lines "To the Reader," and in Daniel's letters to Lord Cranborn (that is, Robert Cecil) and to the Earl of Devonshire.

In brief, if the preceding analysis holds, what has been considered "the serious flaw" of the play need not point to Daniel's interest in Essex. The criticism that "the spectator or reader does not know (as he does, for example, with *Sejanus* or the *Jew of Malta* or Frowde's *Philotas*) where to give his sympathy" is certainly sound,[29] but that feature of the drama need not be explained only by the supposition that the author wished to refer to the Essex case but also wanted to be able to defend his play. It can be explained also by the fact that the drama is of a different type than *Sejanus* or the *Jew of Malta* or Frowde's *Philotas*, by the consideration that it is, and was meant to be, a play of ideas, just as other plays of a similar nature were written by Daniel's associates in the Wilton circle, and just as in Elizabethan political thought simple maxims of state might always be doubtful unless carefully balanced with one another in their application. The basic *desideratum*, once more, is the need for wisdom, especially the detached wisdom of a Chalisthenes.

Fulke Greville, for example, would destroy his *Antony and Cleopatra* (1600-1601) rather than have it misinterpreted by false application, and he would write about his closet dramas that he preferred a "generall scope of profit, before the self-reputation of being an exact Artisan in that Poeticall Mystery." To him, "a perspective into vice, and the unprosperities of it" was "more acceptable to every good Readers ends, then any bare murmur of discontented spirits against their present Government, or horrible periods of exorbitant passions among equals."[30] To him, and apparently to Daniel in this play, ideas seem to have provided the tension necessary for drama; they, and not events or characters, were of primary importance. Especially in such surroundings as that originally envisaged by Daniel might a playwright's audience be interested in the equivocal nature of conventional precepts and in the way in which they could be turned, especially in the process of an oration or a debate, first in one direction and then in another. Such a play might well afford a "perspective into vice" and be designed to be intellectual and speculative only.

From such a point of view, what seems to need explanation is that the Essex affair was uppermost in someone's mind as late as 1604-1605. It has always been easy, however, to apply Essex's story to plays.[31] After all, it did show the course of a perilous treason. Although a Robert Cecil-Craterus application might explain the delator's attitude, perhaps one need look no further than the fact that the closing years of one ruler's reign and the beginning years of another's were conventionally considered to be the time most dangerous for the welfare of a monarchy;[32] and at such a time, delation might have been taken quite seriously, and even encouraged.

As has been mentioned here repeatedly, *Philotas* was defensible. No matter how concerned the authorities may have been in evaluating its occurrence as a relatively isolated phenomenon or as a planned ramification of discontent, they could not grant any playwright the ability to foresee events. In this respect, Daniel's point about the date of writing the first three acts may have seemed a sound one. By reference to the "ordynary" profit, it is a point that the Lord Chamberlain's men may also have made about the composition of *Richard II ca.* 1594-95. Furthermore, some of those examining Daniel probably believed in the idea that he insisted upon—that concepts related to the problem of rule and to the conduct of illustrious persons were universally valid.[33] When Daniel emphasized the frailty of greatness and the perpetual workings of ambition, he also argued, in effect, that our earlier A plus D did not have C as a point of reference; and Robert Cecil, at any rate, was "fully satisfyed."[34]

Although an author would undoubtedly prefer not to undergo such an experience as Daniel's, the fact that a play like *Philotas* could be defended successfully seems important; for it is concerned much less with the ideal of order than with an aspect of the problem of order that arises from the nature of high place and involves the difficult application of sound precepts about the conduct of the one and the few. If, then, one should hesitate to refer to a specific situation in analyzing the purpose of this speculative, debate-like play, one might also hesitate to see any purposeful topicality in a drama that may reflect concepts otherwise applicable to Elizabethan events simply because the English history being dramatized, like the classical history of Philotas, could be interpreted differently even while it showed the perpetual validity of political commonplaces. Nor need a dramatist have had too much trouble with censorship and delation if he were thoughtful and sufficiently skillful. In this instance, at any rate, the authorities seem to have conceded that a dramatist was not a willful Clinias and that he probably was not an unwitting one; for Daniel seems to have been concerned with conflicting aspects of certain ideas, with the conflicting relevance of political commonplaces, and with the conflicting interpretation of events. At least some of the authorities themselves may well have believed his commonplaces to be perpetually valid.

# VI

# Shakespeare's Deposition of Richard II

WHEN ONE TURNS to the plays of Shakespeare that are frequently mentioned in connection with censorship, an easy transition from Daniel's *Philotas* is afforded by the nature of the Essex affair at the turn of the century. Placed in nominal custody during the preceding year, Essex was removed from his offices in June of 1600; and in that year also, the first quarto of *2 Henry IV* was printed. In it some 168 folio-lines in scenes involving the rebels are missing,[1] and in some copies of that text (Q1a), all of Act III, scene i, as well. When, however, the first scene of the third act appears in other copies (Q1b), it agrees closely with the corresponding scene in the folio and refers, among other things, to Richard's deposition. Thus its absence, as well as that of the majority of the other missing lines, has been construed sometimes as resulting from censorship, and it has been suggested that the licenser whose hand may be apparent in these omissions probably was the press-censor rather than anyone connected with the office of the revels.

The longest passage of the eight that are omitted outside of Act III, scene i, is thirty-seven lines devoted to dialogue between Westmoreland and Mowbray (IV, i, 103-39). With this exception, these omissions involve only the speeches given to a single person, and each comprises the major portion of a speech, except for one entire speech of twenty-four lines given to the Archbishop of York (I, iii, 85-108). One passage is four lines long, another is fourteen, and the remainder are only twenty to twenty-five lines in length, the longest again being given to the Archbishop (IV, i, 55-79).

A natural beginning, then, in considering the possible censorship of this quarto, would be to examine the 108 lines that make up Act III, scene i, particularly since one critic has suggested that the censorship of this scene can be understood if one reads the text as it is now printed (i.e., the text of Q1b and F) and mentally substitutes "Essex" for "Northumberland," "Queen" for "King," and "Cecil" for "Warwick." An understanding of the problem, however, involves the nature of the text of Act III, scene i, as it appears on some of the eight pages that distinguish Q1b from Q1a. The circumstances apparently connected with the printing of these pages and the logical inferences therefrom seem particularly revealing.

In the first place, as the gatherings indicate, an insertion, not a deletion, occurred. Except at the end, Qa shows a normal gathering of four leaves (or eight pages) to each signature letter: A-K4, L2. In Qb, instead of leaves E3 and E4, a complete sheet of four leaves appears, and the first three leaves are signed E3, E4, E5; thus the gathering of Qb appears as A-D4, E6, F-K4, L2. The text appearing on E3 and E4 of Qa (the ending of Act II, scene iv, and the beginning of Act III, scene ii) is reproduced with slight variants on the first leaf and the last two leaves of this added sheet. Consequently, on the recto of E3 of Qb and through the first nineteen lines of the verso, the last prose lines of Act II, scene iv (ll. 369-421) are found, and after the last two lines of E5r (a stage direction), the text of E5v-E6v of Qb gives the lines of prose that begin Act III, scene ii (ll. 1-114). The first scene of the third act, then, appears in Qb with line twenty of E3v and runs through line thirty-three of E5r.

The point at issue is when this cancel was made. Since the careful study of Dr. McManaway,[2] there seems to be little doubt that it occurred soon after the printer, Valentine Simmes, finished with Qa and, of course, the corresponding sheets of Qb. Simmes was one of the less prosperous printers and is nowhere listed as having more than one press. He had been in trouble with the authorities frequently, the last time apparently in 1599, and in 1595 he had had his press confiscated and his type melted down. It is fair to assume that when the omission was discovered, if it were to be rectified, Simmes would have had to interrupt the printing of the quarto or defer the printing of sheet E3-E6 until that of L was completed. The latter, simpler alternative seems the more likely, and a comparison of sheet E3-E6 with the others confirms this likelihood and indicates also that a relatively short period of time intervened between the printing of the other sheets and E3-E6.

Such a conclusion results from considering the running titles, the type, the "spelling habits" that appear in the printing, and the paper used. In printing Qa and the corresponding sheets of Qb, only five running titles were needed for the first signature (that is, for the first sheet of eight pages). Thereafter, two sets of four each were used in regular sequence; e.g., that on B1r appears on C1r, D1r, E1r, etc. In the half sheet L, L2 is blank, L1v has no running title, L1r has that which appeared last on K2r (although any one of the others available undoubtedly could have been used). As has been indicated, Qb agrees exactly with Qa in this respect, except for E3-E6. For that sheet, eight entirely new running titles appear. From this, one may infer that the type used in printing the rest of the quarto, including, of course, that used for the two sets of running titles, had been distributed before a compositor set the cancel sheet.

Such an inference accords with the conclusion to be drawn from comparing the text on E3-E6 of Qb with that which also appears on E3-E4 of Qa (the prose lines concluding II, iv, and beginning III, ii). In these two printings of the same text, the very great number of differences in the individual types and in corresponding spaces shows that no part of the original setting of E3 and E4 of Qa was transferred to a different chase and used in printing E3 or E5-E6 of the new sheet in Qb.

The "spelling habits"—spelling, punctuation, mechanical tricks, etc.—that appear in Qa, in the corresponding sheets of Qb, and in sheet E3-E6 indicate that the compositor of Qa, and the corresponding sheets of Qb, also set the cancel sheet. Among various considerations, the following are typical and perhaps the most noticeable. Although the use of parentheses is a fea-

## SHAKESPEARE'S DEPOSITION OF RICHARD II 149

ture of "theatrical" punctuation in general, this compositor shows a fondness for them, not only in treating run-over lines, but also in substituting them four times for commas in the reset text. He also shows a marked preference for lower case type in setting marginal stage directions and for initial capitals in setting centered ones.

Finally, the paper used for Qa seems to have been a job lot of seven or more varieties, at least one with no watermark. Three watermarks can be fairly well identified, however, as distinguishing paper made in 1599 and 1600. Thus it is very much to the point that the paper of the cancel sheet in copies of Qb seems to be the same.

Consequently, the cancel sheet E3-E6, which distinguishes Qb from Qa, seems to have been printed soon after the rest of the sheets and to have been set by the compositor who set the rest of the first quarto. That is, although the type used had been distributed, both the cancel sheet and the other sheets probably were set by some one with distinctive "spelling habits" when a supply was still available of "a single variety of paper closely resembling, or identical with, some of that used in Qa."

In view of such positive evidence, a number of explanations which have been offered for the omission of Act III, scene i, now seem improbable. Although there is no need to review all of them here, a few should be mentioned in that they call attention to features of the printing, and of the text involved, that have not been mentioned so far. Pollard, for example, would explain the omission as a printing house error; for he called attention to what appeared to be the alternating appearance, in runs of three pages, of italic and of mixed roman and italic type. Since a triplet of printed pages would equal 108 lines (3 x 36), and since the 54 lines to a page of the Shakespearean portion of *Sir Thomas More* equal 108 lines to a leaf, the alternating triplets suggested to him that in printing Qa "there was one compositor whose box was well supplied with italics and another who was running short of them." These two compositors, in dividing the manuscript leaf by leaf, might well have lost, or overlooked, one which contained the lines, slightly over a hundred, of the text of Act III, scene i. Aside from the evidence noted above that indicates only one compositor at work, the explanation of alternating triplets may well be that a shortage of italics normally occurred in any three pages when the text of the preceding pages demanded an abnormal number of italics. Indeed, this is what seems to have happened, and its occurrence also agrees with what is known of Simmes's none too opulent establishment in 1600.

The correspondence between the length of Act III, scene i, and the probable number of lines to a leaf of manuscript, however, has been noted also by Professor J. Dover Wilson, who consequently suggests that a single leaf was accidentally left behind at the playhouse; thus it was not seen by the licenser. The latter part of his suggestion involves a situation and inferences therefrom that are difficult to envisage; but the first part is certainly tenable, particularly if the copy given Simmes were foul papers (as seems likely from other considerations) and perhaps not stitched as a promptbook. In such circumstances, a manuscript sheet might well be overlooked, or lost, and its absence not noted until E of Qa, at least, had been printed, but most likely, not until the type for the printing of A-L had been distributed. At that time, the missing scene might be supplied from the overlooked leaf or from the promptbook. Although the possible inference from its length certainly should be kept in mind, whatever may have caused the omission of the scene has generally been connected, however, with the other missing lines. It is this consideration that militates against the last suggestion, which would disconnect the omission of Act III, scene i—a Lancastrian manuscript leaf (a pro-Henry interpretation of Richard's deposition)—from the rest of the omissions.

For each of the other passages, the omission of which affects either the sense or the continuity of the drama, an Elizabethan book-censor's possible objections have been advanced by Professor Hart.[3] Although his explanation of objections to Act III, scene i, and of its subsequent appearance does not stand up, his basic position is revealed by his suggestion that E3-E6 could have been inserted "several years" after 1600, when the events that made the censor of books suspicious had receded from memory. Although this emphasis upon current events is certainly sound, what has just been noted—that the cancel sheet in all probability was printed very soon after the printing of the other sheets—diminishes the likelihood of his suggestion that in 1600 suspicion would result if one mentally substituted "Queen" for "King," "Cecil" for "Warwick," and "Essex" for "Northumberland" in reading the text of Act III, scene i.[4] Since it has been made, however, it is worth noting that such a picklocking tendency proceeds on the assumption of the present ruler's being equated with a past ruler, regardless of what happens to be the past ruler's name; and this, of course, seems to accord with Barlow's, Lambarde's, and Elizabeth's turn of thought in the particular circumstance of a *Richard II* performance plus revolt. It is also worth noting, nevertheless, that if such a substitution and such a tendency were likely in 1600, or relatively soon thereafter, they were not feared by whoever caused the insertion of the cancel sheet.

Of course, the scene beginning the third act, or some comparable scene representing King Henry, might have been censored and then revised in the form in which it is printed. Why the printing of the quarto would proceed in the meantime is a fair inferential question.

Why Simmes failed to advertise the insertion, which must have been of considerable expense to one in his circumstances, is also a fair question; and this failure to note the insertion, taken in conjunction with all of the omissions, points to the major alternative of self-censorship by author, actor, publisher, or printer and, more particularly, to "timidity" on the part of publisher and printer only—a possibility that accords with Simmes's earlier troubles with the authorities. Such an explanation also has the advantage of providing an interested person to procure the correction by a cancel sheet of the major omission, while allowing the much smaller omissions, if indeed they were noticed, to stand because their correction would involve for printer or publishers a greater expense and many more difficulties by far than did the cancel. In other words, "if the printer or publishers did not voluntarily prepare the cancel, it is at least possible that Shakespeare or a representative of the Lord Chamberlain's

Men," upon seeing what Simmes had printed, effected the insertion of sheet E3-E6; and "it is as likely that the publishers omitted" the scene and the other speeches "through timidity as that the censor forbade" their publication.[5]

In all of the preceding possibilities one conclusion seems inescapable, although it has received little, if any, consideration. Whether censored and rewritten, accidentally misplaced in theater or printing house, omitted through self-censorship and timidity, in all probability Act III, scene i, of *2 Henry IV* was inserted soon after the printing of the other sheets; hence its political implications, if any, were apparently considered thoroughly defensible.

It is just possible that a portion of the scene could be specified as an answer to possible censorship or fear of censorship. One speech enunciates a general concept, considered valid by the educated, which, although not identical, is akin to an idea Daniel was to insist upon in his defense of *Philotas*:

> *War.* There is a history in all men's lives,
> Figuring the nature of the times deceas'd;
> The which observ'd, a man may prophesy,
> With a near aim, of the main chance of things
> As yet not come to life, which in their seeds
> And weak beginnings lie intreasured.
> Such things become the hatch and brood of time;
> And by the necessary form of this
> King Richard might create a perfect guess
> That great Northumberland, then false to him,
> Would of that seed grow to a greater falseness,
> Which should not find a ground to root upon
> Unless on you.
> *King.* Are these things then necessities?
> Then let us meet them like necessities.
>
> (III, i, 80-93)

Although phrased so that it agrees with its immediate context, the thought expressed in the preceding lines can be construed as a particular expression of the general concept that history may provide a mirror for the present, a concept also reflected in the letter Daniel wrote to Cecil. *Philotas* was based on the "storie" and "the vniuersall notions of the affayres of men, w$^c$ in all ages beare the same resemblances, and are measured by one and the same foote of vnderstanding." "No tyme but brought forth the like concurrencies, the like interstriuing for place and dignitie, the like supplantations, rysings & overthrowes, so y$^t$ there is nothing new vnder the Sunne. . . ."[6]

In striking contrast with Daniel's defense, Shakespeare's lines are an integral part of the play. Indeed the probability connected with the printing of Act III, scene i—as well as the majority of the preceding possibilities—assumes that the scene as it appears in Qb had been there for performance since its composition *ca.* 1597-98. Thus the scene apparently caused no trouble either before or after its publication. One great advantage of Shakespeare's lines over Daniel's defense, then, might well have been that they would be performed in the theater, and thus they might negate on the spot any objections forming in the mind of a potential informer whose critical picklocking or attention was not entirely lulled by the poetry and characterization of the scene.

In the performance of that scene, after a dramatic and poetic representation of the cares of kingship had been seen and heard, an impersonal, physical change and recurrence would be specified of "the book of fate." Such a turn of thought introduces the brief somber example of a youth viewing both the past and the future of his life. It is then that the reference to Richard's deposition occurs: ten years ago Richard and Northumberland were "great friends," two years after they were "at wars"; eight years ago Northumberland was the man "nearest" Henry's "soul," and Richard's forceful censure of Northumberland, with only implicit censure of Henry, is quoted. It is followed immediately by Henry's denial of ambition and his reference to a "necessity" that "bow'd the state" so that he and "greatness were compell'd to kiss." The lyrically somber note is continued in Warwick's speech, and the concept of change is widened again by a consideration made applicable to the affairs of states and capable of being called a repetitive change when applied to the king's references to recent history. In such a manner, Warwick's lines quoted above fill out the context of the historical allusion, a context also involving the concept of necessity and completed by Henry's words,

> Are these things then necessities?
> Then let us meet them like necessities.
> (ll. 92-93)

Although the impersonal change of mountains, continent, and ocean is not referred to again, in the final lyrical development of this wide "revolution of the times" (l. 46) even the idea of recurring change in history appears as but one manifestation of

> ... the main chance of things
> As yet not come to life, which in their seeds
> And weak beginnings lie intreasured.
> Such things become the hatch and brood of time....
> (ll. 83-86)

The phraseology, though not the idea, is akin to that which Shakespeare was to use when he drew upon a Christian tradition about origins, nature, and creation in the writing of *Lear* and, particularly, of *Macbeth*.[7] Here, however, necessity and the king's health break in to close the scene and the beginning of the epitasis of the play. For the current weight, given conventionally and in an entirely orthodox manner, to a cyclical change, the mutability of men's wits, and their relationship to "necessity," one needs only to remember Smith and Hooker.

Also in contrast to Daniel's *Philotas* is the fact that the ideas in Shakespeare's scene are connotative rather than argumentative. In addition, they support the portrayal of weary king and comforting but wise counselor. In the momentary world of the theater, any speculation evoked by such lines and their play of ideas would have been turned not simply to the deposition of Richard but also to an impersonal regard of change and vicissitude that includes a physical world, as well as a historical one, and embraces "the hatch and brood" of time itself. Such a connotative process is followed immediately by an emphasis and an action (ll. 92-108) congruent with the idea that "these unseason'd hours perforce must add" to the king's illness (also, e.g., II, ii, 32-65). The rush of rebellion, about which the king is concerned, had just drawn his son away from the immediately preceding comic scene, and after Act III, scene i, there would also appear another comic scene, with Falstaff on his antic way to quell revolt. In brief, both the context of the scene and the scene itself may have dispelled critical speculation in the momentary world of the theater.

One would expect drama concerned with disputation and ideas to arouse speculative or critical faculties that might carry with them the suspicion that a play or a scene had an argumentative or topical import. But in Shakespeare's developing scene the conviction of effective poetry not only is devoted to characterization but also stands almost as its own excuse; certainly it must have contributed to the binding power that any effective theatrical performance may have upon its audience as they see and hear characters in action. Such an effectiveness, perhaps, may actually be shown by the apparent failure of the dialogue in the theater to arouse any politic picklock; while outside of the theater, Warwick's lines alone could be pointed to, if necessary, as expressing within the scene an idea more general, more impersonal, and more innocuous than the kindred idea to be utilized by Daniel in his successful defense.

Aside from such considerations the first scene of the third act in *2 Henry IV* is a splendid beginning to what a Renaissance artist and educated critic might consider to be the epitasis—the "busie parte"—of the play. A conscientious playwright, more concerned with the printing of his plays than a previous generation of critics would allow, might have effected its insertion for reasons essentially artistic.[8]

In view of the scope of this present study, further consideration of Shakespeare's poetic capabilities in this scene, especially as they cannot be separated from its theatrical effect, must be neglected for another facet of the preceding discussion; for the fact that the scene refers favorably to Henry's part in the deposition of Richard is sometimes related to another possible instance of Shakespeare's plays being affected by Elizabethan censorship, namely, the omission of the ceremony of deposition in the 1597 quarto (Q1) of Shakespeare's *Richard II*. As will be pointed out later, the lines of that ceremony, in all probability, were written, however, during the composition of the play (this time, *ca.* 1595) and had continued to be acted thereafter. It seems likely, indeed, that one occasion of their performance explains some peculiarities of the text when, in 1608, the deposition proper first appeared in print (Q4) and was so advertised on the title page.[9]

As a consequence, it is possible that readers of the 1600 Qb of *2 Henry IV* would find in Act III, scene i, a reference to what they might have seen and heard upon the stage if they had attended a performance of *Richard II*.[10] They might also have noticed, and certainly the author and actors would know, that the printer of the 1600 quarto of *2 Henry IV* had also printed the first quarto of *Richard II*.[11] In 1597, then, Simmes was three years nearer his earlier punishment when he had had his press confiscated, his apprentice removed, and his type melted down because of his unlicensed printing of a popular school text. In spite of its severity, however, the 1595 punishment did not involve, as did Simmes's 1599 brush with the authorities, the printing of satires and epigrams, and hence the printing of what referred, or might be thought to refer, to contemporary persons and current events—a fact that might have determined, in part, the nature of his possible timidity in 1600.

Be that suggestion as it may, during the middle months of 1597, a clash occurred between the authorities and the theatrical world, one so vigorous that it was remembered in theatrical circles for years.[12] On July 28 of that year, the playhouses were closed because of the performance of the *Isle of Dogs* by the newly reorganized Pembroke's Men. Some of the actors and Ben Jonson, a co-author of the play, were seized and imprisoned. Nashe, who also had a hand in writing the drama, fled London; and on August 15, the Privy Council ordered Richard Topcliffe *et al* to pursue the matter further.

It was noted at that time that one of the players "apprehended & comytted to pryson . . . was not only an Actor, but a maker of *parte* of the said Plaie," and "ffor as moche as yt ys thought meete that the rest of the Players or Actors in that matter shalbe apprehended to receave soche punishment as theire Leude and mutynous behavior doth deserve," Topcliffe, Thomas Fowler, Richard Skivington, Dr. Fletcher, and Mr. Wilbraham were "to exami*n*e those of the plaiers that are comytted . . . what ys become of the rest of theire ffellowes that eith*er* had theire p*ar*tes in the devysinge of that sedytious matter, or that were Actors or plaiers in the same, what Copies they haue given forth of the said playe, and to whome, and so[c]h oth*er* pointes as you shall thincke meete to be demaunded of them, wherein you shall req*uire* them to deale trulie as they will looke to receave anie favor." The investigators were also ordered to "p*er*vse soch papers as were founde in Nash his Lodging*es*." Not until October 3, were warrants signed for Jonson's release and that of the actors Gabriel Spencer and Robert Shaw.[13]

The publication of the first quarto of *Richard II*, entered in the Stationers' Register on August 29 and appearing later in the same year, was carried out in this theatrical turmoil when Shakespeare's company was one of the two allowed to reopen their doors after the performance of the *Isle of Dogs*. In such circumstances, it may well have seemed discreet or necessary to all concerned to omit from the printed version of the play the ceremony of a deposition during which an English ruler surrendered his regalia. The situation, at any rate, deserves further attention, particularly as it illustrates the previous point about censorship and an artistic dramatization of history much more fully than could the consideration of a single scene.

Since all quartos of *Richard II* earlier than 1608 omitted Richard's appearance in Act IV, scene i, not simply the two versions of the deposition should be considered, but also the immediately preceding appearance of Richard at Flint Castle (III, iii) must be examined carefully. In the three quartos before 1608, as far as the appearance of the king was concerned, this Flint Castle scene alone showed Richard and Henry face to face after Henry's return, and it consequently preceded the king's next appearance when he and his queen were parted, an episode treated with increasing pathos. Logically, within the confines of a practical brevity, one should begin with Act III, scene iii, at least; and in analyzing these scenes, examples will be encountered again of the way in which a dramatist might well diminish the probability of a scene's being censured by the critical scrutiny of a politic picklock watching its performance or a licenser reading the text. In this instance, moreover, attention will be focused not simply upon an idea lyrically expressed but upon some images that probably conveyed "public" meanings.

If one considers first what must have been theatrically noticeable during the performance of the Flint Castle episode, he will be struck by the fact that Shakespeare unmistakably indicates the major features of its stage action. The entrance *"with drum and colours"* of three central characters—Bolingbroke, York, and Northumberland—and the later entrance of Percy, presumably from a different direction (ll. 1-19), mark the introduction to the forward movement of this scene. Percy's report and the consequent statement of Bolingbroke's terms (ll. 20-61) then inaugurate the action. Henry's emissary, Northumberland, crosses the stage toward Flint Castle. There is a *"Parle without, and answer within: then a flourish."* Richard enters *"on the walls"* with his followers, and the ruler's appearance is commented upon by the watching Bolingbroke and York (ll. 62-71). The first encounter between Northumberland and Richard follows, in which Richard seizes the initiative because Northumberland has not bent his knee. After three speeches, Northumberland crosses the stage again (ll. 125-26), this time from Flint Castle to Bolingbroke. After that he returns to Flint Castle (ll. 172-75). As this action is taking place, Richard and Aumerle comment in turn upon the situation and upon the waiting Bolingbroke until Northumberland, upon his return, curtsies. The concluding portion of the scene centers upon Richard's visible descent: Northumberland returns a second time to Bolingbroke and comments on Richard, the opposing leaders encounter one another as he who has been on the lower stage kneels.

All this is very obvious, of course. The artistry of the scene, however, demands and repays a detailed consideration; for the skill with which such basically simple and obvious stage-crossings and actions support and arise from certain speeches and are denied by other speeches is a feature of Shakespeare's technique in this portion of the drama—a technique based upon a conflicting historical tradition inherited by Elizabethans, upon obviously conflicting imagery, and upon conflicting meanings of an image conventional to the age. One of the effects of such a thoroughly qualified artistry, moreover, is interpreted by one of the participants in terms conventional to current beliefs about the nature of the passions of men.

When one begins a detailed consideration of the scene, two features emerge from the opening of the Flint Castle episode. The first is that Shakespeare briefly reflects contrasting Richardian and Lancastrian interpretations of history.[14] This is characteristic of the drama as a whole. The second is that Shakespeare effects a dramatic distinction between Bolingbroke and Northumberland. This will be intensified later in the play.

The opening speech of Act III, scene iii, then, refers to what had been dramatized in Act II, scene iv:

> So that by this intelligence we learn
> The Welshmen are dispers'd, and Salisbury
> Is gone to meet the King, who lately landed
> With some few private friends upon this coast.
>
> (ll. 1-4)

In the earlier scene, as is usual when he wishes to heighten an effect, Shakespeare had played upon the mythical thinking of his age, and the emphasis of that short development had fallen upon sublunary phenomena, described by the Welsh captain and believed to be portentous of a "fearful change":

> The bay-trees in our country are all wither'd
> And meteors fright the fixed stars of heaven;
> The pale-fac'd moon looks bloody on the earth
> And lean-look'd prophets whisper fearful change;
> Rich men look sad and ruffians dance and leap,
> The one in fear to lose what they enjoy,
> The other to enjoy by rage and war.
> These signs forerun the death or fall of kings.
>
> (II, iv, 8-15)

By opening the Flint Castle episode with a reference to the dispersal of the Welsh, Shakespeare also refers to an emphasis that will be consistent with the way in which Bolingbroke now appears briefly in the light of a Lancastrian historical tradition which considered him a figure of destiny whose rise was caused, to a degree at any rate, by a supraterrestial force. In other words, the choice of a beginning for the introductory dialogue of Act III, scene iii, agrees with the concluding lines of that dialogue that immediately precede Percy's entrance:

*York.* Take not, good cousin, further than you should,
Lest you mistake the heavens are o'er our heads.
*Boling.* I know it, uncle, and *oppose not myself
Against their will.*

(ll. 16-19)

Such an emphasis, though it be brief, is part of a noticeable feature of Shakespeare's artistry whereby the materials of Tudor history are utilized to effect an artistic complexity that is as unique as it is interesting; and this can be illustrated, as it bears upon the present situation, by noting that throughout the drama Richard consistently refers to Bolingbroke in a manner which reflects the unfavorable accounts of Yorkist historians—a manner directly antithetical to what has just been noted. Richard refers to himself, however, especially as he is falling, in a manner which reflects the sympathetic portrayal of a martyr king that had been developed primarily by French chroniclers. Although Bolingbroke, in contrast, does not consistently refer to Richard in a manner which reflects the unfavorable accounts of Lancastrian historians, at this point in the drama Shakespeare uses for the rising Henry's portrayal one aspect of the technique he uses to portray the falling Richard; thus during the brief introduction to the action of the Flint Castle episode, this rising figure refers to himself in a manner which reflects an extremely favorable, Lancastrian interpretation of his career. Such a brief development accords not only with the emphasis already noted in the Welsh scene but also with other features of a pro-Henry historical tradition that have appeared in the play-world

—most immediately in the dramatization of the execution of parasites.

Such an emphasis, even within these very few lines, conflicts directly with the attitude expressed in York's warning that has been quoted above ("Take not, good cousin . . ./Lest you mistake the heavens are o'er our heads"). This attitude will be intensified later in this scene when Shakespeare has Richard express the politically religious aspect of Renaissance kingship that he has evoked consistently but to which he has not adhered with consistent vigor. Even the few introductory lines, then, posit a celestial force for both opposed figures as their meeting approaches. Such an artistry is obviously well conceived, not simply for these introductory lines but, as we shall see, for other portions of the drama as well.

Related to this consideration of Bolingbroke's not opposing the heavens' will is the second point that becomes apparent in the introductory dialogue to the Flint Castle episode—the dramatic distinction which Shakespeare effects between Bolingbroke and Northumberland and which arises from York's censure of the two figures. York's angry words would balance completely the reflection of Bolingbroke as a child of destiny were they directed fully and solely at Henry. Instead, they arise from the words of Northumberland, who thereby appears much more censurable than Bolingbroke could in the immediate, though brief, dialogue heard by the audience:

*North.* The news is very fair and good, my lord.
Richard not far from hence hath hid his head.
  *York.* It would beseem the Lord Northumberland
To say King Richard. Alack the heavy day
When such a sacred king should hide his head!
  *North.* Your Grace mistakes; only to be brief
Left I his title out.
  *York.*                    The time hath been,
Would you have been so brief with him, he would
Have been so brief with you, to shorten you,
For taking so the head, your whole head's length.
  *Boling.* Mistake not, uncle, further than you should. . . .
(ll. 5-15)

While Bolingbroke appears as a slightly interceding figure in dialogue carried on by others, Northumberland begins to bear the reprehensible onus that might always emerge in representing a driving force turned against an English ruler. Certainly the force of the doctrine underlying York's lines might have been extended in the direction of the words Marlowe gave to Mortimer:

> For howsoever we have borne it out,
> 'Tis treason to be up against the king.[15]

Instead, the present situation anticipates what will be developed much more fully in the remainder of this scene and especially in the complete deposition scene. Therein, just as the conflicting attitudes of a historical tradition inherited by Elizabethans will be intensified, so too will the theatrical differentiation between Bolingbroke and Northumberland, until the northern Earl becomes the efficient, and thereby the theatrical, cause of an incident that seems to bait Richard.

To return to the beginning of the busy part of the Flint Castle scene, with Bolingbroke's terms and the first encounter between Northumberland and Richard an audience would hear lines that both anticipate and deny the possibility that the scene will dramatize a heroic challenge and encounter.

In the phrasing of Bolingbroke's terms a partial challenge is effected, for the alternative offered to Richard's removing the sentence of banishment and restoring the lands of Lancaster is expressed in words conventional to heroic conflict. The audience would hear of the "rude ribs of that ancient castle," of a "brazen trumpet," and of how Bolingbroke will

> . . . lay the summer's dust with showers of blood
> Rain'd from the wounds of slaughtered Englishmen. . . .

Such a "crimson tempest" can "bedrench" the "fresh green lap of fair King Richard's land." An audience would also hear of "the noise of threat'ning drum," "tattered battlements," and "fair appointments." The suitability of such language to a theatrically heroic vein is obvious, but it has been qualified by other words: by "allegiance and true faith of heart," by Richard's "most royal person," by the phrases "at his feet to lay my arms and power," by "stooping duty," and "tenderly shall show."

As a result, the opening lines of the summarizing statement of Henry's speech paradoxically express a peaceful thought in terms of the "thund'ring shock" of contraries:

> Methinks King Richard and myself should meet
> With no less terror than the elements
> Of fire and water, when their thund'ring shock
> At meeting tears the cloudy cheeks of heaven.
>
> (ll. 54-57)

Yet the powerful speaker's interpretation of that image of conflict continues the words that have anticipated his later kneeling action (ll. 35-36), for he represents himself only as the "water," now "yielding," and even weeping.

> Be he the fire, I'll be the yielding water;
> The rage be his, whilst on the earth I rain
> My waters. . . .
>
> (ll. 58-60)

It is ironic that Bolingbroke's interpretation of the "thund'ring shock" is now applicable to a falling and not a reigning king, and it is equally ironic that Richard's first reaction of rage, which accords with Bolingbroke's interpretation, counters in kind the forceful and defiant aspect of Henry's terms. An audience would hear once more of "the purple testament of bleeding war," of "Ten thousand bloody crowns of mothers' sons," of "scarlet indignation," and of "pastures' grass" bedewed "with faithful English blood":

> We are amaz'd; and thus long have we stood
> To watch the fearful bending of thy knee,
> Because we thought ourself thy lawful king;
> And if we be, how dare thy joints forget
> To pay their awful duty to our presence?
>
> . . . .
>
> Tell Bolinbroke—for yon methinks he stands—
> That every stride he makes upon my land
> Is dangerous treason. He is come to open

The purple testament of bleeding war;
But ere the crown he looks for live in peace,
Ten thousand bloody crowns of mothers' sons
Shall ill become the flower of England's face,
Change the complexion of her maid-pale peace
To scarlet indignation, and bedew
Her pastures' grass with faithful English blood.
(III, iii, 72-100)

Other things being equal, such a speech might well have promised fulfillment of anticipations aroused by a number of previous developments. Apparently the opposition between Richard and Henry, which had been emphasized since the ruler's departure for Ireland, is coming to a head in spite of Richard's earlier dismissal of his forces. Before then, an audience had twice been cheated of watching actual combat on the stage, and now such apparent vigor on the part of Richard might also build upon the experiences of regular theater-goers who had witnessed in other plays the rhetorical encounters between leaders of opposing forces before a crucial struggle, even perhaps those conventional but memorable encounters in *Edward II* and *Woodstock,* to say nothing of those in poorer dramas and unhistorical plays. The vitality of such a minor tradition, both dramatic and non-dramatic, in which there might be fighting against a world of odds, does not need to be enlarged upon.

In addition, Shakespeare draws now upon the politically religious aspect of Renaissance kingship, and thus celestial imagery returns strongly—on Richard's side only, however. "Armies of pestilence" are being mustered by "God omnipotent" in "his clouds" as Richard in turn develops rhetorical contraries, based, in this instance, upon Northumberland's neglect of "the fearful bending" of his knee, an "awful duty" demanded by the regal "stewardship" that has been made by "the hand of God."

A simple melodramatic context, compatible with heroic bravings, never becomes dominant, however; for the second aspect of Bolingbroke's partial challenge, not represented at all by Northumberland's failure to bend the knee, is developed in the duke's answer to Richard's forceful speech:

> The King of heaven forbid our lord the King
> Should so with civil and uncivil arms
> Be rush'd upon! Thy thrice noble cousin
> Harry Bolingbroke doth humbly kiss thy hand. . . .
>
> (ll. 101-4)

When Richard accepts this speech and Henry's terms, and as a consequence sends a welcome to Bolingbroke, an apparent resolution to the potential conflict is reached.

In this respect, it is worth noting that imagery connected with the heavens had appeared earlier in the scene in a context varying from that of Richard's forceful speech and varying also from that of Bolingbroke's statement about the heavens' "will." Upon Northumberland's first stage-crossing and the appearance of Richard after two "parles" and a flourish, Shakespeare had Bolingbroke comment on the king, as Richard is later to comment on Bolingbroke; and Shakespeare's use of celestial imagery in Henry's remark again showed the artistry characteristic of this scene, an artistry that accords with the fact that the peaceful resolution just mentioned will, in turn, be strongly qualified. In that comment of Bolingbroke's, since Richard was a "blushing discontented sun" (l. 63)—and thereby the Richard-sun figure of Salisbury's speech in the Welsh scene reappeared—Bolingbroke and his forces, by his own words, were "the envious clouds" that "dim" and "stain the track" of a sun-king's descent (ll. 65-67). Although the six lines are too brief to bear much weight by themselves (and certainly in the Elizabethan theater too brief to be cogitated into an explicit moment of honesty in the course of silent hypocrisy), they do anticipate the later technique of the scene. Although they agree with Salisbury's figure in the Welsh scene, even more to the point is the fact that here the rising figure momentarily wrests the emphasis from his Lancastrian attitude toward one potentially Richardian.

Similarly, to a much greater degree, Richard will wrest the subsequent development of the scene from one of a simple, even heroic, world-picture favorable to himself to one that is con-

166        THE PROBLEM OF ORDER

sistently and finally equivocal, from a speech of defiance with a peaceful resolution that accepts the rights of descent to speeches of lamentation and appropriate actions that deny the other speeches and actions in the latter part of the scene. By such a development an attribute of this ruler is emphasized which is antithetical to a vigorous, forceful rule that can animate a commonweal.

As an illustration of these last statements, one should note that the emphasis started by Bolingbroke's comment about a blushing sun and envious clouds was developed briefly but strongly by York's lines which followed immediately and which drew their dominant image from the planes of correspondences in the simplified world-order that Richard is inclined to rely upon:

> Yet looks he like a king! Behold, his eye,
> As bright as is the eagle's, lightens forth
> Controlling majesty. Alack, alack, for woe,
> That any harm should stain so fair a show!
>
> (ll. 68-71)

The "eagle's eye," the "lightens forth," and the "controlling majesty" are obviously in the nearly constant vein of York's other speeches during this portion of the drama. With the concluding sentence, they give to Bolingbroke's own potentially Richardian emphasis an unequivocal, admonitory force that is given its most intense expression in Richard's speech wherein Northumberland is berated and Bolingbroke accused of treason. From such a point of view, it can be said that a dramatic process with a Lancastrian focal point in a speech by Bolingbroke (ll. 18-19) gives way to an antithetical emphasis with its focal point in the first long speech by Richard (ll. 72-100). There then follows the resolution of potential conflict that has been noted above.

Yet in accordance with this shifting development, after a peaceful resolution apparently has been reached, and even before Northumberland has finished crossing the stage from Richard to Henry, Shakespeare returns briefly to a note of heroic defiance. He now modifies it, however, by Aumerle's wise alternative (ll. 127-32), and he forcefully overrides it by Richard's lamenting, instead of his vigorous, return to an oversimplified world-picture. As a result of this last fact, although the waiting figure of Bolingbroke is again represented in the light of Yorkist chroniclers, Richard begins to appear in this scene as the pathetic king of his immediately preceding appearance:

> O God, O God! that e'er this tongue of mine
> That laid the sentence of dread banishment
> On yon proud man, should take it off again
> With words of sooth! O that I were as great
> As is my grief, or lesser than my name!
> Or that I could forget what I have been,
> Or not remember what I must be now!
> Swell'st thou, proud heart? I'll give thee scope
>     to beat,
> Since foes have scope to beat both thee and me.
>                                   (III, iii, 133-41)

Instead of having a vigorous, admonitory force, these lamenting lines have a pathetic force; and by giving the lament to Richard instead of to an observer, Shakespeare repeats a technique started in Act III, scene ii. Here the ruler not only denies the validity of the apparent resolution to the conflict but he denies also Aumerle's wise alternative, an alternative smothered by Richard's expression of sorrow which swells to a fully developed speech before the king turns to the forward action of this stage-world upon Northumberland's return from Bolingbroke.

Although this subsequent speech by Richard (ll. 143-75) still has regal overtones, particularly from the parts of successive contraries ("gorgeous palace," "gay apparel," "figur'd goblets," "sceptre," "subjects," "large kingdom"), it nevertheless ends by denying the submission in Northumberland's previous speech and even in Northumberland's obeisance:

> Most mighty prince, my Lord Northumberland,
> What says King Bolingbroke? Will his Majesty

Give Richard leave to live till Richard die?
You make a leg, and Bolingbroke says ay.

(ll. 172-75)

It is this feature of Shakespeare's artistry that will reappear more strongly in Richard's speeches which develop from Bolingbroke's kneeling, and from Bolingbroke's expression of dutiful submission in accordance with the terms apparently accepted by Richard:

*Boling.* Stand all apart,
And show fair duty to his Majesty.
My gracious lord,—
*K. Rich.* Fair Cousin, you debase your princely knee
To make the base earth proud with kissing it.
Me rather had my heart might feel your love
Than my unpleas'd eye see your courtesy.
Up, cousin, up; your heart is up, I know,
Thus high at least, although your knee be low.
*Boling.* My gracious lord, I come but for mine own.
*K. Rich.* Your own is yours, and I am yours, and all.
*Boling.* So far be mine, my most redoubted lord,
As my true service shall deserve your love.
*K. Rich.* Well you deserve; they well deserve to have
That know the strong'st and surest way to get.

(ll. 187-201)

At this point in the play, by Richard's speeches, Richard is the fallen ruler. By Bolingbroke's speeches, Richard is a gracious, "redoubted" ruler who will receive true service. By Richard's speeches, Bolingbroke is the proud, powerful, and ambitious politician of Yorkist chroniclers; but by Bolingbroke's speeches, Bolingbroke is the Lancastrian nobleman. Thus the scene has run its course through varying developments that are consistent in their constant qualification. Alternating historical emphases and conflicting imagery gave way to an emphasis upon potential conflict that was denied by a peaceful resolution, and that resolution in turn was ultimately denied by Richard's censuring laments. The antithetical attitudes just indicated then close the scene. They are so closely juxtaposed that for all intents and purposes they fuse with one another, and that fusion accords with the way in which two attitudes toward kingship have been kept alive. Even as Richard lacks the vigorous and wise attribute of a merited name whereby a commonweal must be animated constantly, his right by inheritance, by the hand of God, by a simplified world-order, is expressed forcefully.

The ambiguity of this last consideration is apparent also in the only speech of Richard's that has not so far been mentioned, for it, too, shows a fusion of opposite meanings and illustrates the final ambiguity of this scene. Richard's comment on the stage situation just before he descends begins with a reference to the myth of Phaëthon: "Down, down I come; like glist'ring Phaëthon. . . ." All myths might have a "public" meaning dependent upon the moral conventionally attached to their "story," and thus the Phaëthon myth usually was conceived of as showing the unfortunate results of a dangerous or unskillful grasping of power by those who suffered from an unwarranted affection and ambition or by those who lacked the skill and art necessary to manage what they had undertaken. The idea, the narrative, and the falling image of Apollo's son became one of the poetic coins current during the period. It was put into circulation, in grammar schools and elsewhere, by Ovid's *Metamorphoses* with commentary, by Erasmus' *De Copia*, by reference lexicons, by Comes' *Mythology*, by emblem books.[16]

When applied by a ruler to one under him, the myth would be appropriate to an unwarranted ambition, and so Shakespeare uses it in the *Two Gentlemen of Verona* when the duke condemns and banishes Valentine:

> 'Tis so; and here's the ladder for the purpose.
> Why, Phaëthon,—for thou art Merops' son,—
> Wilt thou aspire to guide the heavenly car
> And with thy *daring folly* burn the world?
> Wilt thou reach stars, because they shine on thee?
> Go, *base intruder! overweening slave!*
> Bestow thy fawning smiles on equal mates. . . .
>
> (III, i, 152-58)

Essentially in this same category is the application of the fable in *3 Henry VI* to aspiring and bloody Richard Plantagenet now about to be killed by the Lancastrians, led by Northumberland and Clifford:

> *North.* Yield to our mercy, *proud Plantagenet.*
> *Clif.* Ay, to such mercy as his ruthless arm
> With downright payment show'd unto my father.
> *Now Phaëthon hath tumbled from his car,*
> And made an evening at the noontide prick.
>
> (I, iv, 30-34)

The myth, however, could be applied also to more than one person involved in the complexities of rule, particularly when the figure of Apollo was emphasized, and it could refer not simply to ambition but to a lack of skill as well. Thus in *Gorboduc* implications of a parent's excessive affection ("tender minde," "parciall eye") and of ambition ("proud son"), as well as implications of an unwise use of princely power ("rasshely"), appear in the first chorus:

> Oft *tender minde, that leades the parciall eye*
>   Of *erring* parentes in their childrens loue,
> Destroyes the wrongly loued childe thereby.
>   This doth the *proude* sonne of Apollo proue,
> Who, *rasshely* set in chariot of his sire,
> Inflamed the parched earth with heauens fire.
>
> (ll. 13-18)

When applied to a ruling figure alone, the lack of skill apparent in the "folly" of the duke's speech and in the "erring" and "rasshely" of the immediately preceding quotation probably would be emphasized;[17] and so Shakespeare uses the myth, shifting in a *gradatio*-like manner from Phoebus to Phaëthon to Henry but relying upon the conventional moral, when his dying Clifford criticizes Henry VI and his failure to rule as a king should:

> And who shines now but Henry's enemies?
> O Phœbus, hadst thou never given consent
> That Phaëthon should check thy fiery steeds,

Thy burning car never had scorch'd the earth!
And, *Henry, hadst thou sway'd as kings should do,
Or as thy father and his father did,*
Giving no ground unto the house of York,
They never then had sprung like summer flies;
. . . . . . . .
And thou this day hadst kept thy chair in peace.
(*3 Henry VI*, II, vi, 10-20)

Shakespeare's use of the myth in Richard II's speech seems purposefully contrived to utilize the double edge that its meaning might have if it were applied to a situation involving both ruler and an opposed, rising figure. To do this, Shakespeare omits any use of an implied, reprehensible tenor-vehicle like Henry VI–Phaëthon and utilizes instead the tenor-vehicle of falling Richard-Phaëthon and the censurable vehicle of "unruly jades."

To perceive his artistry in this respect, an artistry that allows antithetical meanings to exist concurrently and that thereby fuses the antithetical attitudes heretofore juxtaposed, demands considering Richard's speech both by itself and in its context. When considered solely from Richard's point of view, its emphasis is surprisingly consistent. Within his speech alone, the reference is phrased with emphasis upon "unruly jades" and upon "traitors," and thereby the Phaëthon figure appears much less reprehensible than it does in any of the preceding examples.

Down, down I come; like glist'ring Phaëthon,
Wanting the manage of unruly jades.
In the base court? Base court, where kings grow base,
To come at traitors' call and do them grace.
In the base court? Come down? Down, court! down, king!
For night-owls shriek where mounting larks should sing.
(III, iii, 178-83)

From Richard's point of view, it is possible that Shakespeare may have had in mind a distinction between "unruly jades" and aspiring "traitors." In some current interpretations of the myth, such as that edited by Thomas Thomas, the first printer for

Cambridge University, a distinction was made between the signs of the zodiac (the ambitious) and the horses of the sun (the common people). The terrifying nature of the Scorpion, the Crab, and so on, was said to represent *"homines invidi et factiosi"*; and it was the alarming appearance of these envious and factious ones, along with Phaëthon's lack of skill, that caused the steeds—the common people, accustomed to being ruled by a competent and experienced governor—to show their fierceness.[18]

If Shakespeare had such a distinction in mind as he here continued the celestial imagery in this portion of the drama, he may have associated Richard's "unruly jades" with lines in the immediately preceding scene. At that time, Scroop spoke of the "hard bright steel" and the many nameless "hearts harder than steel" that opposed Richard: the "arm'd" "White-beards," the "boys, with women's voices," the "beadsmen," the "distaff-women" who "manage rusty bills" against the king's "seat" (III, ii, 104-20). One is also reminded of the opening lines of this scene that referred to the Welsh who could not be restrained from dispersing. To Richard, the "jades" might be the people; the "traitors," Bolingbroke and Northumberland in particular, would be *"homines invidi et factiosi."*

In the play-world, however, the Welsh had believed Richard dead, and the armed commons had flocked to the figure they consistently favored. If such a distinction as that just noted were in Shakespeare's mind, it might be conceived of as according with Richard's blindness to his sins of government, with the lack of skill pointed out in moralizations of the myth, and with Richard's later denouncement of all his subjects as "beasts."[19]

Yet in spite of what has just been noted, from the point of view of an audience, "unruly jades" would be directed most obviously at all on the lower stage; thus the censure of the moral and the myth would seem to be directed at those whom both the audience and Richard could see—at the figures of both Bolingbroke and his supporters. Thereby, paradoxically enough, the vehicle-tenor of "glist'ring Phaëthon"-Richard could again make Richard at least obliquely at fault, much more so, certainly, than the earlier "envious clouds" had criticized Bolingbroke. In the first place, the category of unskilled and hence censurable rulers mentioned in moralizations of the myth might have force within the speech itself, particularly for educated Elizabethans. Even more important is the fact that it obviously has force in the immediate context of the entire speech; for at this particular moment in the play-world, there is not simply a possible disjunction between Richard's use of the reference and its conventional interpretation that makes the Phaëthon figure blamable, but, much more noticeably, there is a disjunction between his speech and the context of his speech. Northumberland, before these lines of Richard's, had shown the deference that the king had demanded. Bolingbroke, after Richard's speech, will kneel and speak in terms of duty and deference. Thus Richard's words in their context confirm the figure of a culpable, unskilled Phaëthon-Richard even as he persists in predicating pride to a kneeling Bolingbroke. If the irony of the scene is that of hypocrisy, it is at best only partially so; for even more than to Bolingbroke's words is irony applicable to Richard's final words which deny, as the submissive signs and speeches of Bolingbroke do not, the figure of Richard, a king in the simplified picture of world-order.

A purposeful artistic ambiguity that would not only juxtapose but also fuse opposites seems to be at work, as Shakespeare dramatizes the history of a reign that had been recounted and interpreted with the greatest of differences and had been so bequeathed to the Elizabethans. At this point in the play-world, the effect of imagistic reference and context must have been apparent to anyone in the theater, whether or not he was aware of the conventional interpretations of a myth, as he may well have been if he had attended a grammar school or even if he were simply a Londoner and a regular, alert theater-goer.

Shakespeare's technique can be described in a number of ways, each of which accords with the others in that each indicates how thoroughly qualified his artistry is here. The concept of Richard as a pitiable martyr is utilized by Shakespeare to effect the descent of this king who insists upon a world-order that gives substance to the very concept of a martyr king. Yet such a concept, when expressed by Richard himself, results in lament-like, censuring speeches that would normally be expected to appear only after a fall. They seem incongruous when a ruler encounters overt signs of submission resulting from the immediate solution to a potential conflict—a solution, moreover, that also recognizes the rights of descent upon which Richard's world-order is based. From another point of view, a relatively conventional situation of challenge that has resulted in a peaceful solution continues with the figures on the lower stage but is denied by the entirely discordant context of lamentation, fall, and censure that is expressed, and insisted upon, by the figure on the upper stage who literally descends only to find submission offered him by the persons whom he meets. Furthermore, this denial of what is otherwise theatrically apparent is expressed at the moment only by Richard, even with the lamentor's conventional reproach of the "high" heart of the causer of the fall; and it is persevered in even while the principal opposing figure continues kneeling in accordance with the resolution that ended for him the possible warlike encounter with which the busy part of the scene began. Ironically, in Gaunt's earlier words, Richard seems "possess'd now" to depose himself.

Finally, from the point of view emphasized in the preceding paragraphs, the effect of the Flint Castle episode appears to have been designed so that it would fuse antitheses. The two groups of words and images in Bolingbroke's partial challenge had been antithetical. Also antithetical was the emphasis of Richard's lamenting lines as they followed hard on the heels of his "heroic" speech, and even details not so far mentioned are consonant. Witness Richard's references to Aumerle's weeping (l. 160) and to York's tears (ll. 202-3); but witness, too, the sentence

> Well, well, I see
> I talk but idly, and you laugh at me.
>
> (ll. 170-71)

From the time of Richard's descent, the two interlocking figures concurrently deny one another's words and actions, only to agree to a return to London with any future intent left unexplicit and, to that degree, unresolved. The effect, although produced by the conventional, has resulted from an unconventional coalescence and is too ambiguous for any simple or theatrical frame of reference, or for any literary frame of reference, other than its own. In the total sweep of the play, in view of what had been dramatized already, the effect of the scene confirms the censurable intent of the Phaëthon-Richard image; but by individual speeches, Richard's right is emphasized.

As such an effect is being developed, Shakespeare draws upon a generally accepted belief about the nature of the passions of men when he has Northumberland report to Bolingbroke that "Sorrow and grief of heart" make Richard "speak fondly, like a frantic man" (ll. 184-85). For the educated once more, such words might evoke another frame of reference in no way discordant with what has been pointed out. For Richard's actions —however unique and ambiguous their effect might be as they appeared in the momentary world of the dramatic scene—could be glossed by a reflective educated person drawing upon information in Batman, De la Primaudaye, or related treatises. In such a circumstance, Northumberland's comment might well have been considered as indicating explicitly how sorrow, one of the affections or passions of the soul, was said to arise from the soul's irascible power and to draw with it attendant perturbations, grounded not on Reason but following the dangerous and unreliable dictates of "Fantasie," which is "a sodaine and tumultuous judgement." Thus man's soul might be filled "with endlesse trouble and disquietnes" and he might indeed appear "fondly, like a frantic man." For "fancie beeing very turbulent and skittish" draws "to it selfe confusedly some shew and apparence of opinion and judgement, whereby it deemeth that which is offered vnto it to be either good or bad," but "deemeth" incorrectly or unsubstantially. Consequently it "is the cause that wee liue in the middest of marueilous troubles in respect of our affections of feare, of desire, of sorrow, of ioy, and that one while we weepe, and sodainly wee laugh againe."[20]

From such a point of view another corresponding aspect of the scene emerges; and once more, in dramatic literature especially, a note of familiarity might be struck with a uniquely varied effect. Never had a "distracted" passive protagonist spoken so lyrically and with such rhetorical logic—a logic suitable to himself alone, however, not to the surrounding figures; and as a result, an anticipation of the passive protagonist's turn to an active counter-design might possibly arise and be confirmed by Richard's words (ll. 127-30), by Aumerle's counsel (ll. 131-32), and even by the "fond" ending of the scene.[21] Thus the possibility of future action on Richard's part might have been faintly underlined by the king's franticness—though in this respect the Renaissance insisted that a basic precept *de regimine principum* was the necessity for a ruler to command his affections or passions.[22]

Within the theater, the conclusion of the Flint Castle episode must have produced an ambiguous effect with an unusual artistry deeply etched by the lyricism given Richard. Outside of the theater, one can see how its printed or written text might accord even with a critical scrutiny proceeding upon a divine rightist's sympathy for Richard's anger and frustrating sorrow. Such a point of view would be substantiated not simply by a psychological reference but also by that aspect of an imagistic reference that Richard had emphasized. It would be substantiated also by the insistence upon Richard's right that the other relatively long speeches of the scene provided. Like the preceding scenes, the episode affords little that would remain constant for delation. It presents a historical incident that, within the main course of Richard's fall and Bolingbroke's rise, had no settled factualness;[23] but from the lines and actions of such a dramatization, it would be most difficult to develop any one "dangerous" point. Other lines, or even the same lines in a different light, would militate strongly against any "seditious" interpretation.

There is no need to turn to a fear of censorship in order to account for Shakespeare's artistry that fuses the disparate, which already existed in his historical materials and which is always inherent, at least potentially, in any action of men. Whether or not *Richard II* was performed before Sir Robert Cecil on December 9, 1595, at Sir Edward Hoby's house,[24] the dramatization of the Flint Castle episode seems thoroughly accordant with Sir Thomas Smith's statement that about such "doubtful and hasardous" matters only the wise can judge "according to the purpose of the doers" and "the estate of the time then present."[25] Although from such a point of view and upon such an occasion, Shakespeare's play, no less than Daniel's, might have been considered suitable to provoke the Elizabethan "habit of mind fostered by the debate," in the public theater the equivocal ending of the Flint Castle episode might well have heightened an interest in the stage-world, especially in what would have to happen by incident only, if not by the protagonist's turn from a passive to an active figure, to clarify such an ending.

After the Flint Castle episode, Shakespeare's audience would next encounter the major figures in the deposition scene, although before then they would have seen and heard the garden scene, with its consistent note of sorrow and "the heavy thought of care" and with its turn from censure to pity:[26]

> Hold thy peace.
> He that hath suffer'd this disordered spring
> Hath now himself met with the fall of leaf.
>
> (III, iv, 47-49)

When one considers the deposition scene as first printed, however, and then analyzes its fuller form, it is noticeable that, in contrast with the shorter scene, the longer one shows a continuation and development of the artistry that is characteristic of the conclusion to the Flint Castle episode; whereas the most noticeable feature of the shorter deposition is that it fluctuates between antithetical attitudes.

This shorter version presents three incidents, each of which might well stand by itself: the incident of the quarreling nobles, that of Bolingbroke's ascent to "the regal throne," and that of the Abbot of Westminster's plot. The connection among the three is effected almost entirely by the fact that, with the exception of York (whose entrance marks the end of the first division), the participants in the two latter incidents are drawn from the first. The only other cohesive effect between the first two episodes is what might result from the juxtaposition of contrary words: of Henry's regal "we," followed by York's "Great Duke of Lancaster" (IV, i, 106-7). At any rate, in the dramatization of the second and third incidents the appearance of contrary emphases in alternating succession reminds one of a feature of Marlowe's artistry in *Edward II*.[27] The preceding statements, however, obviously need to be elaborated.

The challenge of recrimination and counter-recrimination in the representation of quarreling nobles is developed from the same grounds as that of the earlier quarrel between Bolingbroke and Mowbray. It is now performed with Henry in a dominant position, which roughly parallels Richard's earlier one, but the question of guilt is again left unresolved. Indeed, this seems characteristic of the entire episode. Any explanation of Bagot's presence or of his accusation of Aumerle, also an erstwhile supporter of Richard's, is smothered by Henry's command that Bagot refrain from taking up Aumerle's gage (IV, i, 30). It is also overriden by the subsequent alignment of Fitzwater, Percy, and the nameless lord against Aumerle and then against Surrey. But that alignment also ends undramatically with the news of Mowbray's death in exile. The episode focuses attention on Aumerle, who in later scenes is to appear in a stronger theatrical light than he has so far received. With the matter that immediately follows, it also brings Carlyle once more to the audience's attention (e.g., ll. 91-100); but these 106 lines—the major portion of the shortened deposition scene—are less artistically purposeful in the stage-world of *Richard II* than are any of the other incidents Shakespeare chose to dramatize in this play.

With York's entrance, as was indicated above, the scene turns to a simple representation of the event that caused the "blood of English" to "manure the ground" and "future ages" to groan. The Lord Appellants' "days of trial" are forgotten. Of the figures who entered at the beginning of the scene only Bolingbroke and Carlyle have speaking parts in this incident. It is not surprising, then, that the words and the theatrical position given Bolingbroke, as well as the speeches given Carlyle, indicate what major emphasis there is here.

Bolingbroke's dominance had been established in the immediacy of the theater by the first incident, wherein he appeared in a controlling and commanding position. In the shortened version of the scene, however, any impression that Henry is hypocritical probably would be less easily forgotten than in the fuller version, in which, presumably, it would be subordinate to the emphasis that dominates the scene once Richard appears. Such an impression, at any rate, probably would depend most clearly upon the lines which close the quarrel:

> Repeal'd he [Norfolk] shall be,
> And, though mine enemy, restor'd again
> To all his lands and signories.
> (ll. 87-89)

> Sweet Peace conduct his sweet soul to the bosom
> Of good old Abraham!
> (ll. 103-4)

An impression of hypocrisy may also have been derived, though much more indirectly, from Bolingbroke's use of the royal "we" (l. 106) immediately before York's contradictory "Great Duke of Lancaster" (l. 107). Yet any partiality of an Elizabethan audience for a regal mercy might be brought to bear upon the first of the lines quoted above—a regal mercy to be extended to Aumerle in succeeding scenes and explicitly extended here to Norfolk, as it was not extended willingly to the banished Hereford even when he became Lancaster. In such a manner a simple, forthright interpretation of those speeches might be substantiated. Similarly, the explicit force of the lines that follow "Great Duke of Lancaster" with their emphasis upon descent might well substantiate in the world of the theater both Bolingbroke's preceding dominance and his use of the royal "we":

> Great Duke of Lancaster, I come to thee
> From plume-pluck'd Richard; who with willing soul
> Adopts thee heir, and his high sceptre yields
> To the possession of thy royal hand.
> Ascend his throne, descending now from him;
> And long live Henry, fourth of that name!
> (ll. 107-12)

What follows is Bolingbroke's visible ascent; and the dramatization, as mentioned above, is one in which contrary emphases alternate. York's lines about Richard's "willing soul" in adopting Bolingbroke "heir" and yielding the "high scepter" to Lancaster's now "royal hand," the last two lines quoted above, and Bolingbroke's

> In God's name, I'll ascend the regal throne,
>
> (l. 113)

agree with Northumberland's arrest of a treasonable Carlyle (ll. 150-53) and with Henry's lines that immediately follow in the shortened version:

> Let it be so, and loe on Wednesday next,
> We solemnly proclaime our Coronation,
> Lords be ready all.[28]

Interpolated in such speeches and their accompanying action, however, is Carlyle's relatively long protest against Henry's ascent, a protest that repeats the theme and is phrased in the words of Richard's earlier "heroic" speech at Flint Castle. For that matter, the bishop repeats the idea he expressed in the first lines that Shakespeare gave him in the play (III, ii, 27-32). Such an attitude is then renewed in the third incident. At that time, Carlyle, the Abbot of Westminster, and Aumerle remain on stage to end the scene. Since there has been no strong cohesive element achieved by the dramatization of Richard's appearance, one is left with a reflection of historical traditions that can be described briefly as Lancastrian (ll. 107-13), Richardian and Yorkist (ll. 114-49), Lancastrian (ll. 150-53 and ll. 319-20), and Yorkist (ll. 321-34).

In a Lancastrian context, "My Lord of Westminster" was apparently Lancastrian, thus Northumberland seemed to rely upon him when Carlyle was arrested:

> My Lord of Westminster, be it your charge
> To keep him safely till his day of trial.
>
> (ll. 152-53)

But at the close of the scene, that is, in the third Yorkist incident, he is Richardian and Yorkist:

> My lord,
> Before I freely speak my mind herein,

> You shall not only take the sacrament
> To bury mine intents, but also to effect
> Whatever I shall happen to devise.
> I see your brows are full of discontent,
> Your hearts of sorrow, and your eyes of tears.
> Come home with me to supper; [and] I'll lay
> A plot shall show us all a merry day.[29]
>
> (ll. 326-34)

As unemphasized as Bolingbroke's preceding "hypocrisy" is any irony inherent in this final grouping of characters, in which a churchly prophet leaves the stage with those who by plots would disturb a kingdom and make the bishop's woeful prophecy come true in search of their "merry day." Once more, the usually explicit nature of Elizabethan drama, and particularly the lines phrased poetically in the second incident, would probably militate against such a reaction; but it is inescapable that the alignment of the abbot accords with the alternating emphases just noted and with the consideration that the shortened scene reminds one of an earlier dramatic artistry.

More important than what has just been considered is the fact that, by length of speech and by effective poetic lines, the second episode is developed with emphasis upon the simple world-picture that had supported Richard's heroic speech in the Flint Castle episode and will accord with the development of the third situation. It is this effectiveness that might well have dominated the balancing but brief vigor of Bolingbroke, which in turn accords with his forceful dominance in the first situation. Presumably, such an emphasis by speech and poetic line would be more readily perceived by a reading than by a theatrical audience, and in such a manner the scene was printed in a year of turmoil and official scrutiny. As a work of art, however, it leaves much to be desired, even though a succession of varying emphases larger than that noted above is also apparent: theatrically dominant Bolingbroke in the first episode; ascending Bolingbroke, but poetically dominant Carlyle in the second; theatrically dominant Carlyle and colleagues in the third. Such a development (which includes the smaller alternation of contrary emphases just noted) also reminds one of any naïve theatrical world wherein the author rests upon an immediate theatrical expression as its own excuse.

Any simple Elizabethan world-picture, however, is quite inadequate to represent the concept supporting the dominant poetry of the full deposition scene, just as it is inadequate for the theatrically valid vigor of Bolingbroke. This can be illustrated by the added material that appears even before Richard enters. In the first place, after the Richardian Carlyle has been arrested for a Lancastrian treason, in the full deposition scene attention is turned immediately to the "common's suit" (ll. 154-57), and in subsequent lines this suit will appear not simply as a possible reflection of Holinshed's statement that the commons favored Henry but, more obviously, as an insistence that Richard read "this paper" listing the "accusations" and "crimes" which, publicly confessed, make "the souls of men" deem Richard to be "worthily depos'd."[30] Even here in these few lines the desire is that the deposition shall proceed "in common view" so that there may be no suspicion (ll. 155-57). In the second place, between York's exit and his re-entrance with Richard, the dominant and forceful Bolingbroke of the quarreling incident again appears:

> Lords, you that here are under arrest,
> Procure your sureties for your days of answer.
> Little are we beholding to your love,
> And little look'd for at your helping hands.
> *Re-enter* York, *with* Richard.
>
> (ll. 158-61)

With Richard's entrance, the "busy," climactic portion of the scene begins, and Shakespeare achieves in its dramatization an emphasis thoroughly harmonious with the final effect of the Flint Castle scene and also with the censure and pity of the garden scene. His brief representation, at the beginning of the Flint Castle episode, of a contrast between Bolingbroke and Northumberland is continued and intensified, as is his composition of most of Richard's speeches in a Richardian and a Yorkist vein of history and in the manner of laments associated with the fall of the illustrious. In addition, though, he now places Richard, intermittently but paradoxically, in one strain of the Lancastrian tradition that represented him as willingly resigning the throne in public.[31] The result is that lamenting speeches—which here, as in the Flint Castle episode, are given almost exclusively to Richard—become part of a ritual of deposition performed by Richard himself. Even from such general remarks, the cohesive artistry of the full deposition scene and of the Flint Castle episode is obvious. When seen in such a light, the artistry of Shakespeare's deposition can be analyzed rather fully, although it is illustrated here by considering only four aspects of this dramatization that did not appear in print until the publication of the fourth quarto (1608).

The first consideration concerns Shakespeare's handling of Henry. By the length and number of the speeches given Richard, Shakespeare has so manipulated this scene, with the additional matter connected with "the commons' suit," that the relative silence of Bolingbroke has a Lancastrian force. Previously in this scene, during the transfer of regalia, Bolingbroke's three brief lines, one of them a question (ll. 190, 194, 200), are concerned with his refusal to be a struggling participant in the ritual of deposition; they rest upon York's report of Richard's willingness to dethrone himself (ll. 107-12) and upon York's kindred answer to Richard's introductory speech (ll. 177-80). In the contention between Northumberland and Richard, the first of Henry's two brief lines grants Richard's request for a mirror (l. 268), the second would silence Northumberland (l. 271). At this last point in the scene, although the ceremony of deposition had been lengthened by Richard's poetic speeches and reproaches—which strongly qualify the effect of his willing participation—those very speeches, building upon his previous "frantic" passiveness, may well have increased his pathetic appeal. As a consequence, Henry would appear as the intercessor between a pitiable Richard and Richard's "Fiend" who is insisting upon a public confession of those accusations and "grievous" crimes committed "Against the state and profit of this land" (ll. 155-57, 222-27, 270-72). From such a position, Shakespeare then has Richard represent Bolingbroke as a silent spectator to a moral mirror episode that here, as elsewhere in Elizabethan thought and literature, was considered to be especially suitable for principal rulers. Henry, in brief, acts upon the words of York, ignores Richard's censure, while saving a weeping Richard from fully condemning himself for violating the purpose and nature of a commonweal. He then listens, with only one brief correction, to Richard's exposition of his sorrow. In other words, as the emotional force in the play runs from criticism of Richard (II, i) to pathos for Richard (especially in the fifth act), Bolingbroke's position accords with such a movement.[32]

Obviously involved with this aspect of the portrayal of Bolingbroke is the impression created by the appearance of Richard, whose speeches and actions within this deposition scene effect successive shifts in emphasis. Those variations appear in Richard's lamentation and censure of his own fall (ll. 181-221) and are intensified during his contentious dialogue with Northumberland (ll. 222-75). They lead, of course, into the mirror episode, which is considered below.

In comparison with the effect of Shakespeare's handling of Henry, the effect developed by Richard's lines is a good deal more complex. Essentially Lancastrian by their continuity with York's statement about Richard's "willing soul" are his opening lines:

> Alack, why am I sent for to a king
> Before I have shook off the regal thoughts
> Wherewith I reign'd?
>
> (ll. 162-64)

But a qualified movement in the opposite direction is immediately begun, ending with the close of this introductory speech (particularly lines 174-75). Such a development is momentarily stopped in turn by York's third speech, which emphasizes Richard's "own good will," his "tired majesty," and his "resignation" of his "state and crown" (ll. 177-80). An opposite movement begins immediately, however, and culminates in the lines that accompany the visible tipping of the crown grasped by opposing figures. It is then that Shakespeare returns to Richard's "high" frame of reference for Bolingbroke.

That bucket down and full of tears am I,
Drinking my griefs, whilst you mount up on high.
(ll. 188-89)

Stopped again by Henry's statement, "I thought you had been willing to resign" (1. 190), this variable movement then turns—by a momentary emphasis on "griefs" and "cares," which accords with York's "tired majesty"—to a Lancastrian culmination in

God save King Henry, unking'd Richard says,
And send him many years of sunshine days!
(ll. 220-21)[33]

Briefly, the preceding emphases are Lancastrian (ll. 162-67), Richardian (ll. 167-76), Lancastrian (ll. 177-80), Richardian (ll. 181-90), and Lancastrian (ll. 190-222).

With the transfer of regalia completed,[34] this movement of successive emphases starts once more after the "accusations" and "crimes" of the "commons' suit" are mentioned.[35] It is then that Northumberland takes York's dramatic position as the third figure involved in the dialogue. As a consequence, the next movement toward censure is pointed strongly at Northumberland, overrides a line by that earl (1. 243), but comes to rest upon the Yorkist note:

Good king, great king, and yet not greatly good. . . .
(1. 263)

Such a development is stopped by a Henry who opposes an insistent Northumberland; and these varying emphases then culminate in a Richard reproving himself as the cause of his own fall in a context other than that of violating his simplified world-order. Previously, in lines that preceded the culminating censure that rested on Henry (". . . *and yet not greatly good*"), Richard had accused himself of treason defined in the light of his personalized divine-rightist logic:

I find myself a traitor with the rest;
For I have given here my soul's consent
To undeck the pompous body of a king;

> Made glory base, and sovereignty a slave,
> Proud majesty a subject, state a peasant.
>
> (ll. 248-52)

Now at the conclusion of contention with Northumberland, which involves not simply speeches but an action that Richard wishes to avoid, Richard blames himself again; but this time, by being connected with the commons' suit and the satisfaction of the ruled, his censure of himself takes on a Lancastrian color, involving something other than a ruler's own state and logic, even though Richard continues to personalize his concepts:

> *Boling.* Urge it no more, my Lord Northumberland.
> *North.* The commons will not then be satisfi'd.
> *K. Rich.* They shall be satisfi'd. I'll read enough,
> When I do see the very book indeed
> Where all my sins are writ, and that's myself.
>
> (ll. 271-75)[36]

At the moment, an oversimplified divine-rightist attitude has given way to one more nearly accordant with the age's Aristotelian definition of a commonweal. From a modern point of view, it is difficult to think of any sixteenth-century composition that in such a short space might be said to embody so neatly the inevitable and perilous eddy produced by those cross-currents of political thought and Elizabethan compromise outlined in the preceding chapters. Yet within the theater, any such conscious speculation probably would be restrained by the attention focused upon the stage action and upon this dramatic portrayal of forceful, contending, wavering, and weeping persons.

As has been noted above, part of the artistry which effects this result and which has been considered here as the second aspect of the scene seems to be produced by alternating emphases; but this aspect of Shakespeare's artistry is much more concise than it was in Marlowe's comparable drama, and it is accomplished primarily by the speeches of one figure alone. After the strong Lancastrian emphasis of "God save King Henry, unking'd Richard says, / And send him many years of sunshine days!" (ll. 220-22), a Richardian and Yorkist emphasis has been developed with great intensity (ll. 223-63), to be succeeded once more by the Lancastrian stopping point just noted (ll. 263-75).

Such a development centering in the figure of Richard is interlocked, obviously, with the speeches and relative silence of Henry and is consistent with the demonstrable ambiguity of the mirror episode into which it leads, an episode that produces an effect thoroughly consonant with that of the ending to the Flint Castle scene, although such an effect is again intensified.

The mirror episode can serve as the third illustration of Shakespeare's artistry in the full deposition scene, for the various meanings of a mirror may well have influenced Shakespeare to include the incident in his dramatization. As with all popular symbols, however, especially those having a wide range of possible meanings, the intent to be conveyed will be determined by the context. In the visual arts, Jan van Eck, for example, had framed a mirror with scenes of the Passion to delimit its meaning.[37] In Shakespeare's dramatization a moral is attached explicitly to the incident (l. 290); while the connection of the mirrow with truth, and with brittleness also, must have been fairly obvious: the mirror will show Richard himself, but Richard, his majesty, and his glory are "crack'd in an hundred shivers" (ll. 265-67, 273-75, 287-89). In the mirror are reflected Richard's sins and follies, his being beguiled by flatterers and by a false magnificence (ll. 275, 279-85); and in this respect, the episode leads into a differentiation between shadow and substance (ll. 292-98). As other writers have noted in part, Shakespeare seems to have developed the episode in accordance with this group of ideas, which here constitute the context of a symbol and specify the traditional meanings now being attached to it.

In the iconography of the period, the mirror of Prudence or Wisdom often occurs—for example, in the representations of Truth. It might also appear as an attribute of Vainglory and Pride.[38] With an awareness of such conflicting meanings, one thinks immediately of a process of thought underlying the sequence of the pageants for Elizabeth's coronation. In the second of those pageants, the moral of which was to be inculcated later by contrasting commonweals, Time and Truth reveal how the "seate of worthie governance" was upheld, among other things, by Wisdom treading upon Folly and Vainglory; and twice, at least, the ruler was warned about adulation and flattery. Such a process of thought partially agrees with the preceding meanings, even though they are antithetical, and agrees also with the meaning a mirror might have as a mirror for magistrates. With the difference between shadow and substance, one thinks of Macrobius' mirror; and "when the King dashes the mirror to the ground and comments upon the brittleness of glory, we remember the figure of *Fortuna Vitrea* and those representations of the goddess where, as in Bellini's painting, she holds in her hand a brittle globe of glass."[39]

Utilizing all of these public meanings, Shakespeare develops a unique scene once more. Richard's "Proud majesty" (1. 252) surveys itself and speaks of the flattery conventionally associated with pride of life in high station; and the truth is apparent in such a comment, just as pride is apparent in the reference to the magnificence of a royal household and the sun-like countenance of majesty—a countenance wrested, however, so that it "fac'd so many follies" and was at last "out-fac'd."

> Give me that glass, and therein will I read.
> No deeper wrinkles yet? Hath sorrow struck
> So many blows upon this face of mine,
> And made no deeper wounds? O flatt'ring glass,
> Like to my followers in prosperity,
> Thou dost beguile me! Was this face the face
> That every day under his household roof
> Did keep ten thousand men? Was this the face
> That, like the sun, did make beholders wink?
> Is this the face which fac'd so many follies,
> That was at last out-fac'd by Bolingbroke?
> A brittle glory shineth in this face;
> As brittle as the glory is the face,
> For there it is, crack'd in an hundred shivers.
>
> (ll. 276-89)

These aspects of Truth—that is, this perception of Folly and Vainglory on the part of Proud Majesty—keep the episode from being developed only within the limits determined, for example, by the nature of the mirror in Macrobius[40] and keep it from being a simple representation of Donne's later statement that a "glass is not the less brittle, because a king's face is represented in it; nor a king the less brittle, because God is represented in him."[41] The name of "king" as a merited name also comes into play. Although Richard's constant association of his sorrow with his erstwhile majesty carries with it at least an oblique censure of Henry, this truth of a lack of merit is linked with the truth of the brittleness of glory, whereupon Richard moves into a rhetorical position from which he indicates, like the interpreter of a pageant, that new majesty may learn from old and, like Prudence, look before and after. Thus the widespread mirror tradition applicable to magistrates also finds its way into the preceding context of meanings, especially when the mirror is dashed to the ground:

> Mark, silent king, the moral of this sport,
> How soon my sorrow hath destroyed my face.
>
> (ll. 290-91)

It is not entirely adequate to emphasize the second of the conflicting mirror meanings noted above and to point out that for "the spectator into whose memory these meanings flashed Richard would become the embodiment of Pride and Vainglory and also a travesty of Wisdom and Prudence, as indeed he is."[42] In such a commentary, the rhetorical movement whereby a moral would be pointed for the observing "silent king" is too easily ignored, a moral that embodies the truthful idea not only of the brittleness of glory but also of the way in which a lamenting, fond, and frantic Richard had been outfaced by Bolingbroke so that in sorrow a Wisdom "who knows herself" now speaks, and a Prudence "who looks before and after" is not entirely absent from Richard himself.

Yet, once more, it would be a mistake not to indicate that the contrary emphasis pointed out in the preceding quotation is also present; for Richard's sorrow remains essentially personalized, reproaching, and concerned with the state of sovereignty alone, rather than with the state of the body politic outside the court or the state of "children yet unborn." His actions, and not simply his "sorrows," have shown this in more ways than one. The point is made by Bolingbroke, when Shakespeare turns to conventional associations related to substance and shadow. Richard's sorrow has not destroyed his face; the shadow of his sorrow has destroyed what was the shadow of his face.[43] Thus an idea expressed earlier in the play by a "caterpillar" speaking of a perspective glass can be said to be applicable to Richard's view of himself, which

> ... look'd on as it is, is nought but shadows
> Of what it is not.
>
> (II, ii, 23-24)

For to Richard, the substance of his fall—that which has shattered his "brittle glory"—is expressed most frequently by his censure of others and most noticeably in this scene when he leaves the stage with a new image congruent with his earlier lines that had accompanied the tipping of the crown:

> Conveyers are you all,
> That rise thus nimbly by a true king's fall.
>
> (ll. 317-18)

In a contrary sense of the phrase, and in a context different from that of Bushy's perspective glass (II, ii, 14-27), Richard looks "awry" and falsely sees only the form of fallen majesty, not Gaunt's "tenement or pelting farm" with a state of law that is "bondslave to the law" (and hence a state that violates the very definition of any commonweal) and not the gardeners' land of weeds or of a "disordered spring." His final condemnation here, separated from its next appearance by only some fifty lines, falls upon his former subjects; and when he refers to them again they will be, not former inhabitants of a "pelting farm," nor simply "conveyers," but "beasts":

> A king of beasts, indeed; if aught but beasts,
> I had been still a happy king of men.
>
> (V, i, 35-36)[44]

So it is true that this Richard who was not a king by continuous regal action is also a travesty of Wisdom and Prudence.

# SHAKESPEARE'S DEPOSITION OF RICHARD II 191

In brief, contraries once more co-exist. In addition to what has been noted, the historical truth of Carlyle's prophecy and the truth of Richard as a king by succession are both oblique and explicit within the scene. Such a truth exists with the opposing fact that Richard had not curbed his affections, had allowed and produced a disordered land and a commons' suit, and now truly sees his face, "the very book" wherein all his sins are writ and that is himself. Such a Richard caused Richard's "brittle glory" that could stand as an explicit mirror for others.

Although there is no persistent shifting between contrary emphases, the mirror episode, like the entire scene of Richard's appearance, is protean. From Richard's entrance to his exit, the dominant effect is strikingly akin to that of the Flint Castle episode after Richard's Phaëthon speech; and such an effect is created by an artistry which, in contrast with Bushy's glass, *unites* "many objects" in "one thing entire" and which, in the mirror episode, solidifies a co-existence of many meanings, including antithetical ones.

Since this seems true of the mirror episode, as it was also true of the Phaëthon speech, one might be justified in pointing out, for the fourth and last consideration, how the effect of some other words and images accords with this fusion of antitheses.[45] In this respect, Richard's Christ images are as revealing as they are noticeable. In his introductory speech, for example, Richard had moved to a condemnation of "these men"—Judases (ll. 168-70), who had flattered and betrayed him. Some of them were obviously the same lords "under arrest" for their "days of answer" to whom Bolingbroke was little "beholding." But by Richard's reference to Judas, Shakespeare had returned to a general frame of reference from which one of Carlyle's warnings had been drawn—that England shall

> . . . be call'd
> The field of Golgotha and dead men's skulls.
> (ll. 143-44)

In Richard's speech, however, the innocence implicit in any such figure connected with Christ appears only as the extravagant statement that Richard is more sinned against than was the Saviour.

> Yet I well remember
> The favours of these men. Were they not mine?
> Did they not sometime cry, "All hail!" to me?
> So Judas did to Christ; but He, in twelve,
> Found truth in all but one; I, in twelve thousand, none.
> (ll. 167-71)

Exaggeration, and to that degree travesty, tends to turn the truth awry. Similarly, in contentious dialogue that ends with an admission of guilt, the image reappears in lines which proceed upon the valid assumption that an inferior owes a duty to his superior. In this instance, Shakespeare has had Richard, in his usual manner, link his concept of kingship with the book of heaven, in which the warrant of an oath is now cracked and the oath itself marked "with a blot" and damned (ll. 229-36). Then, as Richard's censure increasingly develops a Yorkist emphasis, Richard returns to a Christ image, now implicit in his reference to the "Pilates" who wash their hands, "Showing an outward pity," but explicit in the reference to Richard's "sour cross" (ll. 239-42). Yet, however applicable the truth under such exaggeration may be, the idea of any reciprocal duty is completely absent; and the wrested logic in the juxtaposition of Richard upon his "sour cross" and Richard's reproving himself, which immediately follows, is preserved in its awryness by the fact that his self-censure here is the result of giving his

> ... soul's consent
> To undeck the pompous body of a king....
> (ll. 249-50)

Although Christ images do not appear in the remainder of the scene, there does appear a process of thought that had been joined with them in Richard's first speech. When he referred to his Judases, Richard had already equated a subject's state with that of a flatterer—

> I hardly yet have learn'd
> To insinuate, flatter, bow, and bend my knee.
> (ll. 164-65)

It is to this frame of reference that Shakespeare returns when the contentious dialogue between Richard and Northumberland moves into the mirror episode and Richard upon viewing his image compares this "flatter'ring glass" to his "followers in prosperity"; the truth is again expressed, but Richard's earlier, awry attitude will be intensified when Shakespeare redevelops this thought process during Richard's dialogue with Bolingbroke.

> "Fair cousin"? I am greater than a king;
> For when I was a king my flatterers
> Were then but subjects; being now a subject,
> I have a king here to my flatterer.
>
> (ll. 305-8)

With such a jibing, but nonetheless twisted, reference, Shakespeare moves Richard to his final forthright denunciation of all on the stage as "conveyers," and to a concomitant reference to himself as "a true king," which is followed by Henry's

> On Wednesday next we solemnly proclaim
> Our coronation. Lords, be ready all.
>
> (ll. 319-20)

Perhaps the preceding discussion, as well as that of the mirror episode, has been extended unrealistically. Yet as long as such considerations substantiate and are not used to determine a major emphasis, they seem permissible. In this instance, they seem to point to a final consideration. Probably the equivocal, and dominantly sorrowful, emphasis of Richard's appearance in three brief dramatic spectacles (the transfer of regalia, contention with Northumberland, and the mirror episode) would not have been dispelled by the fourteen lines spoken after Henry's exit. That ambiguity may well have carried into the forecast of woe for England and a plot for "a merry day."

In the complete deposition scene, the theatricality of quarreling nobles and a dominant Henry, the vigorous protest of Carlyle, the action with scepter and crown, the insistence of Northumberland, the shattering of the mirror, the possibility of a plot in favor of the relatively passive, "frantic" figure, and especially the constantly effective lament-like lyricism given to this fallen figure undoubtedly produced a major emphasis from which the pathos of parting (V, i, 37 ff.) and of York's description of Richard (V, ii, 23-40) would seem to emerge naturally. Henry will then be separated from Richard as he extends mercy to Aumerle, and Richard with a final lyricism will speak of how he had "not an ear" for "the concord" of his "state and time" and did not hear his "true time broke." In such circumstances, an incident of "love to Richard" will hold the stage (V, v, 67-97) before he meets his death with a vigor heretofore lacking. Protest at such a murder is reflected upon the stage only in Exton's words (ll. 114-19), in Henry's denunciation of the murderer (though Henry did wish Richard dead), and finally in this present ruler's "sullen black incontinent" that "blood should sprinkle" him to make him grow (V, vi, 45-52). Such a theatrical paradox, in which stage protest at the death of a ruler finds its strongest expression in the woe of his opponent, is, nevertheless, harmonious with what has preceded—with the Lancastrian features in the portrayal of Henry throughout the drama, the complete absence of soliloquies for this rising figure, and his position in the Northumberland-Richard contention during the deposition scene.

As regards the censorship and publication of the full deposition scene, it is pertinent to note, once more, that the emphasis by speech falls on a Richardian interpretation of history. Such an emphasis is always more evident to a reader than is an emphasis by action or even by brief explicit line, which here, in general, falls in a contrary direction. The historical truth of Carlyle's prophecy alone, coming upon the heels of a representation of quarreling noblemen, may well have carried sufficient weight to keep the play from being considered seditious; and, as far as one knows, no trouble with the authorities was connected with its publication.

As regards its performance, it has already been noted that what variation there is between the full deposition scene in the fourth quarto and in the first folio may well indicate that the quarto version was derived from a theatrical performance. Within the walls of a theater, the constant action, as well as the compelling lyricism of the scene and its promise of further action in favor of Richard, may well have restrained any tendency toward delation on the part of those who watched its performance even in a year of official scrutiny and theatrical turmoil. Certainly the scene is capable of effecting the temporary cessation not only of disbelief but also of speculation, both of which demand a considerable degree of detachment.

Moreover, Shakespeare could have expected his artistry to be supported by that of the Lord Chamberlain's actors, and the weight of patronage aside, such a fact seems important. Even when one allows for an individual "bent," each of the major actors in Shakespeare's company was apparently able to handle successfully a great variety of roles. Augustine Phillips perhaps was assigned the parts of Holofernes, Edward IV, Gratiano, Cassius, as well as Henry IV. John Heminges may have had the parts of Boyet, Glendower, the Chief Justice, and Julius Caesar. Henry Cundall possibly played Northumberland, Antonio in *The Merchant of Venice,* and Antony in *Julius Caesar*.[46] The skill of Burbage became almost proverbial. Certainly, as others have pointed out, it seems a fair conclusion that such actors could become Shakespeare's competent instruments, whose "bent" need not have controlled his art. Even when one allows for the difference in comic artistry which Kemp and Armin presumably showed, yet Armin would advertise himself as one who many times had played the role of Dogberry, a role which probably was designed originally for Kemp.[47] In spite of the transitoriness of acting, the point is not unrelated to Shakespeare's enduring artistry. Directly connected with what has been the major concern of this chapter is the fact that in *Richard II* one finds at least two roles that could support the mature and purposeful complexity of the drama and its attendant conviction of reality, particularly if both parts were acted with something approaching an effective appeal to an audience's sympathies. From such a point of view one may draw support for a similarly complex intent that would increase the dramatic power of a play when later in the century Shakespeare wrote his *Julius Caesar*.[48] In both instances, to emphasize an ethical dichotomy does injustice to Shakespeare's art.

Be the capability of his actors as it may, the striking similarity between the full deposition scene and the end of the Flint Castle episode seems to indicate not only that both scenes were composed at the same time but also that Shakespeare's artistry was purposefully equivocal. Nor need such an intent be explained only by a desire to escape trouble with a licenser, for in his representation of the deposition of Richard, Shakespeare is working with political commonplaces, just as he had in the past, although now he works much more skillfully.

As it was noted at the beginning of this section, the process of thought sketched in the first portion of this essay seems to have provided Shakespeare in the early history plays with some ready-made concepts acquired at first or second hand.[49] These he used in such an obvious way that they need little comment. The total sweep of the *Henry VI* trilogy and *Richard III* amply shows the mutability of man's wit and the concomitant changes in government comparable, for example, to changes in Rome, though they were neither as severe nor as lasting. Thus the favor of God, extended to even an earlier England, might seem to have been apparent when the first of the Tudors won the throne from a thoroughgoing tyrant. No one can deny the reflection of the emotional Tudor myth in such a dramatization. The course of the action, however, might also have been intellectualized by considerations embodied in Smith's sketch of different types of states and their relationship to one another or by the political commonplace that emphasized man's fallibility, perverseness, and the decay or change of states. In that panorama, there appears also the virtue of the many of the Bury St. Edmunds Parliament, a virtue which, because of the corruption of the few, could sustain a weak ruler and precipitate a new series of events. The vice of the many as shown in Cade's revolt was then dramatized almost immediately. Similarly, the virtue of the few in war and in council and the vice of the few in faction and in the devious ways of ambition allow for the development of many scenes. Nor can the ruler be left out. Henry VI's failure to heed good advice leads to his wedding with one of Sidney's "Heroicall minded" ladies, who shows the disposition toward absolutism conventionally associated with the French, and hence not too foreign to those from Anjou. This ruler also fails to support

Gloucester until it is too late; for in general he shows a lack of that vigor so prized by Sidney, and both before and after Gloucester's death he fails to exercise Hooker's "power, even power of dominion" that rests in "the person of a king." In brief, the attributes of vigor and of Christianity are divided between York and Henry, instead of being combined, as was necessary for effective rule. A similar division of necessary attributes produces the conflict and the tragedy of *King John*. In this instance, a rightful succession (Arthur) is separated from a forceful possession (John); and although that forceful possession shows a secret villainy, it does not rely, as does Arthur's right, upon both a foreign and a Catholic power.

As Shakespeare came to the writing of *Richard II*, he utilized another variation within the conventional process of thought sketched earlier, and he thereby gave to his play one aspect of its unique nature. In a manner comparable to what has been noted about the first tetralogy, when the large canvas of the history plays is considered, the result of deposing a ruler who was king by lineal descent accords with the Elizabethan world-picture; yet as *Richard II* was performed by itself (as it must have been, regardless of what preceded it on a previous afternoon and what might follow it on a later one), in more ways than one did Richard "undeck the pompous body of a king." The idea that the sacred name of "king" is not simply inherited, but merited as well, is certainly validated, even as the right and power of lineal descent is expressed by Carlyle and others.

In other words, the two scenes considered here not only utilize at least two aspects of their literary milieu but also employ at least two concepts about rule. On the one hand, Shakespeare brings to bear upon the Flint Castle episode and the full deposition scene an Elizabethan's sensitiveness to the fall and lament tradition and his possible predilection for a simple world-order. On the other hand, Shakespeare utilizes the appeal of a theatrical vigor and a contemporary audience's dislike of a rule that made England a "tenement or pelting farm." In this last instance, a Renaissance preference for a forceful, catalytic rule would be evoked—a rule which was curative and which was not unmerciful, one which was supported by the vast majority of commoners and of noblemen, among whom York finally appeared, and one which was linked with the common's suit. In that they were of the many, the commons could be conventionally conceived of as wavering, but as a body in Parliament, they were not the unruly multitude or the undisciplined many-headed. Their predilection in rule might be conceived of, conventionally, as favoring the vigor and force necessary to produce a prosperous stability;[50] and in Parliament the public action of an entire realm was effected. Hence the description in the fourth quarto of the full deposition scene as "the Parliament Sceane" is revealing in that it substantiates one emphasis Shakespeare brought to bear upon his play, and such a description is confirmed by the initial stage-direction of the shorter deposition scene in the 1597 and 1598 quartos, *"Enter Bull(ingbrooke) with the Lords to Parliament,"* as well as by that in the first folio, *"Enter as to Parliament."*[51] As conflicting meanings of an image and a symbol co-exist, so conflicting attitudes toward kingship are constantly kept alive, and Shakespeare's drama is thereby intensified.

Although this is no place to discuss the artistry of the entire play, yet one should note also that even in Shakespeare's representation of Bolingbroke alone, there is an inescapable ambiguity that must have been purposeful. While Richard constantly places Bolingbroke in the Yorkist historical context of an ambitious, unscrupulous nobleman, Henry in open dialogue that reflects the debate form (II, iii, 81-171) and in lines about himself constantly speaks in a Lancastrian vein, representing himself as an excellent nobleman, grievously wronged. Once there is even a reflection of the extreme Lancastrian position that looked upon Henry as a child of destiny who saved England from a most degenerate state. By the usual "rules" of Elizabethan drama, such conflicting attitudes would be clarified by soliloquies. But as in *Philotas,* soliloquies are almost completely absent. In fact, there is only one true soliloquy in *Richard II*; and since that is given to Richard, Henry remains silent in this respect.[52] Thus although the evils of the time then present are made clear, the motive of the principal doer—that is, Smith's second consideration whereby the wise may judge of disobedience and of changing the rule in a state—is never completely resolved. In the deposition scene, consequently, a "silent" but forceful Bolingbroke and a lyrically lamenting and censuring king, "possess'd" to depose himself, solidify a dominant aspect of Shakespeare's artistry.

That Shakespeare's capabilities were not restricted by Elizabethan censorship, that no record has survived, save one, of the play being delated, that the players who performed *Richard II* on the eve of Essex's revolt were acting again within ten days of their examination by the Privy Council can be explained, in large part, by the nature of Elizabethan political commonplaces and by the way in which they appear in a drama whose author also skillfully uses the literary tools of his trade. Although those tools have not been the primary concern of this study, Shakespeare's use of them illumines the way in which his recreation of Richard's deposition reflects the omnipresent problem of order. To the Elizabethans, the problem involved not simply the actions of the many and the few but the actions of the one as well; and the Elizabethan Parliament, not the ruler alone, was conventionally recognized as representing the force of the whole, determining the succession, and controlling men's estates. Acting with a Christian vigor in accordance with the conventional definition of a commonweal, and hence acting for the good of the whole, also involved accepting what that commonweal had established as its form and its law. The sacred name of "king" was not only inherited but also merited, and the problem of order became intense and perilous when those two attributes were not united in one person. Drawing upon conflicting images, conflicting meanings of one image or symbol, and conflicting speeches and actions, Shakespeare intensifies his play-world in the scenes just considered and fused their contraries, including those which reflect political commonplaces, into "one thing entire" though equivocal. By that equivocality, his representation of Richard's deposition expresses concisely but forcefully the unresolved nature of the crux noted at the beginning of this section, a crux that needed no resolution in the political thought of those who rejoiced in the reign of Gloriana and who felt that her unenvious love was not "countervailed" and that she, in contrast to earlier rulers, did do her duty in that state of life to which it had pleased God to call her.

As it was noted at the beginning of this study, Shakespeare's contemporaries knew that not all nations, and not all Englishmen, had been as fortunate as they. Sometimes the truths of political commonplaces had conflicted and could not be resolved. Nor for a dramatist, and especially an Elizabethan one, was such a resolution needed. The crux could aid in making a drama absorbing, especially one that would recreate and thereby interpret history. In *Richard II,* the unique contexts that Shakespeare created effected an equally unique characterization; and thereby his artistry at least approached the practice of Pontano, Comines, and Guicciardini. Outstanding historians, these men were concerned primarily with war, with its unexpected contingencies, such as those of the weather or of rumor, and with the supernatural phenomena that seemed to indicate the processes behind appearances. But while allowing for circumstances beyond man's ken and control, Comines and Guicciardini so described the wisdom and folly, the virtues and vices, of the principal men engaged in such conflicts that personalities became real, and none could escape the sense of the participants' individualities.[53] This, too, one sees in Shakespeare's play, especially in his silent Bolingbroke and lamenting Richard. As a consequence, unless the critic or reader can be satisfied only with dichotomies, he should be thankful that the process of thought here considered contributed to such a result and that *Richard II* is as much of a problem play as any of the later "problem comedies."[54]

# Notes

## Chapter I

1. *Iustiniani Digesta* (I. 4. 1), ed. Theodore Mommsen, in *Corpus Iuris Civilis*, I (Berlin, 1920). See Otto Friedrich von Gierke, *The Political Theories of the Middle Ages*, tr. Frederic W. Madden (Cambridge, 1922), pp. 39, 42-43, 147, 150; and the quotations given by Fritz Kern, *Gottesgnadentum und Widerstandsrecht im früheren Mittelalter* (Darmstadt, 1954), p. 213, n. 461; also R. W. Carlyle and A. J. Carlyle, *A History of Medieval Political Theory in the West* (Edinburgh, 1936), VI, 15-16, 19-20, 152-56, 300, 323. J. W. Gough, *The Social Contract* (Oxford, 1957), p. 21: ". . . it was a maxim of Roman Law that, by the *lex regia*, the authority of the emperor himself was derived from the people." On the relationship between the social contract and the governmental contract, see Gough, pp. 37-40. About the social contract he writes as follows: "Popularized, like its great rival, in the age of the Renaissance despots, and to a great extent, in fact, a protest against the overweening powers they claimed to hold, it grew from ideas already current in the Middle Ages, which can be traced back to that very Investiture Contest between Popes and Emperours which also brought the claims of divine right into prominence" (p. 2); see also John Neville Figgis, *The Divine Right of Kings* (Cambridge, 1922), pp. 38 ff.
2. Gierke, *Pol. Theories*, pp. 32-33, 44-45. For the expression in England that the king may not violate positive law, since positive law declares divine or natural law, see Charles H. McIlwaine, *The High Court of Parliament and Its Supremacy* (New Haven, 1910), pp. 66-74; see also Stanley Burton Chrimes, *English Constitutional Ideas in the Fifteenth Century* (Cambridge, 1936), pp. 59-61; note, however, below, p. 20, n. 36. See the examples in Carlyle, *Hist. Med. Pol. Theory* (Edinburgh, 1927), I, 240 ff.; Gough, *Social Contract*, pp. 25-26; Chrimes, *Eng. Const. Ideas*, pp. 18-19.
3. *The History of the World* (London, 1614), I, 294.
4. W. S. Holdsworth, *A History of English Law* (Boston, Mass., 1923), II, 408; Charles H. McIlwaine, *The Growth of Political Thought in the West* (New York, 1932), p. 361; Chrimes, *Eng. Const. Ideas,* pp. 59-61; H. D. Hazeltine's preface to S. B. Chrimes's edition of the *De Laudibus Legum Angliae* (Cambridge, 1942); Max Adams Shepard, "The Political and Constitutional Theory of Sir John Fortescue," *Essays in Historical and Political Theory in Honour of Charles Howard McIlwaine* (Cambridge, 1936), pp. 289-319; George L. Mosse, "Change and Continuity in the Tudor Constitution," *Speculum*, XXII (1947), 18-28; Caroline A. J. Skeels, "The Influence of the Writings of Sir John Fortescue," *Transactions of the Royal Historical Society*, Series 3, X (1916), 77-114; R. W. K. Hinton, "English Constitutional Doc-

trines from the Fifteenth Century to the Seventeenth. I. English Constitutional Theories from Sir John Fortescue to Sir John Eliot," *EHR*, LXXV (1960), 410-25. Hinton would modify the views of McIlwaine and Chrimes in the direction of Plummer's view, i.e., that Fortescue foreshadows a nineteenth-century constitutional concept, "the accepted hallmark of which was parliamentary sovereignty." For an interpretation of Fortescue's immediate purpose and of "attitudes that conditioned his ideas," see Arthur B. Ferguson, "Fortescue and the Renaissance: A Study in Transition," *Studies in the Renaissance*, VI (1959), 175-94. See also below, chap. II, n. 96.

5. For a brief description of Reginald Pole's point of view, expressed in his *Pro Ecclesiasticae Unitatis Defensione* (Strassburg, 1555), see Winthrop S. Hudson, *John Ponet (1516?-1556): Advocate of Limited Monarchy* (Chicago, 1942), pp. 174-75.

6. *A History of Greater Britain as Well England as Scotland, 1521*, tr. Archibald Constable (Scottish Hist. Soc., 1892), pp. 82, 158, 213-15.

7. See Hudson, *John Ponet*, pp. 189-90. Hudson is discussing John Aylmer's *An Harborowe for Faithfull and Trewe Subjectes* (Strassburg, 1559); Lawrence Humphrey's *De Religionis Conservatione et Reformatione Vera* (Basel, 1559); and John Hale's oration. See also A. F. Scott Pearson, *Thomas Cartwright and Elizabethan Puritanism, 1535-1603* (Cambridge, 1925), pp. 419-21, as well as pp. 42-45, 142; M. M. Knappen, *Tudor Puritanism* (Chicago, 1939), pp. 173-76. For difficulty which Cartwright later encountered in connection with the idea of an Aristotelian "mixed" state, in this instance that of Sparta, see Scott Pearson, *Cartwright*, pp. 333-35.

8. C. W. Previté-Orton, "Marsilius of Padua," *Proceedings of the British Academy*, XXI (1935), 156.

9. *De Regimine Principum*, I. vi. *Saint Thomas Aquinas on the Governance of Rulers*, tr. Gerald B. Phelan (New York, 1938), pp. 55-61. On this passage, see Gough, *Social Contract*, p. 37, as well as one aspect of Ponet's thought (his scale of revolt), below, pp. 78-79; and for advice to Mary that she not proceed without Parliament in matters of religion, see Richard W. Dixon, *History of the Church of England* (London, 1891), IV, 15-17.

10. *The Two Liturgies . . . with Other Documents Set Forth . . . in the Reign of King Edward VI*, ed. Joseph Ketley, Parker Soc., 1844, p. 123. See also pp. 495 ff., as well as pp. ix-xi; and, for the Ponet Catechism, pp. xii, 544-71. For the use of catechisms in the schools, see the footnote immediately following.

11. *A Catechism Written in Latin by Alexander Nowell . . . with the Same Catechism Translated into English by Thomas Norton*, ed. G. E. Corrie, Parker Soc., 1853, pp. 130, 132-33. "Let them [the grammar-school pupils] say *Nowels Catechisme*, or the *Palatinate Catechisme* on Saturdaies. By this meanes they will become familiary acquainted with the Latine and Greek Tongues." T. W. Baldwin, *William Shakspere's small Latine and lesse Greeke* (Urbana, 1944), I, 457, quoting from C. Hoole.

12. As quoted by E. M. W. Tillyard, *Shakespeare's History Plays* (New York, 1946), p. 19. As it has been noted above, the author emphasizes this process of thought; see also his other quotations.

13. *Robert Laneham's Letter*, ed. F. J. Furnivall, New Shakesp. Soc., Series VI, no. 14, pp. 54-55. As it might be expected, this follows his rhapsody on "the dignitée of onehod" (pp. 53-54).

14. As quoted by Arthur O. Lovejoy, *The Great Chain of Being* (Cambridge, Mass., 1936), p. 68 (i.e., *Paradiso*, XXIX, 130-45; XIII, 56, 58-63).

15. Further details for this and the paragraphs that follow immediately will be found in Tillyard, *Shakespeare's Hist. Plays*, pp. 6-7, 10-20. Variations are found constantly in the literature of the period—e.g., in regard to the

"hierarchy" apparent in man's brain—but as a general picture what is sketched below seems a fair one.

16. As given by Lovejoy, *Great Chain of Being*, p. 63 (i.e., *Comment. in Som. Scip.*, I, 14, 15).

17. Certain features of this statement are discussed below. See, e.g., the contrast between Hooker's and Ponet's treatment of the law of nature and the law of reason; yet the simplified process of thought here indicated appears so frequently as to almost preclude glossing. Note, on the one hand, the basic design of John Bale's *Three Laws* and, on the other, the way in which Sir John Hayward brings the Golden Rule into his discussion as late as 1603: "God in the creation of man, imprinted certain rules within his soul, to direct him in all the actions of his life; which rules, because we took them when we took our being, are commonly called the primary law of Nature: of which sort the canons account these precepts following. To worship God: to obey parents and governors, and thereby to conserve common society: lawful conjunction of man and woman: succession of children: education of children: acquisition of things which pertain to no man: equal liberty of all: to communicate commodities: to repel force: to hurt no man: and generally, *to do to another as he would be done unto*. . . . Out of these precepts are formed certain customs, generally observed in all parts of the world; which, because they were not from the beginning, but brought in afterward . . . are called the secondary law of nature, and by many also the law of nations." Quoted by Theodore Spencer, *Shakespeare and the Nature of Man* (New York, 1943), p. 15. The italics are mine. The relationship of such a discussion to the catechistical matter quoted above is obvious.

18. J. E. Neale, *Elizabeth I and Her Parliaments, 1559-1581* (London, 1952), pp. 172, 284, and *passim;* below, pp. 16-17, 27.

19. See below, pp. 42, 56.

20. Willard Farnham, *The Medieval Heritage of Elizabethan Tragedy* (Berkeley, Cal., 1956), p. 332, quoting Sir Francis Hubert's *the Historie of Edward the Second*.

21. See below, pp. 17-18.

22. Quoted by Baldwin, *Shakspere's small Latine*, II, 587.

23. Nowell, *Catechism*, p. 131. The italics are mine.

24. *Summa Contra Gentiles*, tr. English Dominican Fathers (London, 1923), II, 106-7 (II. 45).

25. Conyers Read, *Lord Burghley and Queen Elizabeth* (London, 1960), pp. 325-26 (Burghley's "Advice to Queen Elizabeth in Matters of Religion and State," MS Harl. Misc., VII, 57).

26. Conyers Read, *Mr. Secretary Walsingham and the Policy of Queen Elizabeth* (Oxford, 1925), III, 241 (MS Galba C xi, f. 292).

27. Such a commonplace certainly precludes glossing; yet see Robert Cecil's comment on the popular agitation against monopolies: "We being here are but the popular branch, and our liberty the liberty of the subject; and the world is apt to slander most especially the ministers of government." J. E. Neale, *Elizabeth I and Her Parliaments, 1584-1601* (New York, 1958), p. 386; Sir Simon D'Ewes, *A Compleat Journal of the Votes, Speeches, and Debates Both of the House of Lords and House of Commons throughout the Whole Reign of Queen Elizabeth* (London, 1693), p. 651.

28. Neale, *Eliz. and Parl., 1584-1601*, pp. 172-73. This distinction between types of government, in relationship to the validity of revolt, is especially interesting in that it appears in a speech animated by a belief in God's immediacy in human affairs and His punishment of a nation for their sins. It illustrates neatly the polemical force of political *thought*, rather than political *theory*.

29. Neale, *Eliz. and Parl., 1584-1601*, pp. 174-75, 180-81.

30. Neale, *Eliz. and Parl., 1559-1581*, pp. 105, 155-57, 335, and *passim*. See also Richard T. Vann, "The Free Anglo-Saxons: A Historical Myth," *JHI*, XIX (1958), 264; and Neale, *Eliz. and Parl., 1584-1601*, pp. 319-20; *Eliz. and Parl., 1559-1581*, pp. 419-21. For the respect that Elizabeth, and even Whitgift, showed for agitation in Parliament, see Neale, *Eliz. and Parl., 1584-1601*, p. 358.

31. For Wentworth, see Neale, *Eliz. and Parl., 1559-1581*, pp. 318-32; *Eliz. and Parl., 1584-1601*, pp. 154-58, 164. For the quotation from Aristotle, see *The Works of Aristotle*, ed. W. D. Ross (Oxford, 1921), X, 1329 a-b (*Politica*, VII. 10). In 1576, Wentworth was greatly concerned that Elizabeth had not proceeded against Mary Queen of Scots and had repressed the Puritans. On the first day of the session, begun quite decorously, he rose to make a motion about liberty of speech and began to criticize Elizabeth sharply for her treatment of bills against Mary passed by the previous Parliament. In view of previous references here to the necessity for good advice and hence the danger of flattery, the Germanic theory of kingship, and the House of Common's sensitiveness to their prerogatives, and in view also of subsequent references to Bracton, some of the points in the course of his argument deserve brief notice. Before being stopped, he had proceeded upon the following grounds: "Sweet indeed is the name of liberty and the thing itself a value beyond all inestimable treasure"; free speech in Parliament, moreover, is what distinguishes that "honourable Council" from "a very school of flattery and dissimulations." Giving heed in Parliament to rumors of the sovereign's pleasure or displeasure and bringing messages "commanding and inhibiting" are, consequently, "traitorous and hellish." Such actions "through flattery" seek "to devour our natural Prince." This was substantiated by the following argument. The ruler, as Bracton shows, is under no man "but under God and under the law because the law maketh him a king"; he is "God's vicegerent here upon earth . . . to execute and do His will, the which is law and justice"; thereunto "was her Majesty sworn at her coronation" as he had heard "learned men in this place sundry times affirm." Since the Queen "is the head of the law and must of necessity maintain the law," and since "Free speech and conscience in this place are granted by a special law, as that without the which the Prince and State cannot be preserved or maintained," all who attempt to restrict that freedom are culpable. In view of the matter at hand, then, "none is without fault: no, not our noble Queen." She has "commited great faults—yea, dangerous faults to herself and the State" by opposing herself to "her nobility and people." Also "all messengers, tale-carriers, or any other thing" do "infringe the liberties of this honourable Council," a body that is "incorporated into this place to serve God and all England, and not to be time-servers and humour-feeders." He, consequently, would censure also those who vote with the "best sort" in spite of their earnest speeches; for it is "a shameful thing to serve God, their Prince, or country with the tongue only and not with the heart and body." When he was stopped as he began to censure Elizabeth's treatment of bills against Mary, he delivered all of his oration to the Committee of the House appointed to examine him and made up of privy councilors and other officials; there he answered a charge of uttering rumor himself about the Queen's "misliking of religion and succession" by refusing to answer the committee if they questioned him as "Councillors" rather than "as committees from the House": "For I am no private person: I am a public, and a counsellor to the whole State, in that place where it is lawful for me to speak my mind freely. . . ." See also Christopher Hatton's speech noted below, chap. I, n. 36.

32. *The Fourth Part of the Institutes of the Laws of England* (London,

1817), p. 1. See also the earlier definition of Parliament in a phraseology reminiscent of Smith's (below, p. 31): "the highest and most honourable and absolute court of justice in *England,* consisting of the King, the lords of parliament, and the commons." *The First Part of the Institutes of the Laws of England* (Dublin, 1791), p. 109 b (II. 10. 164).

33. Cited, e.g., by Wallace Notestein, "The Winning of the Initiative by the House of Commons," *Proc. Br. Academy,* XI (1924-25), 126.

34. See, e.g., Chrimes, *Eng. Const. Ideas,* pp. 76, 140-41; A. F. Pollard, *The Evolution of Parliament* (London, 1920), pp. 231-32; *Tudor Constitutional Documents, 1485-1603,* ed. J. R. Tanner (Cambridge, 1951), pp. 580-82.

35. For the statement by Sir Thomas Smith, see *De Republica Anglorum,* ed. L. Alston, with a preface by F. W. Maitland (Cambridge, 1906), p. 48; and below, pp. 31-32. In this respect, see also Franklin Le Van Baumer, *The Early Tudor Theory of Kingship* (New Haven, 1940), pp. 126-27, 210. Notestein also points out aptly that Westminster was not far removed in place and feeling from the streets of the great merchants around St. Pauls. *Proc. Br. Academy,* XI, 129-30. See below, pp. 87, 90; and for an early instance of the circulation of Parliamentary news, H. G. Richardson and G. O. Sayles, "The Parliament of Carlyle, 1307—Some New Documents," *EHR,* LIII (1938), 425-37.

36. See Fortescue's statement "what things soever are either recorded in customs or comprehended in writings, if they be adverse to natural law, are to be held null and void." *The Works of Sir John Fortescue,* ed. Thomas [Fortescue] Lord Clermont (London, 1869), I, 67. See also Christopher St. German: "a law grounded upon a custome is the most surest lawe, but thou must alwaies understand therewith that such a custome is neither contrary to the law of reason, nor to the law of God." This last statement occurs in *The Dialogue in English, betweene a Doctor of Divinitie, and a Student in the Lawes of England* (London, 1593), f. 16, a treatise widely read throughout the century (cf. *STC*). Paul Vinogradoff, "Reason and Conscience in Sixteenth Century Jurisprudence," *Collected Papers* (Oxford, 1928), II, 190-224; S. E. Thorne, "St. German's Doctor and Student," *Library,* 4th Series, X (1929-30), 421-26; Franklin Le Van Baumer, "Christopher St. German: The Political Philosophy of a Tudor Lawyer," *AHR,* XLII (1936-37), 631-51. That Smith is describing, and in effect defending, institutions, manners, and customs accords with such a view, of course, even though he does not develop this specific process of thought. See below, pp. 22-23. Note also Christopher Hatton's speech to Mary Queen of Scots at Mary's trial, in which he asserted that "royal dignity in the case of such a crime as she was charged with would not exempt her from answering, either by Civil Law, or the Common Law, nor by the Law of Nature or of Nations." Read, *Lord Burghley,* p. 353.

CHAPTER II

1. *De Republica Anglorum,* pp. xiii-xvi, 142. For R. B.'s recommendation, see Read, *Walsingham,* I, 428 ff. See also John Strype, *The Life of Sir Thomas Smith* (London, 1698), pp. 112-13; and also, e.g., as regards Osorius, p. 103; see also Mosse, *Speculum,* XXII, 25-26: "Sir Thomas Smith seems to be a step ahead of Jean Bodin."

2. Jean Bodin, *Method for the Easy Comprehension of History,* tr. Beatrice Reynolds, Records of Civilization—Sources and Studies, No. XXXVII (New York, 1945), e.g., pp. 99-100, 264-65. Although Bodin's abuse of female worthies may have injured the reception of his works in England, there is no doubt that they were studied there, especially his *Les Six Livres de la*

*République* (1576). L. F. Dean, "Bodin's *Methodus* in England before 1625," *SP*, XXXIX (1942), 160-66; Celeste Turner Wright, "The Elizabethan Female Worthies," *SP*, XLIII (1946), 640-43. See Gabriel Harvey's comment: "You can not stepp into a schollars studye but (ten to one) you shall litely finde open ether Bodin de Republica or Le Royes Exposition uppon Aristotles Politiques or sum other like Frenche or Italian Politique Discourses." *Letterbook of Gabriel Harvey*, ed. E. J. L. Scott, Camden Soc. Publ., New Series, XXXIII (1884), 79.

3. *De Rep. Angl.*, pp. xiii-xiv, translating a Latin letter in answer to one by Haddon: "And because in my absence I feel a yearning for our commonwealth, I have put together three books here at Toulouse describing it, taking as the title *De Republica Anglorum;* and in this I have set forth almost the whole of its form, especially those points in which it differs from the others. But it differs in almost all; with the consequence that the work has grown larger than I expected. I have written it moreover in the language of our own country, in a style midway between the historical and the philosophical, giving it the shape in which I imagined that Aristotle wrote of the many Greek commonwealths books which are no longer extant. I have furnished fruitful argument for those who would debate after the fashion of philosophers on single topics and raise nice points as to justice and injustice, and whether what is held in England as law be the better, or what is held here and in those regions which are administered in accordance with the Roman Law." He then says that the present form of this treatise is rough scrawls in notebooks and that there are gaps which he plans to complete at his leisure when he returns to England.

4. *De Rep. Angl.*, pp. 20-21.

5. *The Education of a Christian Prince*, tr. Lester K. Born, Records of Civilization—Sources and Studies, No. XXVII (New York, 1936), p. 178; see also Erasmus' opinion of the *De Officiis* (above, chap. I, n. 22).

6. Strype, *Life of Smith*, p. 118; and above, chap. II, n. 2.

7. *Aristotles Politiqves* (London, 1598), pp. 24-30 (on I. iii); see also, e.g., pp. 57-58 (I. viii).

8. The sentences immediately following are based on Hudson's concise and readable account of the Cambridge humanists (*John Ponet*, pp. 4-18, and *passim*) and upon the article on Smith in the *Dictionary of National Biography*. For the close and friendly relationship between Smith and Cheke, in spite of their being in "continual emulation" at Cambridge, see James Bass Mullinger, *The University of Cambridge* (Cambridge, 1884), II, 46. The tutorship of Tudor rulers by this group is well known: Edward VI (Cheke, Richard Cox, Anthony Cooke); Lady Jane Grey (John Aylmer, James Haddon); Elizabeth (William Grindal, through the efforts of Cheke and Ascham, and, after Grindal's death, Ascham himself).

9. *The Six Books of a Commonweale*, tr. Richard Knolles (London, 1606), pp. 3-4 (I. i); and note Smith's comparable concern with the "end" (below, p. 29), in contrast, e.g., with Ponet's emphasis on wealth (below, pp. 70-71).

10. *De Rep. Ang.*, p. 11.

11. See the chapter heading of I. 15. *De Rep. Angl.*, p. 28.

12. Bodin, *Method*, pp. 210, 289, 363, and above, chap. II, n. 2; see also Bodin's discussion of "northerners" (p. 101).

13. Major, *Hist. Greater Britain*, p. 348.

14. *Calendar of Letters and State Papers Spanish, 1568-1579, Elizabeth* (P.R.O., 1894), II, 157; see also Read, *Walsingham*, II, 423 (quoting Stafford on the Westmoreland-Mendoza situation, MS Harl. 288, f. 187).

15. *De Rep. Angl.*, p. 9. The italics are mine.

16. For a concise and lucid exposition of some of these points, which also relates Smith's concept of sovereignty to Bodin's, see Mosse, *Speculum*, XXII, 18-28.

17. *De Rep. Angl.*, p. 29. For the beginnings in the family of a society of freemen and its growth by "provining and propagation," see pp. 22-27. Seeing such beginnings in an extension of the family is, of course, thoroughly conventional. Le Roy, *Arist. Politiqves*, pp. 13-14 (I, ii).

18. *De Rep. Angl.*, pp. 12-13.

19. *De Rep. Angl.*, p. 29.

20. Bodin, of course, is the outstanding exception here. Rule in a mixed state was said to be effected by the one, the few, and the many, of which Venice was an example, as that state was described by Gasparo Contarini, whose work was known in England and translated by Lewes Lewkenor as *The Commonwealth and Government of Venice* (London, 1599). For knowledge of Contarini and other similar works before the end of the sixteenth century, see Zera S. Fink, *The Classical Republicans* (Evanston, 1945), pp. 41-45.

21. E.g., on Sparta and Venice, see Bodin, *Method*, pp. 186-200.

22. *De Rep. Angl.*, p. 14.

23. E.g., *De Rep. Angl.*, p. 19. In addition, Smith writes that since the English ruler has absolute power in matters of foreign affairs, "the kingdome of Englande is farre more absolute than either the dukedome of Venice is, or the kingdome of the Lacedemonians was" (p. 59). Such a turn of thought also shows his awareness of the concept of the mixed state and, possibly, of Bodin's argument as well.

24. *De Rep. Angl.*, pp. 16-17, 18. The italics are mine.

25. *The Bible, That Is, The Holy Scriptvres Conteined in the Olde and Newe Testament* (London, 1599), p. 127 b (I Kings 12:9). See also the marginal notes on I Sam. 8:6 and 11:1; I Kings 21:2; II Kings 9:16 and 22; Ps. 2:10-12; Isa. 10:1-4. Such matter, of course, becomes increasingly important in the next century, when William Prynne, e.g., would cite the notes of the English Bible as confirming his political thought. *The Soueraigne Power of Parliaments and Kingdomes* (London, 1643), p. 148 (Appendix).

26. Bodin, *Commonweale*, p. 184 (II. i); for the books Vives recommended, see Baldwin, *Shakspere's small Latine*, I, 185-99 (More and Mary, p. 187).

27. Above, chap. I, n. 7. In his later difficulties, for example, when Cartwright was far from being in favor, he had to argue with Sutcliffe as to whether or not Fenner (*Sacra Theologia*, 1585) gave the Ephori the right to depose a king. Cartwright, who admired the work, argued that Fenner gave them such authority only when the laws of the land established such a rule as that in "Lacedemonia"; and he denied that he taught that there should be Ephori. Scott Pearson, *Cartwright*, pp. 333-35.

28. I quote from the 1599 Waldegrave edition. Only in dialect and spelling does this portion of the edition vary from the version in MS Royal 18. B. xv and from the 1603 Waldegrave edition. *The Basilicon Doron of King James VI*, ed. James Craigie, Scottish Text Soc., Series 3, no. 16, p. 24. The italics are mine.

29. See the speeches by Throckmorton and Wentworth, noted above, pp. 16-17 and chap. I, n. 31. Nor need such an attitude be necessarily "radical" or "puritanical"; see below, pp. 92-93. Even in James's reign, a reported speech by Edwin Sandys, as it might be expected, can be glossed easily by ideas noted at the beginning of this study. The speech was on impositions, portions of which are reported as follows: "That the King of France, and the rest of the imposing Princes, do also make Laws:—That will, in short time, bring all to a tyrannical Course, where Confusion both to Prince and

People—Death of the last great imposing Prince.—No successive King but First elected.—Election double; of Person, and Care; but both come in by Consent of People, and with reciprocal Conditions between King and People. —That a King, by Conquest, may also (when Power) be expelled." *Journals of the House of Commons from November the 8th 1547 . . . to March the 2d 1628*, reproduced by order of the House of Commons (1803), I, 493 (12 Jac. I).

30. See Allan H. Gilbert, *Machiavelli's "Prince" and Its Forerunners* (Durham, N.C., 1938), pp. 186-96; Sir Thomas Elyot, *The Boke Named the Gouernour* (London, 1537), ff. 165-69v, 235v-237 ("The election of frendes and the diuersitie of flaterers," II. 14; "Of Consultation and counsaylle," III. 27).

31. *De Rep. Angl.*, pp. 14-16. Before he refers to the source of the Pope's claim to power, Smith writes that the tyrannical administrations of many emperors after Caesar and Octavius was grounded upon their claim "by pretence of that Rogation or *plebiscitum*, which *Caius Caesar* or *Octavius* obtained, by which all the people of Rome did conferre their power and authority unto *Caesar* wholly." See above, Chap. I, n. 1.

32. These sentences are drawn from II. 3. *De Rep. Angl.*, pp. 58-63. Smith also cites there the king's right to choose his privy council; his control over coinage; the fact that all writs, executions, and commandments are done in the king's name; and the king's power of wardship and first marriage over all who hold land in chief from him and over all fools, both by nature and sickness. See also, p. 30. As regards the final sentence, note, too, Burghley's statement about "councils": "Her Majesty's Councils consist upon parliament, upon assemblies of judges in courts of justice, in Councils attending upon her person for affairs either foreign or for government within the realm, and other council for revenues of her crown and good order of her tenants, besides sundry others." Read, *Lord Burghley*, pp. 509-10 (second version of "Meditations on the state of England").

33. This dispensing with laws occurs "whereas equitie requireth a moderation to be had." It also involves "paynes for transgression of lawes, where the payne of the lawe is applyed onely to the prince" (p. 61). With this power, I join the "prerogatives royalle," mentioned in the paragraph devoted to wardship (p. 62).

34. *De Rep. Angl.*, pp. 48-49. Quite revealingly, then, this definition of Parliament and the "forme" of holding Parliament (II. 1. 2) precedes the list of the king's powers.

35. *De Rep. Angl.*, p. 58.

36. *De Rep. Angl.*, p. 49; see also p. 126.

37. *De Rep. Angl.*, pp. 52, 55, 62-63.

38. *De Rep. Angl.*, p. 19. Italics are mine. See also Smith's discussion of *praemunire*, pp. 141-42. As it might be expected, Smith does not mention the Magna Carta; see Faith Thompson, *Magna Carta: Its Role in the Making of the English Constitution, 1300-1629* (Minneapolis, 1948), pp. 139 ff.

39. *De Rep. Angl.*, pp. 109-10. In addition to their being imprisoned, Smith notes that both inquests were fined, the fine for the first being "an houge" one.

40. *De Rep. Angl.*, pp. 12-13.

41. This is one of the points in his *De la Vicissitude ou Variété des Choses en l'Univers*.

42. See Brents Stirling's discussion of this passage. *The Works of Edmund Spenser* (Baltimore, 1938), VI, 416-19.

43. *De Rep. Angl.*, p. 33.

44. *The Works of Sir Walter Ralegh* (Oxford, 1829), VIII, 293.

45. See Mosse, *Speculum,* XXII, 18-28, and, e.g., *De Rep. Angl.,* p. 12.

46. See, e.g., the references to "mathematicians," i.e., astrologers, in Valerianus' popular reference work *Hieroglyphica* (Basle, 1556), lib. xliv ("De Stella"), lib, xlviii ("De colv et Fvso"); also above, chap. II, n. 7; and Fink, *Classical Republicans,* p. 91; Bodin, *Method,* pp. 316-19, 342-43. The idea of a decaying world was more widely disseminated in the seventeenth century, though it touched upon the sixteenth. To impermanence in general, stoicism, of course, might be an answer; see Justus Lipsius, *Two Bookes of Constancie, Englished by Sir John Stradling,* ed. Rudolph Kirk (New Brunswick, N.J., 1939), pp. 107-28 (I. xvi-xxii). The translation was published in 1595.

47. *Faerie Queene,* VII, vi, 14, l. 6; III, vi, 47, ll. 4-9; and above, p. 12, n. 16.

48. E.g., Fink, *Classical Republicans,* pp. 2-8 (citing Plato, Aristotle, Polybius, Cicero), 10-21 (Machiavelli), 34-41 (Contarini).

49. As Miss Reynolds remarks, "Racial peculiarities, the influence of the planets, and Pythagorean numbers fit into the pattern of the Platonism of the Renaissance." Bodin, *Method,* p. xiii. See Bodin's fifth and sixth chapters especially (e.g., pp. 148-52, 223-36, and also pp. 316-19). On a much lower level, that history was divided into a series of cycles would also be apparent in that combination of divine numerology, mathematics, and astrology that alarmed England as the prophesied disaster of 1588 approached. Although one may not wish to follow the author's main line of argument, for the impact of Regiomontanus' prophecy on England, see Leslie Hotson, *Shakespeare's Sonnets Dated* (London, 1949), pp. 10-16.

50. Above, chap. II, nn. 19, 20.

51. *De Rep. Angl.,* p. 64.

52. *De Rep. Angl.,* pp. 64-65, 113-14. In certain circumstances, this, too, may check the action of a ruler. If a murderer or manslayer "hath his pardon of the prince, as occasion or the favour of the Prince may so present, that he may have it," yet the aggrieved party can "require justice by grand assise, or battle upon his appeale and private revenge," and "if the defendent either by the great assise or by battle be convinced upon that appeale, he shall die, notwithstanding the Princes pardon. So much favourable our Princes be, and the lawe of our Realme to justice and to the punishment of blood violently shed" (p. 115). As part of his defense of trial by battle, Smith notes that "At the least a common wealth militarie must adventure many things to keepe it in quiet, which cannot seeme so precisely good to them which dispute thereof in the shadowe and in their studies" (p. 114).

53. *De Rep. Angl.,* pp. 12, 88-89, 92. This is quite contrary, of course, to the misuse of this power as in France, which "will be the present ruine (though not at the first apperceived) of the common wealth. Of which the fault may be as well in the commaunders for not making good choice what and howe they commaunde, as in the commaunded, for not executing that which is commaunded" (p. 89).

54. *De Rep. Angl.,* p. 106. This follows a discussion of how and why confession by torture is not esteemed in law courts, "for death our nation doth not so much esteem as a mean torment" (p. 105). "Again, the people not accustomed to see such cruell torments, will pitie the person tormented, and abhorre the Prince and the Judges, who should bring in such crueltie amongst them, and the xij. men the rather absolve him" (pp. 105-6). See above, pp. 24-25.

55. *De Rep. Angl.,* pp. 82-83. Cato is referred to in connection with the statement that going to court should be difficult since "idle, whot heades, busie bodies, and troublesome men" "nourish pleading" (p. 70).

56. *De Rep. Angl.*, pp. 116-18.
57. *De Rep. Angl.*, p. 39. Again, in his immediately preceding defense of gentility, Smith refers to the Roman state (pp. 38-39).
58. Read, *Walsingham*, II, 92-93.
59. Owen Ulph, "Jean Bodin and the Estates-General of 1576," *JMH*, XIX (1947), 289-96.
60. Particularly important in this respect are the Huguenot treatises *Francogallia* by François Hotman (1573) and the *Vindiciae contra Tyrannos* (1579), probably by Languet or Du Plessis-Mornay. E. Armstrong, "The Political Theory of the Huguenots," *EHR*, IV (1889), 13-40; John William Allen, *A History of Political Thought in the Sixteenth Century* (London, 1928), pp. 306-31; Beatrice Reynolds, *Proponents of Limited Monarchy in Sixteenth Century France* (New York, 1931), pp. 41-104. See also the Calvinist Beza's *Du Droit des Magistrate* (1589), the magnum opus of Jean Boucher, *De Justa Henri III Abdicatione e Francorum Regno* (1589), and the writings in the 1590's by Catholic monarchomachi. Gough, *Social Contract*, pp. 59-62.
61. Charles Flinn Arrowood, *The Powers of the Crown in Scotland, Being a Translation of* . . . *"De Jure Regni apud Scotos"* (Austin, 1949), pp. 100-9, 124-34. See also Buchanan's *History of Scotland*, tr. J. Aikman (Glasgow, 1927), xx. 38: "The Scottish nation originally a free people, created themselves kings upon this condition:—That the government being intrusted to them by the suffrages of the people, if the state of the country required it, could be taken from them by the same suffrages; of which law, many vestiges remain even in our day . . . besides, the ceremonies used at the inauguration of our kings, have an express reference to this law; from all which, it is evident that government is nothing more than a mutual compact between the people and their kings." For one aspect of the reception of Buchanan's works in England, see below, p. 92.
62. *De Rep. Angl.*, p. 13.
63. *The Works of That Learned and Judicious Divine Mr. Richard Hooker, in Eight Books of Ecclesiastical Polity* (London, 1676). This is the text used for all subsequent quotations, except for those from the eighth book, for which the text is that of *Hooker's Ecclesiastical Polity Book VIII*, ed. Raymond Aaron Houck (New York, 1931). For the question of the authenticity of the last book, see below, chap. II., n. 85.
64. See above, pp. 5, 13 and chap. I, n. 36.
65. *Laws*, pp. 72-74 (I. iii), 82-83 (I. viii. 9, 10).
66. *Laws*, pp. 82 (I. viii), 84 (I. ix).
67. *Laws*, pp. 94 (I. xii. 1), 96-98 (I. xiv), 136-41 (III. viii, especially "IV," pp. 137-38), 198-99 (V. ix); 3-4 (VIII). See also John S. Marshall, "Hooker's Doctrine of God," *Anglican Theological Review*, XXIX (1947), 81-89.
68. *Laws*, p. 137 (III. viii). Note also how, in an entirely different context, Daniel writes, "Nor can it be but a touch of arrogant ignorance, to hold this or that nation Barbarous, these or those times grosse, considering how this manifold creature man, wheresoever hee stand in the world, hath always some disposition of worth. . . ." *Poems, and a Defence of Ryme*, ed. Arthur Colby Sprague (Cambridge, Mass., 1930), pp. 139-40.
69. *Laws*, p. 82 (I. viii): ". . . Those Laws are investigable by Reason, without the help of Revelation, Supernatural and Divine. Finally, in such sort they are investigable, that the knowledge of them is general, the World hath always been acquainted with them, according to that which in *Sophocles* observeth, concerning a Branch of this Law. *It is no child of two days, or yesterdays birth, but hath been no man knowth how long sithence.*" See also the quotation from Aquinas, p. 142 (III. ix): "*Out of the Precepts of*

*the Law of Nature, as out of certain common and undemonstrable Principles, Mans Reason doth necessarily proceed unto certain more particular determinations: Which particular determinations being found out according unto the Reason of Man, they have the names of Humane Laws, so that such other conditions be therein kept as the making of Laws doth require,* that is, If they whose Authority is thereunto required, do establish and publish them as Laws," to which, however, is added "this Caution concerning the Rule and Canon whereby to make them: *Humane Laws are Measures* in respect of Men, whose actions they must direct; howbeit such Measures they are, as have also their higher Rules to be measured by, *Which Rules are two, the Law of God, and the Law of Nature.* So that Laws Humane must be made according to the General Laws of Nature, and without contradiction unto any Positive Law in Scripture; otherwise they are ill made."

70. See below, p. 55. Thus when writing from a different point of view, E. T. Davis remarks that Hooker "had no clear-cut doctrine of authority either in Church or State because he realized the problem was too complex to allow an easy and a facile solution." *The Political Ideas of Richard Hooker* (London, 1946), p. 98. Nevertheless, Hooker's basic precepts, of course, would be applicable in any particular situation.

71. *Laws,* pp. 85-88 (I. x).

72. See also below, chap. II, n. 88. Earlier, when writing about natural agents, Hooker, for example, had also emphasized the individual's subordination to the good of the whole (*Laws,* p. 74 [I. iii]). Thus, about the heavens, the celestial spheres, and the elements of the world "we must further remember also . . . That as in this respect [i.e., "in themselves"] they have their Law, which Law directeth them in the means whereby they tend to their own perfection; so likewise another Law there is, which toucheth them as they are sociable parts united into one Body: A Law which bindeth them each to serve unto others good, and all to prefer the good of the whole, before whatsoever their own particular, as we plainly see they do, when things natural in that regard, forget their ordinary natural wont: That which is heavy, mounting sometime upwards of its own accord, and forsaking the Centre of the Earth, which to it self is most natural, even as if it did hear it self commanded to let go the good it privately wisheth and to relieve the present distress of Nature in common."

73. *Laws,* pp. 86-87 (I. x), 170-72 (VIII. ii). Hooker obviously has Moses in mind. A portion of the first passage runs as follows: "Howbeit, over a whole grand multitude, having no such dependency upon any one, and consisting of so many Families, as every Politick Society in the World doth; impossible it is, that any should have compleat lawful power, but by consent of men, or immediate appointment of God, because not having the Natural Superiority of Fathers their power must needs be either usurped, and then unlawful; or if lawful, then either granted or consented unto by them, over whom they exercise the same, or else given extraordinarily from God, unto whom all the World is subject." For kings by conquest, also see below, p. 49, and *Laws,* pp. 171-73 (VIII. ii). One should understand, however, that upon such bases as those indicated above, to Hooker the power of parents and husbands and of all superiors made by consent or agreement of a commonweal is a power of God's institution; thus the persons having such power, whether they derive it immediately from God ("mere divine right," as Moses or Aaron) or from nature (as parents), or from the natural course of a commonweal in accordance with its order or nature, derive that power in their persons from Him. Obviously, as F. J. Shirley remarks, this is "not in the least teaching the seventeenth-century view of the divine right of kings," nor is it, as we shall see, enunciating the idea of popular sovereignty.

*Richard Hooker and Contemporary Political Ideas* (London, 1949), p. 99. Shirley's references to Parliament, of course, should be read in the light of the later studies by Neale.

74. See Neale, *Eliz. and Parl., 1559-1581,* pp. 291-317, and *passim;* Scott Pearson, *Cartwright,* p. 104, and *passim* (for a survey of Puritan agitation after the repudiation of cope and surplice in 1565). Scott Pearson's study is particularly useful because of Cartwright's academic attainments and his reputation and because of his repudiation of the radical Puritans, even though anti-Martinists considered the Marprelate controversy to be bred out of Cartwright's terms. See also Bishop Sandys' complaint in 1573 and 1574 that he was being abused by the charge of cruel and unwarrantable persecution. Scott Pearson, *Cartwright,* p. 116. For the linking of Puritanism and Papism, see below, chap. II, n. 81 and pp. 48-49.

75. *Laws,* "Preface," viii, ix; pp. 434-35 (VII. xxiv. 3); see also Brents Stirling, "Shakespeare's Mob Scenes: A Reinterpretation," *HLQ,* VIII (1944-45), 213-40—especially his notice of Bishop Cooper's *Admonition* (London, 1589) wherein it is stated that Martin Marprelate means "Mar-prince, Mar-state, Mar-law, Mar-magistrate" until everything is brought to an "Anabaptistical equality and community" (pp. 217-18), or Stirling's quotation from Bancroft's 1588-89 sermon at Paul's Cross: all lay factions, Arians, Donatists, Papists, Libertines, Anabaptists, the Family of Love are levellers and speak as if they would say in secular terms "my brethern of the poorer sort . . . will you suffer this unequal distribution of worldly benefits?" (pp. 216-17).

76. It is revealing that the Privy Council thought the Hacket affair serious enough to call for a public explanation and in the year following Hacket's examination under torture published the pamphlet *Conspiracy under Pretended Reformation.* Read, *Lord Burghley,* p. 471. See also Scott Pearson, *Cartwright,* pp. 320-24, and Henry Barrow's earlier protest that his adversaries insist that "whatsoever writeth to work a discontent . . . do intend a rebellion" (*A Petition Directed to Her Most Excellent Maiestie* [Middelburg, 1590]).

77. Scott Pearson, *Cartwright,* pp. 328-31, 458-63 (especially pp. 459, 461).

78. C. J. Sisson, *The Judicious Marriage of Mr. Hooker and the Birth of the Laws of Ecclesiastical Polity* (Cambridge, 1940), pp. 45-60, and *passim;* Hardin Craig, "Of *The Laws of Ecclesiastical Polity*—First Form," *JHI,* V (1944), 91-104; Neale, *Eliz. and Parl., 1584-1601,* pp. 280-97.

79. Stirling, *HLQ,* VIII, 119-220, 226-27.

80. Neale, *Eliz. and Parl., 1584-1601,* p. 287; *Eliz. and Parl., 1559-1581,* pp. 291-317; Scott Pearson, *Cartwright,* p. 234.

81. Neale, *Eliz. and Parl., 1584-1601,* p. 282. See also Neale's summary of Sir Francis Hastings' speech against John Bond (p. 403), in which Hastings said he had learned from his Oxford tutor, Dr. Lawrence Humphrey, who was a famous Puritan don, that Puritans were of four sorts: Catholics, Papists, Brownists, and "your evangelical Puritans, who rely wholly upon the scriptures as upon a sure ground."

82. *Laws,* p. 224 (VIII. vi); but note pp. 176 (VIII. ii), 359-60 (V. lxxx), 401-403 (VII. xiv).

83. *Laws,* pp. 182-83 (VIII. ii). Hooker continues the last statement as follows: ". . . which positive laws, whether by custom or otherwise established without repugnancy unto the law of God and nature, ought no less to be of force even in the spiritual affairs of the Church" (see above, chap. I, n. 36 and p. 5).

84. *Laws,* pp. 241-42, 244 (VIII. vi).

85. For the authenticity of this book, see Houck, *Hooker's Book VIII,* p. 13. Houck's conclusions do not disagree with Craig's, *JHI,* V, 91-104, nor with

Shirley's consideration of the authenticity of both the seventh and the eighth books. *Hooker and Cont. Pol. Ideas,* pp. 42-57 (especially p. 52).

86. *Laws,* p. 70 (I. i): ". . . I have endeavoured throughout the Body of this whole Discourse, that every former part might give strength unto all that follow, and every later bring some light unto all before. . . ." Thus in the discussion which follows, note the congruence between matter cited in Book I, part of which has been noted already, Book VIII, and occasionally Book VII.

87. *Laws,* p. 388 (VII. viii); but see also the emphasis upon order in Hooker's definition of "Law," pp. 70-71 (I. ii), 84 (I. ix): "For we see the whole World and each part thereof so compacted, that as long as each thing performeth only that work which is natural unto it, it thereby preserveth both other things, and also itself." Note too, pp. 184-85 (VIII. ii); nor is this passage from Book VII noted by Shirley as being possibly spurious. *Hooker and Cont. Pol. Ideas,* pp. 53-57. See also *Laws,* p. 168 (VIII. ii): "Without order there is no living in public society. . . . Yea, the very Deity itself both keepeth and requireth for ever this to be kept as law, that wheresoever there is a coagmentation of many, the lowest be knit to the highest by that which being interjacent may cause each to cleave unto other, and so all to continue one."

88. *Laws,* pp. 86-87 (I. x), 101-2 (I. xvi). Note also the correspondence between this thought and the force of the power of the whole which Hooker gives to Parliament in Book VIII, above, chap. II, n. 84. See also above, chap. II, n. 72, as well as *Laws,* pp. 86, 88 (I. x), 213 (VIII. iv), 243 (VIII. vi), passages expressing the idea of consent and common advice.

89. For the Spanish Jesuit Molina's *De Justitia et Jure,* see Gough, *Social Contract,* pp. 68-69, wherein, however, the power of the state, which cannot derive from the power of individuals, is called divine. The power of the whole is also implicit, e.g., in the conception of the relationship between subject and ruler as *mutuo consensu ac publice contracta obligatio,* an *obligatio solemni et publico consensu contracta,* a conception expressed by Hugenot writers. The same is obviously true for the insistence in the *Francogallia* upon the subordination of the king's interest to that of the people. See above, chap. II, n. 60.

90. *Laws,* pp. 85 ff (VIII. ii), on the choice by stock, not by twig, wherein Hooker cites, quotes, and refutes matter in the *Vindiciae contra Tyrannos;* or *Laws,* pp. 173-75 (VIII. ii).

91. *Laws,* pp. 177 (VIII. ii), 220 (VIII. v). He had also pointed out in his first book that even though the extension of the family may have caused kingship to be the first kind of government, it is not "the only kind of Regiment that hath been received in the World" and that "the kinds therof being many, Nature tieth not to any one, but leaveth the choice as a thing arbitrary." *Laws,* p. 86 (I. x). Thus he points out that one of the "Laws of making Laws" is the necessity for law-makers to "have an eye to" both the place and the people; and he illustrates his statement by comparing necessary laws where the multitude rules with necessary laws where a few of the wealthiest rule. *Laws,* p. 88 (I. x). Thoroughly congruent with such a process of thought, then, is Hooker's specifying rule by the Aristotelian many, few, and one as the kinds of power into which the power of the whole may be resolved. *Laws,* p. 170 (VIII. ii).

92. *Laws,* p. 178 (VIII. ii). Hooker then quotes Archytas on the four steps necessary for a good society (the King ruling by law, the magistrate following, the subject free, the whole society happy) and their contrary (the king growing a tyrant, the magistrate abhorring guidance and commands, the people "subject under both, have freedom under neither," the whole com-

munity wretched). See the pageantry on Elizabeth's coronation, below, pp. 79-80, as well as *Laws*, p. 87 (I. x): ". . . that for any Prince or Potentate, of what kind soever upon Earth, to exercise the same [i.e., the law-making power] of himself, and not by express Commission immediately and personally received from God, or else by Authority derived at first from their consent upon whose persons they impose Laws, it is no better than meer tyranny."

93. *Laws*, pp. 175-76 (VIII. ii): "May then a body politic at all times withdraw in whole or in part that influence of dominion which passeth from it, if inconvenience doth grow thereby? It must be presumed, that supreme governors will not in such cases oppose themselves, and be stiff in detaining that, the use whereof is with public detriment: but surely without their consent I see not how the body should be able by any just means to help itself, saving when dominion doth escheat. Such things therefor must be thought upon beforehand, that power may be limited ere it be granted; which is the next thing we are to consider." Usually elucidations of Hooker's doctrine present this statement as a major premise rather than as a conclusion. It undoubtedly is a major premise in Book VIII, wherein Hooker is arguing for the English ruler's supremacy in church as well as in state; and it is a major premise in that the *Laws* grew out of Hooker's controversy with Travers and was a document of the early 1590's directed at the Cartwrightian program. But also, each book was conceived of as giving strength to what would follow and light to what had preceded (above, chap. II, n. 86); and since the power and nature of the English Parliament will be enunciated soon as being the power of the whole, that is, the power of the king and all the realm, whereupon the essence of all government depends (above, chap. II, n. 84), Hooker in effect elucidates thereby the way in which the English had thought upon this matter "beforehand." Thus it seems eminently fair to represent this statement as a logical consequence thoroughly congruent with the basic principles enunciated in the first book about the way in which reason perceives the Law of a Commonweal, especially since the following passage obviously serves as a major premise upon which Hooker is now drawing. *Ibid.*, p. 88 (I. x): "And to be commanded, we do consent, when that Society whereof we are part, hath at any time before consented, without revoking the same after by the like Universal Agreement. Wherefore, as any Mans Deed past is good as long as himself continueth; so the Act of a Publick Society of Men done Five hundred years sithence, standeth as theirs, who presently are of the same Societies, because Corporations are Immortal; we were then alive in our Predecessors, and they in their Successors do live still. . . ." To so represent Hooker's thought indicates the many ways in which his treatise, by constantly returning to first principles, represents an Aristotelian method. It also emphasizes the material that was printed in the early 1590's and related to parliamentary action. By doing so, furthermore, one can hardly escape noticing how Hooker's thought varies from the conception of a perpetual corporation such as that apparent in the *Vindicae*, which we know Hooker wished to qualify. At the same time it provides a basis for considering Hooker's thought with Molina's, when that writer was concerned with the question of how a simple association of individuals could create a genuine corporate body with power to coerce those who did not freely join it but had been born in it (see above, pp. 50-51), and with Grotius' thought, when that writer would handle the problem of the will of the majority binding a dissenting minority in a society supposed to rest on individual consent. For the way in which consent is given, see further in *Laws*, pp. 87-88 (I. x), 176 (VIII. ii); for the authority of Parliament over the church in Mary's time, see p. 242 (VIII. vi).

94. *Laws*, p. 173 (VIII. ii).

95. See Edgar M. Carlson, "Luther's Conception of Government," *Church History*, XV (1946), 257-70.

96. Bracton's *jurisdictio* is comparable to Fortescue's *regimen politicum*; his *gubernaculum*, to Fortescue's *et regale*. Thus the Stuarts, e.g., would encroach upon *jurisdictio* with prerogatives of *gubernaculum*. See Charles Howard McIlwain, *Constitutionalism Ancient and Modern* (New York, 1940), pp. 72-94; also G. O. Sayles, *Select Cases in the Court of King's Bench under Edward I*, Seldon Soc., LVIII (1939), III, xliii ff. For Hooker's quotation of Bracton's famous sentence, see below, chap. II, n. 120. For further passages on the king's royal power, see *Laws*, pp. 264-65 (VIII. viii), 289-91 (VIII. ix); and for the king's dependency upon the politic body, p. 175 (VIII. ii).

97. *Laws*, pp. 317-18 (V. lxix), 352 (V. lxxix), 76 (I. v).

98. For Hooker's solution to a possible conflict between the idea of William I's naming himself "Conqueror" (above, chap. II, n. 82) and the idea that the king is head of Parliament, see *Laws*, p. 176 (VIII. ii).

99. Given Hooker's definition of tyranny (above, chap. II, n. 92), see also his comments on Tiberius, pp. 367-68 (VI. vi).

100. *Laws*, p. 85 (I. x).

101. Raleigh, *Works*, VIII, 292.

102. See below, p. 58.

103. *Laws*, p. 91 (I. xi).

104. *Laws*, pp. 78 (I. vii), 87 (I. x).

105. *Laws*, p. 198 (V. ix); see also p. 333 (V. lxxii).

106. *Laws*, p. 340 (V. lxxvi).

107. *Laws*, pp. 199 (V. ix), 363-4 (V. lxxxi).

108. *Laws*, p. 198 (V. ix).

109. "Epistle Dedicatory," pp. 36-37, also paraphrased immediately below.

110. Raleigh, *Works*, VIII, 282.

111. *Laws*, p. 339 (V. lxxvi); see also pp. 337 (VI. iv), 256 (V. xlviii).

112. *Laws*, p. 77 (I. vii).

113. *Laws*, p. 332 (VI. i). The pagination in this portion of the edition is incorrect, though not confusing because of the book and division numbering.

114. "Preface," pp. 53-54.

115. In view of Hooker's process of thought, it seems fair so to apply the phrase. See *Laws*, pp. 382-83 (VII. vi), 249 (VIII. vi). This last passage runs as follows: "There is no remedy all must come by devolution at the length, even as the family of Browne will have it, unto the godly among the people; for confusion to the wise and to the great, the poor and the simple, some Knipperdoling with his retinue, must take the work of the Lord in hand; and the making of church laws must prove to be their right in the end. If not love for truth, yet for shame of so gross absurdities, let these contentions and shifting fancies be abandoned." See also the statement that Calvin himself had denied the capacity of the people to judge of the best in questions of civil polity. Thus Hooker asks why they should "better judge what kind of Regiment Ecclesiastical is the fittest." "Preface," p. 49, citing *Institutes*, IV, xx, 8.

116. See above, chap. II, n. 93, though it is revealing that it is "supreme governors" who will consent. See immediately below.

117. Above, chap. I, nn. 34, 35; and *Laws*, pp. 264-65 (VIII. ix), which reflects a characteristic Elizabethan enthusiasm for the ruler. The English Church is ordered much better than the church in the days of St. Ambrose under Valentinian II "because our laws have with far more certainty prescribed bounds unto each kind of power." "What power the king hath he hath it by law, the bounds and limits of it are known; the entire community

giveth general order by law how all things publicly are to be done, and the king as the head thereof, the highest in authority over all, causeth according to the same law every particular to be framed and ordered thereby. The whole body politic maketh laws, which laws give power unto the king, and the king having bound himself to use according unto law that power, it so falleth out, that the execution of the one is accompanied by the other in most religious and peaceable sort." See also Hooker's emphasis upon the concord and mutual obligation between English ruled and English rulers: the one bound by the law of God to acknowledge the other His lieutenants; the other bound by the law of God to use their power as far as possible to His honor. *Laws*, p. 172 (VIII. ii). See also, his statement that love and fear are the two special affections which make the "good estate of a commonwealth"; the "subject's love for the most part continueth as long as the righteousness of kings doth last; in whom virtue decayeth not as long as they fear to do that which may alienate the loving hearts of their subjects from them." *Laws*, p. 279 (VIII. ix). See above, chap. I, n. 25, and below, on Elizabeth at her coronation and to Mr. Aglionby, pp. 83-84. See also Bodin's position, below, chap. II, n. 125. One of the commonest of historical commonplaces is that the Tudors had at least the tacit acquiescence of the vast majority of the population, which, as in the Confucian tradition, might be said to constitute the mandate of Heaven to rule. Thus, for his age, Hooker is not being too unrealistic even when he writes concerning the revocation of power that it "must be presumed, that supreme governors will not in such cases oppose themselves, and be stiff in detaining that, the use whereof is with public detriment." *Laws*, pp. 175-76 (VIII. ii). See also above, chap. II, n. 93.

118. For Mary and Philip in matters of religion, see Hudson, *John Ponet*, p. 61. While Mary Queen of Scots was alive, at least, no Protestant could rely upon the preceding doctrine of possession; hence, the Bond and Oath of Association. See Neale, *Eliz. and Parl., 1584-1601*, pp. 103-44.

119. *Laws*, p. 416 (VII. xviii); see also the passage quoted above from V. lxxvi (see chap. II, n. 111); and *Laws*, p. 406 (VII. xv).

120. *Laws*, p. 178 (VIII. ii); see also pp. 226, 234 (VIII. vi) and above, chap. II, nn. 92, 94, 98. The first citation in the passage quoted is from Bracton's famous sentence that the king while not below man, must be "sub Deo et sub lege, quia lex facit regem."

121. *Laws*, pp. 239-40 (VIII. vi).

122. See John Strype, *Ecclesiastical Memorials* (Oxford, 1822), II, ii, 365-72, 375, 377; III, i, 280; E. R. Adair, "William Thomas: A Forgotten Clerk of the Privy Council," *Tudor Studies . . . Presented to Albert Frederick Pollard*, ed. R. W. Seton-Watson (London, 1924), pp. 133-60; Hudson, *John Ponet*, p. 173. Yet in spite of his low opinion of popular government (e.g., that of the Swiss), Thomas would allow the multitude to rise against the tyrant.

123. E.g., W. Gordon Zeeveld, *Foundations of Tudor Policy* (Cambridge, Mass., 1948), pp. 178-89.

124. E.g., the dedicatory epistle of Le Roy's translator. *Arist. Politiqves*, sig. Aiijv, and sigs. Bij, Bvjr-v, cii-ciii.

125. See Miss Reynolds' summary about the type of monarch who won Bodin's approval: "While fear of God was an end in itself, it was also the means by which royal power was best held to its task of working for the good interests of the nation" and "Awe of the Deity was to him the most important factor for limiting despotism." Bodin, *Method*, p. xviii.

126. See above, chap. II, n. 106, and *Laws*, p. 189 (V. i): "Concerning Fortitude, sith evils great and unexpected (the true touchstone of constant

minds) do cause oftentimes even them to think upon Divine power with fearful suspicions, which have been otherwise the most secure despisers thereof; how should we look for any constant resolution of mind, in such cases, saving only where unfeigned affection to God-ward, hath bred the most assured confidence to be assisted by his hand?" Since to Hooker, a true fortitude, consequently, can not exist apart from religion, see also his citation of Cicero on religion upholding kingdoms. *Laws,* p. 413 (VII. xviii); see also pp. 189-90 (V. i).

127. *Laws,* pp. 192-93 (V. ii); "wise malignants" in John Keble's edition is glossed "Mach[iavelli] Disc. lib. 1. c. 11-14." Richard Hooker, *Works,* (Oxford, 1888), II, 22.

128. *Laws,* pp. 367-68 (VI. vi).

## Chapter III

1. See Ernest A. Strathman, "Raleigh and the Catholic Polemicists," *HLQ,* VIII (1944-45), 337-58, where the quotations that follow can be found; see also Strathman's "An Epitaph Attributed to Raleigh," *MLN,* LX (1945), 112-13.

2. For further details related to the material of this paragraph, see Neale, *Eliz. and Parl., 1584-1601,* pp. 262 ff.; Lily B. Campbell, *Shakespeare's "Histories": Mirrors of Elizabethan Policy* (San Marino, 1947), pp. 176-81, especially Camden on Essex (p. 178).

3. For a description of Wentworth's tracts, which is a good deal fuller than that which follows, see Neale, *Eliz. and Parl., 1584-1601,* pp. 262-66, 252-57.

4. Scott Pearson, *Cartwright,* pp. 274-75, 334-35.

5. Hudson, *John Ponet,* p. 205.

6. Hudson, *John Ponet,* pp. 64-65.

7. John Foxe, *The Acts and Monuments,* ed. Josiah Pratt (London, n.d.), VI, 558. See also *Holinshed's Chronicles* (London, 1808), IV, 63, and Robert Withington, *English Pageantry: An Historical Outline* (Cambridge, Mass., 1918), I, 192-93, wherein the account by the eye-witness John Elder is compared with that by Foxe.

8. *Shorte Treatise,* pp. 152, 47. Note, too, the signs and portents in the first portion of his "An Exhortation or rather a warnyng to the Lordes *and Commones of Englande," Shorte Treatise,* pp. 147-59, and his references to hiring a shepherd or a horsekeeper, p. 17. I use Hudson's pagination to the facsimile edition in his *John Ponet* and silently expand all contractions.

9. *Shorte Treatise,* pp. 5-6.

10. *Shorte Treatise,* p. 5; and see, above, chap. I, n. 17. By this concept of natural law, Ponet sets forth in reverse a number of natural rights: e.g., "that people have a 'right' to life, to their means of livelihood, to their property, to an equality before the law, to freedom from those petty invasions of personal liberty which are so irritating, and to resist and alter their form of government whenever any of these 'rights' are infringed." Hudson, *John Ponet,* p. 143.

10a. *Shorte Treatise,* pp. 80, 83-84.

11. *Shorte Treatise,* pp. 85-87, 99.

12. *Shorte Treatise,* p. 6.

13. *Shorte Treatise,* pp. 98-99, 99-101. Like the "natural rights" of men, the actions of tyrants are listed constantly; e.g., pp. 35-36, 98-126. See also below, chap. III, n. 25.

14. *Shorte Treatise,* pp. 7-9, 11-13, 42-46. It is interesting to note that in this respect Ponet repeats the conventional statement about a mixed state: "men by long continuaunce haue iudged [it] to be the best sort of all. For

wher that mixte state was exerciced, ther did the common wealthe longest continue" (p. 9).
15. *Shorte Treatise*, p. 11.
16. *Shorte Treatise*, pp. 95-96.
17. *Shorte Treatise*, p. 96.
18. *Shorte Treatise*, p. 107.
19. *Shorte Treatise*, pp. 9-10.
20. *Shorte Treatise*, pp. 25-27; see also pp. 22-23, 27-28, 43, 46, 78.
21. E.g., "Kinges, Princes and other gouernours, albeit they are the headdes of a politike body, yet they are not the hole body. And though they be the chief membres, yet they are but membres: nother are the people ordained for them, but they are ordained for the people." "And men ought to haue more respect to their countrey, than to their prince: to the common wealthe, than to any one persone. For the countrey and common wealthe is a degree aboue the king. Next unto God men ought to loue their countrey, and the hole common wealthe before any membre of it: as kings and princes (be they neuer so great) are but membres: and common wealthes mai stande well ynough and florishe, albeit ther be no kinges, but contrary wise without a common wealthe ther can be no king. Common wealthes and realmes may liue, whan the head is cut of, and may put on a newe head, that is, make them a newe gouernour, whan they see their olde head seke to muche his owne will and not the wealthe of the hole body, for the which he was ordained." *Shorte Treatise*, pp. 108, 61.
22. *Shorte Treatise*, pp. 107-8.
23. *Shorte Treatise*, pp. 108-10.
24. *Shorte Treatise*, pp. 102-5, 110 ff.
25. *Shorte Treatise*, pp. 121-22.
26. *Shorte Treatise*, pp. 101, 116-17, 112-13. Also Denmark "in our dayes did nobly the like acte whan they depriued Christierne [sic] the tiranne, and committed him to perpetual prison" (pp. 101-2).
27. Though John of Salisbury advocated tyrannicide, yet he also admitted that tyrants could be God's instruments. Hudson, *John Ponet*, pp. 157-58; and see *Shorte Treatise*, pp. 70-75, 49, 43, 55. To Ponet, Sodom and Gomorrah and Jerusalem are examples of how vicious states are completely destroyed (p. 117). Note, too, Ponet's description of the West Indies after being subject to Spanish rule and his citation of Peter Martyr (p. 94). Good princes realize that to "doo any thing against Goddes worde, or the lawes of nature" will "make them of kinges no kinges"; and hence the sad fate of Lady Jane Grey, with, of course, an exculpation of Cranmer (pp. 59, 61-62). In all of this, Ponet insists, however, that not only "the doers but also the consentours to euil, shalbe punished" (pp. 61, 64, 51, 53, 178-79, 181-82).
28. *Shorte Treatise*, pp. 11-12.
29. *Shorte Treatise*, pp. 106-7.
30. Hudson, *John Ponet*, p. 176.
31. *Shorte Treatise*, p. 27.
32. "This arte of subtiltie of princes (otherwise called policie) consisteth chiefly in this, for a man to appeare outwardly that he is not inwardly: to saye one thing with the mouthe, and thinke an other in the hart: to smyle vpon him, whose throte he wolde gladly see cutte: and so pretende to the eie all amitie, beneuolence and loue, wher they beare greatest hatred, enuye, and malice, till conuenient tyme maie be had with least daungier, to execute their conceaued mischief." Such subtlety also leads them to hire vile men to do the deeds they can not do alone. *Shorte Treatise*, pp. 127, 129.
33. *Shorte Treatise*, pp. 14-16. See also Ponet's argument that it is not "the mannes warauut that can discharge the, but it is the thing itself that must iustifie

thee" (p. 53). Thus the Queen of England can not give away any part of the realm (e.g. "the towne of Calese and Barwicke"), for though she had it by inheritance, she had it with an oath to keep and maintain it; nor did she have any more right to the realm than did her father who "required" the consent of Parliament to give the crown to Mary; and all who counsel or concur in such action are guilty, even "the deputie and garison" are "traitoures for suffring it to be done" (pp. 67-69). One should also note the Catholic opposition to Mary's policies and especially to Philip. The coronation of Philip was objected to on the following grounds: ". . . we must obey her [Mary] surely in those actes that be paste by parliament and confirmed by the whole realme . . . but I think there is no law confirmed and paste by which the Queene may lawfully disinherit the realme of the crowne." D. M. Loades, "The Authorship and Publication of *The Copye of a Letter Sent by John Bradforth to the Right Honorable Lordes the Erles of Arundel, Darbie, Shrewsbury and Pembroke* (STC 3480)," *Transactions of the Cambridge Bibliographical Society*, III, part II (1960), 160.

34. *Shorte Treatise*, pp. 143-45.
35. *Shorte Treatise*, p. 145.
36. *Shorte Treatise*, p. 169.
37. *Shorte Treatise*, pp. 166-67.
38. *Shorte Treatise*, p. 77.
39. *Shorte Treatise*, pp. 17-20.
40. *Shorte Treatise*, pp. 117-18 (see also p. 13), 111-12, 114-17, 120-26. Ponet also implies the possibility of relief from "judges in common wealthes" (p. 113).
41. Thus he was willing to make concessions about Mary's hearing Mass, for although "to give license to sin, was sin," yet "to suffer and wink at it for a time might be borne. . . ." Gilbert Burnet, *The History of the Reformation of the Church of England*, ed. Nicholas Pocock (Oxford, 1865), V, 32.
42. The following account of the 1558-59 pageants is based upon John Nichols, *The Progresses and Public Processions of Queen Elizabeth* (London, 1823), I, 34-35, 38-58. My numbering of the pageants begins with the one before "the signe of the Egle" (pp. 40-41) and corresponds with that in the contemporary tract reproduced by Nichols (e.g., p. 44).
43. *The Rhetoric of Aristotle*, tr. Lane Cooper (New York, 1932), p. 52 (*Epideictic Rhetoric*, I, 9): e.g. ". . . and we should praise a man even if he had not done a thing, if we were sure he was capable of doing it." Cf. also Quintillian, *Institutio Oratoria*, III, vii, 24-27; viii, 39.
44. Nichols, *Progresses*, I, 47.
45. For these and similar statements, see E. W. Talbert, "The Interpretation of Jonson's Courtly Spectacles," *PMLA*, LXI (1946), 456-58.
46. E.g., the return in 1432 of Henry VI from his coronation in Paris. Withington, *Eng. Pageantry*, I, 141-47. See also Robert Fabyan, *The New Chronicles of England and France*, ed. Henry Ellis (London, 1811), pp. 604-7; *Coventry Leet-Book*, ed. Mary Dormor Harris, E.E.T.S., 135, 138, Part II, 285-92; Part III, 589-92; John Leland, *Collectanea*, ed. Thomas Hearn (London, 1774), IV, 185-90; J. Payne Collier, *The History of English Dramatic Poetry to the Time of Shakespeare* (London, 1831), I, 182-88; *Collections* (Malone Soc.), I, 144-48. For a regular feature of the procession in Lord Mayors' Shows, where by "certayne fygures and wrytinges, some matter touchinge justice, and the office of a maiestrate is represented," see Withington, *Eng. Pageantry*, II, 22, also 16-17, 18 n. 2.
47. Nichols, *Progresses*, I, 311-16.
48. Above, chap. II, n. 30.

49. See especially Withington, *Eng. Pageantry*, I, 98 (the water "Triumph" of 1539).
50. Nichols, *Progresses*, I, 315.
51. Neale, *Eliz. and Parl., 1559-1581*, pp. 191-92, 386-92, 419.
52. Neale, *Eliz. and Parl., 1584-1601*, p. 428. The italics are mine.
53. Neale, *Eliz. and Parl., 1584-1601*, p. 431.
54. Neale, *Eliz. and Parl., 1584-1601*, p. 389 (the version in Stowe MS 362, fols. 169-72).

## Chapter IV

1. Neale, *Eliz. and Parl., 1584-1601*, pp. 339-41.
2. See Harold George Fox, *Monopolies and Patents: A Study of the History and Future of the Patent Monopoly*, University of Toronto Studies, Legal Series, extra vol. (Toronto, 1947), pp. 51, 65-66, 79-81, 82-83.
3. Fulke Greville, *Life of Sir Philip Sidney*, with an introduction by Nowell Smith (Oxford, 1907), p. 61.
4. There was also the 1598 Folio with "sundry new additions." Both folio texts, however, tack onto the "New Arcadia" the concluding books of the "Old Arcadia," which seems to have circulated rather widely in manuscript.
5. See Greville's description of the purpose of the *Arcadia*: "first, on the Monarch's part, lively to represent the growth, state, and declination of Princes, change of Government, and laws: vicissitudes of sedition, faction, succession, confederacies, plantations, with all other errors, or alterations in publique affaires. Then again in the subjects case; the state of favor, disfavor, prosperitie, adversity, emulation, quarrell, undertaking, retiring, hospitality, travail, and all other moodes of private fortunes, or misfortunes," so that a man "might (as in a glasse) see how to set a good countenaunce upon all the discountenances of adversitie, and a stay upon the exorbitant smilings of chance." *Life of Sidney*, pp. 15-16.
6. In writing this paragraph and in discussing Sidney's concepts of the origin and nature of government, I have been indebted greatly to William Dinsmore Briggs, "Political Ideas in Sidney's *Arcadia*," *SP*, XXVIII (1931), 137-61; "Sidney's Political Ideas," *SP*, XXIX (1932), 534-42. My emphasis varies from Briggs's chiefly in that the following discussion focuses upon aspects of the English scene which have been elucidated since those studies. For Spenser's "Puritanism," see Virgil K. Whitaker, *The Religious Basis of Spenser's Thought*, Stanford University Publications, University Series, Language and Literature, VII, No. 3 (Stanford, 1950).
7. See especially below, pp. 103-6.
8. For Beale's treatise on the state of the church, see Neale, *Eliz. and Parl., 1584-1601*, pp. 66-68. For his activity in subsequent Parliaments, see pp. 267-68, 277-78, and *passim*.
9. In brief, what is true for much sixteenth-century literature, is true here: the possible applications exist within the generalities, but that an application may be possible should not exclude consideration of the generality.
10. Here and elsewhere quotations are from *The Complete Works of Sir Philip Sidney*, ed. Albert Feuillerat (Cambridge, 1912). The emphasis in the meaning of "vertue" seems always to be clear by the context; the following passages, for example, move from an emphasis on an amoral forceful accomplishment to one on moral goodness. "But the Princes using the passions of fearing evill, and desiring to escape, onely to serve the rule of *vertue*, not to abandon ones selfe, lept to a ribbe of the shippe, which broken from his fellowes, floted with more likelyhood to doo service . . ." (I, 194). The unknown Black Knight in battle rained blows, wounds, and death, for "his

quicknes" was "more forcible then his force, and his judgment more quick then his quicknes. For though the sword went faster than eyesight could follow it, yet his owne judgment went still before it"; and thus although he was "followed by none, and adorned by nothing; so far without authoritie, that he was without knowledge," yet *"vertue* quickly made him knowne, and admiration bred him such authoritie, that though they of whose side he came knew him not, yet they all knew it was fitte to obey him: and while he was followed by the valiantest, he made way for the vilest," (I, 392). Pyrocles-Zelmane says to Amphialus, "I have long desired to know you, heretofore I must confesse with more good will, but still honoring your *vertue,* though I love not your person . . ." (I, 225). When his widowed mother agrees that Musidorus should travel for "the increase" of his "worthiness," "here-to did *Musidorus* owne *vertue* (see how *vertue* can be a minister to mischiefe) sufficiently provoke him: for indeed thus much I must say for him . . . that well-doing was at that time his scope, from which no faint pleasure could with-hold him" (I, 160). When the Princes made promises, "their *vertue*" promised that they should be kept (I, 194). By stories of worthy rulers, the young princes were moved "to do nobly . . . the beautie of *vertue* still being set before their eyes" (I, 190).

11. See the citation of Baumer above, chap. I, n. 35.
12. Briggs, *SP,* XXIX, 537.
13. For Smith, see the paragraph immediately following; for Walsingham's comment on the French in the Netherlands, see above, pp. 38-39.
14. Greville, *Life of Sidney,* pp. 97-98, 95. The italics are mine except for *"French Grandees"* and *"per saltum."*
15. Greville, *Life of Sidney,* pp. 54, 52-53. Smith's thought and Hooker's have already been discussed. Mildmay also defined Parliament in words nearly identical with Smith's, "the highest Court and Council of the realm." His concern for the authority of Parliament is apparent, e.g., in his argument that a dangerous precedent may be set for the "authority of proclamations" to extend "to greater matters than these are [i.e., disorders in apparel]," and in his statement to the Lords about Stourton's restitution in blood: that the Commons would leave to their posterity "the liberties of their House" "in the same freedom they received them." Neale, *Eliz. and Parl., 1559-1581,* pp. 331, 354-55, 357-59.
16. Greville, *Life of Sidney,* pp. 51-55.
17. See Sidney, *Works,* IV, 237-242. Note the nearly identical description of Philisides (IV, 67-68) and of the unnamed shepherd at the close of the first book in the revised *Arcadia* (I, 132). See also II, 74. The text of this song I quote, however, from the revised *Arcadia* (I, 132 ff.).
18. I, 134.
19. I, 135-36.
20. *Shorte Treatise,* p. 160.
21. *Laws,* pp. 86-87 (I, x).
22. II, 194.
23. Above, chap. I, n. 31.
24. II, 201. Except for the proper names, the italics are mine.
25. II, 176-77.
26. See also Hatton's speech at the trial of Mary, above, chap. I, n. 36.
27. II, 168.
28. II, 170.
29. I, 408.
30. Greville, *Life of Sidney,* pp. 85, 95-98, 102, etc.
31. I, 201-2 (italics mine). Musidorus thus becomes a lawmaker in the

best, widest, and, to the Renaissance, well-nigh eternal sense of that word. Le Roy, *Arist. Politqves*, sig. B6; see also Sidney, *Works*, II, 157.

32. I.e., "by all the desire of that people" after the king was slain (I, 204). In addition, Pyrocles gives this Princess in marriage to a nobleman who was an old friend of his father Euarchus, and thus both are endowed with the crown.

33. II, 158-59, 154.

34. II, 118.

35. II, 131.

36. These are Musidorus' words, quoted above, chap. IV, n. 28; but see such descriptions of Basilius or addresses to him as II, 99-100; I, 19, 314-15, 467-68. See also II, 75: ". . . the Princes persons; being in all monarchall governments the very knot of the peoples welfare," etc.

37. II, 130-31. This idea, i. a., motivated interest in the Venetian government, i.e., in the mixed state with its ancient example in Sparta. Fink, *Classical Republicans*, p. 32.

38. I, 371-72.

39. I, 371.

40. Although the aged gentleman of the blood royal in Phrygia, for example, had "past his time in modest secrecy," since he had been hated by his tyrannical cousin, and although he therefore kept "from entermedling in matters of government," he had done as much as he could, as much "as the greatnesse of his bloud would suffre him" (I, 201-2).

41. See Pyrocles-Daiphantus among the Helots (I, 46-47) and the description of Laconia as "unhappy" with its "unnatural" war (II, 152). See also, I, 317.

42. II, 100.

43. I, 468.

44. In this celebrated case, note the following: "The third platform is the government of God himself over the world, whereof lawful monarchies are a shadow. And therefore both amongst the Heathen, and amongst the Christians, the word, *sacred*, hath been attributed unto kings, because of the conformity of a monarchy with a divine Majesty: never to a senate or people. And so you find it twice in the lord Coke's Reports; once in the second book, the bishop of Winchester's case; and his fifth book, Cawdrie's case; and more anciently in the 10 of H. VIII. fol. 18. *Rex est persona mixta cum sacerdote;* an attribute which the senate of Venice, or a canton of Swisses, can never challenge. So, we see, there be precedents or platforms of monarchies, both in nature, and above nature; even from the monarch of heaven and earth to the king, if you will, in an hive of bees. And therefore other states are the creatures of law: and this state only subsisteth by nature." *The Works of Francis Bacon*, ed. James Spedding, Robert Leslie Ellis, and Douglas Denon Heath (London, 1858), VII, 645.

To Sidney, a monarch may become the devil's agent, in which case, obviously, he no longer embodies divine authority. See Greville, *Life of Sidney*, p. 116: "Tyrants be not nursing Fathers, but step-fathers; and so no anointed deputies of God, but rather lively Images of the dark Prince, that sole author of dis-creation, and disorder, who ever ruines his ends with over-building." The discussion concerns the way in which Sidney, "our unbelieved *Cassandra*," had observed the "limitless ambition of the *Spaniard*" to have chosen "that uttermost Citadell of bondage, I mean the Inquisition of *Spain*, for her instrument" to root out "all seeds of humane freedom . . . with fatal dissolution to itself."

45. II, 131.

46. II, 145.

47. I, 202.
48. About Euarchus in particular, see I, 184-87; also above, pp. 61, 57. Note also Sidney's comment on Euarchus: that "one mans sufficience is more available than ten thousands multitude" (II, 157). In this last instance, of course, one is concerned again with the law-giver in the widest sense of that word. See above, chap. IV, n. 24. See also the quotations above, chap. IV, n. 33. Such virtue, i.a., destroys the evils of oligarchy (I, 185-86).
49. That is, the disciplined and substantial people (nobles, senators, men of virtue and wisdom). Gough, *Social Contract*, p. 59.
50. I, 318-19, 319-24; see also I, 311; II, 119; or the giants of Phrygia (I, 204-5).
51. I, 319. Note, too, the rhetorical ability of Plexirtus (I, 213).
52. I, 314.
53. I, 46-47, 39. For the subsequent violation by the ruler of these terms and Euarchus' avoidance of the Helots' country, see II, 152.
54. I, 185-86.
55. II, 131, 146.
56. II, 148-49; I, 186.
57. I, 373 and 386, 222-23, 394, 373, 68, 263, 98-99, 450, 494.
58. Although Amphialus and the vicious Plexirtus are different, the precept *qua* precept is enunciated as valid (I, 293).
59. Greville, *Life of Sidney*, p. 15.
60. I, 211. The friend, of course, of these two friends is Plexirtus. See also I, 212.
61. It is his proud mother, of course, who stirs up Amphialus' rebellious ambition, etc.
62. I, 196-97, 199-200. This tyrant also relies upon his guard and upon soldiers, just as Plexirtus kept Paphlagonia "by force of stranger souldiers in *Cittadels*, the nestes of tyranny, and murderers of libertie" (I, 209). See above, on Ponet's thought, chap. III, n. 25.
63. I, 202-4.
64. I, 242-50.
65. I, 330-31, 332-33.
66. I, 326.
67. I, 22, 117-18, 123. Note also the comparison and contrast between Gynecia and Cecropia (I, 19-20, 125; II, 94) and see above, pp. 111-12.
68. II, 152. See also Briggs, *SP*, XXVIII, 149; and note how Buchanan specifies even the negligence of an hereditary king, along with his violence and his fraud, as being something for which the sovereignty of the people provide a remedy (above, p. 39).
69. I, 25, 167 (the maxim taught by "the mountie at a Hearne"), 510; also I, 326, 468-69, and *passim*.
70. This is said specifically about Andromana (I, 278).
71. I, 356. See also "the rule of vertue" (I, 194); Pyrocles' "naturall hunger" for "high honor" (I, 205-6); Philanax's activity even though Basilius persists in his foolishness (I, 510); Euarchus' vigor in preparing for attack (II, 149-50).
72. I, 186-87. By contrast, Cecropia, e.g., speaks of "the sweetnesse of authoritie" (I, 364).
73. I, 373.
74. I, 486, 26.
75. II, 156-57.
76. II, 198.
77. I, 332; see also I, 298 ff.
78. I, 373; see also I, 22: Basilius' "office" should be "not to make men,

but to use men as men are." As Sidney moves out from, and returns to, princely attributes, he also specifies minor aspects of such an art. Thus, in accordance with the thought of both Hooker and Machiavelli, he writes as follows about Euarchus' temporary rule of Arcadia and the ceremony which he used: "For *Euarchus* did wisely consider, the people to be naturally taken with exterior shewes, farre more then with inward consideracion, of the materiall pointes. And therefore in this newe entrie into so entangled a matter, he would leave nothing which might be eyther an armour or ornament unto him, and in these pompous ceremonyes he well knewe a secreat of government much to consist" (II, 167).

## Chapter V

1. For a brief discussion of this point, see below, pp. 196-98. It is discussed more fully, however, in the study referred to in the preface to this work, wherein one can also find a consideration of the plays mentioned in the next sentence.

2. Here and in all subsequent quotations from Shakespeare, I use, for the reader's convenience, *The Complete Plays and Poems of William Shakespeare*, ed. William Allan Neilson and Charles Jarvis Hill (New York, 1942)—unless otherwise noted. All italicized lines are mine.

3. *Ben Jonson*, ed. C. H. Herford, Percy and Evelyn Simpson (Oxford, 1938), VI, 17: "The Indvction," *Bartholomew Fair* (1614), ll. 135-48. Unless it is otherwise noted, this edition is used throughout. For an argument that "application" was a favorite pastime of patrons of private theaters, see William A. Armstrong, "The Audience of the Elizabethan Private Theatres," *RES*, N.S. X (1959), 234-49. The evidence is based heavily upon Jonson's comments. See also the first two chapters of C. J. Sisson, *Lost Plays of Shakespeare's Age* (Cambridge, 1936), particularly p. 79.

4. For these and similar remarks, see Campbell, *Shakespeare's "Histories,"* pp. 23-41, and the first chapter of Irving Ribner, *The English History Play in the Age of Shakespeare* (Princeton, 1957).

5. Leonard F. Dean, "Sir Francis Bacon's Theory of Civil History Writing," *ELH*, VIII (1941), 183; and for "ruminated history," Bacon, *Works*, IV, 310. A valuable supplement to Dean's study is that by Vincent Luciani, "Bacon and Guicciardini," *PMLA*, LXII (1947), 96-113.

6. Its "pretence original" was like Tyler's in that it was said to be "for the King"; yet it was a rebellion, for its "pretence final" was still a "pretence." Stirling, *HLQ*, VIII, 231-32 (wherein the emphasis is placed upon earlier historical incidents being "applied topically" or "printed as of interest" to Elizabethans and Jacobeans, p. 233). See also *Calendar of State Papers, Domestic, 1591-1594* (London, 1867), pp. 75-76 (wherein the Hacket incident is likened to "that matter of John of Leyden"); and *C.S.P., Dom., 1598-1601* (London, 1869), p. 599. In view of what might be called a conventional picture of perilous ambition or of revolt (above, pp. 58-59, 97-98, 104-5) it is interesting to note how some of Leicester's activities in the Low Countries seem to follow that conventional process of thought, which, quite understandably, because of its workability, seems to have been conceived of as valid. Thus Leicester would stir up trouble by using the proletariat of the large cities, mostly the small craftsmen, against the aristocratic merchant class. Read, *Walsingham*, III, 158-59; see also III, 249-50.

7. See the proclamation closely following Essex's revolt (Feb. 15, 1601) which speaks of the "great multitude of base and loose people . . . listening after news and stirs" and "ready to lay hold of any occasions to enter into any tumult or disorder." Stirling, *HLQ*, VIII, 222.

8. The quotations immediately following are taken from Nichols, *Progesses*, III, 552-53. Usually only Elizabeth's question through her next response to Lambarde is quoted.

9. Neale, *Eliz. I and Parl., 1559-81*, pp. 16-29 and *passim*.

10. For the 1599 date, see *A Transcript of the Registers of the Company of Stationers of London, 1554-1640*, ed. Edward Arber (London, 1876), III, 134 (Jan. 9, 1599); and for further details about the treatment of Hayward, his book, and those connected with its publication, see Leo Kirshbaum, *Shakespeare and the Stationers*, Ohio State Univ. Grad. School Monographs, Contrib. in Lang. and Lit., No. 15 (Columbus, 1955), pp. 51-52.

11. *C.S.P., Dom., 1598-1601*, p. 404.

12. When, for example, Elizabeth is said to have asked if treason were not apparent in the history, Bacon answered that although he could find no treason, yet the borrowings from Tacitus might be grounds for prosecuting Hayward for felony. Bacon, *Works*, VII, 133 (*Apophthegms*, 58).

13. About the instances of censorship cited by Evelyn May Albright in her *Dramatic Publication in England, 1580-1640* (New York, 1927), the following considerations seem pertinent: that matter in *Sir Thomas More* was ordered revised, for example; that Middleton's *Game at Chess* referred to contemporary events and persons; that Charles I might consider a portion of a drama "too insolent and to be changed" does not mean that the author of the "original" scene in *Sir Thomas More* intended to refer to any particular riot (see, e.g., *The Book of Sir Thomas More*, ed. W. W. Greg, Malone Soc., 1911, p. xix); or that the lines Massinger wrote and Charles objected to were meant to refer to the royal imposition of taxes (the thought and phraseology of the lines can be paralleled quite easily elsewhere). And the *Game at Chess*, after all, is unique in the process of its entire five acts. Riots have occurred in all generations; rulers, like foreign ambassadors, censors, and delators could be excessively touchy. Furthermore, given the conventions of Elizabethan political thought, with its constant references to the one, the few, and the many and its recognition of potential beneficence and viciousness in each of the components of a commonweal, certain patterns, which are essentially political but which are also both obvious and natural, may emerge from any play-world and be part of an audience's theatrical heritage. As such, they should be considered along with the structural movements and the more purely literary motifs that may also appear in any given play; and thus one might well doubt a topical or doctrinal intent in, for example, a drama by Beaumont and Fletcher wherein the ruler and the powerful few are corrupt and the true ruler is restored with the aid of the many. See Mary Grace Muse Adkins, "The Citizens in *Philaster*: Their Function and Significance," *SP*, XLIII (1946), 203-12. My point is that the nature of such a state's corruption finds a natural corollary in the nature of that state's beneficence; thus the appearance of the sensible many may result simply from a conventional, theatrical process of thought and need not have been designed at all to apply to Stuart England and the developing struggle between king and parliament, any more than the good sense of the many in *Richard III* need be applied to Elizabeth's England and to the activity of representatives of the many in her parliaments.

To illustrate the point of differentiation being considered with another example, notice how Parsons' argument for the lawfulness of the deposition of Richard II in his *Conference about the Next Succession* (above, pp. 66-67) accords perfectly with his attacks and those of other Catholics upon Elizabeth's "corrupt" court, a court that for them violated the most elementary requisites for good rule, namely, good counsel, good counselors, and a true religion. Yet similarly and in interesting detail, though without a religious purpose, Walsingham would refer to the Scottish court and Scottish policy during his embassy to James in 1583. Thus his report of his conversation with that ruler reveals a situation both interesting and amusing; for although Walsingham and other members of Elizabeth's government, when the Ruthven raiders had been in control, were opposed to the policy they were now advocating, in 1583 they feared the influence of Esmé Stuart. As a consequence, in his second conference with James, Walsingham advised the king to ask the Parliament, shortly to be held, about his counselors. In support of this advice he cited the Elizabethan maxim that "the assembly of state in Monarchies did especially serve to consult of such remedies as might best serve to cure the diseases of the same." With a constant emphasis upon the necessity for advice and counsel drawn from the assembly of 'state, he then continued with another valid precept, encountered also in the *De Republica Anglorum*, in the *Laws of Ecclesiastical Polity*, in the *Arcadia*, in a slightly different form in *Gorboduc*, and elsewhere. Because a regency had existed in Scotland for forty years "the reverence of the authority of a king was taken away, so as every great personage within his realm did think himself as it were exempt from the ordinary obedience of common subjects." In this particular instance, moreover, the Scotch ruler should realize that "young princes were many times carried into great errors upon an opinion of the absoluteness of their royal authority and do not consider, that when they transgress the bounds and limits of the law, they leave to be kings and become tyrants." In a manner comparable to the arguments of both Smith and Sidney, Walsingham also pointed out that when rulers were carried into the error of "the absoluteness of their royal authority" by ambitious counselors, many had been deposed, both Scotch and English. The shades of Major and Buchanan might well have hovered over this conversation, but the specific incident Walsingham cited was English, namely, the deposition of Edward II: "That as subjects are bound to obey dutifully so were princes bound to command justly; which reason and ground of government was set down in the deposition of Edward the Second, as by ancient record thereof doth appear." Read, *Walsingham*, II, 216-18.

It is not surprising that James considered Walsingham "a very Machiavelli" and that he insisted, even though he said he had told his subjects differently, that Walsingham had not given him "faithful counsel"; for whether or not Walsingham had counseled James to "use religion for his people's obedience" (II, 221), Walsingham had struck directly at James's divine-rightist theories—expressed, however, in the first conference of 1583 only by James's saying "with a kind of jollity" "that he was an absolute king" (II, 213).

Obviously the differences between Parsons' and Walsingham's purpose is great, but both utilize a conventional process of thought. For both individuals the immediate event and then the precept take precedent over history. As a consequence, then, because history was so used does not mean that history plays and a similar process of thought in those dramas have an ultimate point of reference comparable to that of either Walsingham or Parsons. I emphasize this point because of Campbell, *Shakespeare's "Histories."*

14. For Daniel's difficulties, see *The Tragedy of Philotas*, ed. Laurence Michel, Yale Stud. English, CX (New Haven, 1949), pp. 36-37, although I cannot agree with Michel's emphasis upon the Essex affair in his analysis of the play. The quotation is from Daniel's letter to Devonshire, printed by Michel, along with its summary in the *Calendar of State Papers* (pp. 37-39).

15. For Jonson's difficulties, see *Ben Jonson*, I, 36-39; II, 4-5, 31; III, 606.

16. For Daniel's use of North's translation of Plutarch and of Quintus Curtius' *De Rebus Gestis Alexandri Magni Regis Macedonum* in the original, see *Philotas*, pp. 67-68. The treatment of Philotas' silence about the con-

spiracy (see the resumé below) is more favorable to Philotas than are the words of either of Daniel's sources. "Philotas would not let him [Cebalinus] speak with the king (but why, no man could tell) telling them that the king had greater matters in hande, and was not at leisure." *Plutarch's Lives . . . Englished by Sir Thomas North,* Tudor Translations (London, 1895), IV, 355. "Philotas, after strongly commending him [Cebalinus], at once went into Alexander, and having talked with him for some time about other matters, reported nothing of what he had learned from Cebalinus. Toward evening the young man met Philotas in the vestibule of the royal apartment, as he was coming out, and asked him whether he had done what he requested. Philotas alleged that the king had had no time to talk with him, and went away. On the following day Cebalinus was on hand when Philotas came to the royal apartment, and reminded him, as he entered, of the matter which he had communicated to him the day before. Philotas replied that he was attending to it, but did not even then disclose to the king what he had heard." *Quintus Curtius,* tr. John C. Rolfe, Loeb Classical Libr. (Cambridge, Mass., 1946), II, 65 (VI. vii. 19-21).

Similarly, at the trial before the assembled soldiers, the words Daniel represents as being in the letter intercepted between Parmenio and Philotas are *"So shall you do what you intend to do,"* (V, ii, 1311), a statement more ambiguous, and less applicable to a conspiracy, than the words of his source: "thus we shall accomplish what we have planned" ("sic enim quae destinavimus efficiemus") (VI. ix. 14). In Daniel's play the earlier words quoted from Parmenio's letter are simply "Make thyself less *Philotas* than thou art" (I, i, 1); nor does Daniel reflect the earlier conspiracy against Alexander with which Philotas is charged (VI. ix. 17). Furthermore, Daniel does not represent Philotas as swooning or as not venturing "to lift his eyes or to open his mouth" when charges have been made against him, "either through consciousness of guilt or beside himself and thunderstruck by the greatness of his peril . . ." (VI. ix. 32-33). In this respect, Daniel also omits Bolon's speech with details unfavorable to Philotas (VI. xi. 1-7).

Finally, in treating a third important incident, found this time in Plutarch but not in Quintus Curtius, Daniel represents Philotas' words calling Alexander a "young man" as occurring only on one occasion, as being motivated by a "iolly" heat of the moment (I, ii, 302-27), and as being reported to the conqueror only when Craterus uses them as fresh grounds for arguing that Philotas should be watched (II, i, 545-49). In Plutarch, those and similar words were reported to the ruler over a period of time during which Alexander did not accuse Philotas "though he had manifest proofe and cause" (*Plutarch's Lives,* p. 355). Daniel's treatment of this incident, indeed, can be construed as reflecting upon the integrity of Craterus, although such an interpretation, as will be pointed out later, can be negated by other considerations.

As regards the characterization of Alexander, Daniel's treatment of that ruler contrasts strikingly with Curtius' statement that after conquering the Persians, Alexander fell into their vices—banqueting all night, for example, entertaining troops of harlots, and becoming increasingly irascible as a result of the discontent arising therefrom (VI. ii. 1-4). Since Daniel also draws the Antigona plot from Plutarch, it is Philotas, as a consequence, who seems to have so succumbed, rather than Alexander; for Antigona is a Persian "curtizan" (cf. I, ii). Indeed, a general conception of Alexander's conduct which accords with Curtius' words would be well known, presumably, from the account of Alexander found in the dictionary that was recognized as the basic Latin-English thesaurus and used widely throughout England. Thus Cooper writes that, although Alexander was the "one most excellent" of the "many noble princes" given that name, and although he was "brought vp by Aristotle in learning" and at an early age had "enterprised to conquer all the worlde," yet his great accomplishments in a relatively little space of time led only to moral degeneration and death. "But when he had pacified the world from all rebellions, he fell into such crueltie and pride (sleying his most trustie counsailours in his furie, and commanding himselfe to be called a God) that he became odious to his owne people: who desiring his destruction, at the last when he was in his most glorie at the Citie of Babylon (where he abode the Ambassadours from all realmes) at supper with one of his phisitions, was poysoned by drinking out of a cup, which was supposed to be made of an horses hoofe, and was thought to be done by the deuise of Aristotle, sometime his maister, and Antipater his lieutenant in Macedonia, whom a little before he had grieuously threatned. Thus Alexander, abounding in excellent vertues and notable vices, after most happie fortune, by his outragious pride and crueltie shortned his life, being at his death little aboue xxxiii. yeres old, which was afore the incarnation of Christ . 322 yeares."

17. II, ii, 628; III, iii, 1042-43; see also III, i, 873.

18. See the chorus between Act III and Act IV and the chorus of V, i (ll. 1132-35, 1819-20, 1843-49). They are discussed more fully below.

19. E.g., the passages cited in Gilbert, *Machiavelli's "Prince,"* pp. 54-55; the popularity of Seneca's *De Beneficiis*; and *Philotas,* II, i, 441-52 (Alexander and Philotas); ii, 602-7 (Philotas and the Captain); III, i, 923-33 (Alexander and Parmenio).

20. The statements occur in "The Apology." *Philotas,* pp. 155-56. The second also appears in both the letter to Robert Cecil, Lord Cranborne, and to the Earl of Devonshire (p. 38).

21. The quotations are again from "The Apology" and again a portion of the idea (three acts written before "my L. of Essex troubles") reappears in the letter to Devonshire. *Philotas,* pp. 156, 138.

22. Madeleine Doran, *Endeavors of Art* (Madison, 1954), pp. 310-22.

23. E.g., below, p. 141, as well as the correspondence between Chalisthenes' speeches in I, i, and the concern of Alexander in II, i. Note also I, i, 160-63 and II, i, 463-82. For full discussion of these parts of a drama, see T. W. Baldwin, *Shakspere's Five Act Structure* (Urbana, 1947).

24. *The which may teach vs to observe this straine, / To admire high hills, but liue within the plaine.*

25. In II, i; III, i; III, iii.

26. On its first appearance, the chorus describes itself as *"the Chorus of the vulgar,"* who see and censure all that great men do and say. Though they be considered ignorant, they are *"capable of truth"* in that they know when actions are performed well and when they lack the *"grace that makes them proue the best in show."* They judge by *"th' events"* what plots have existed and *"how they all without do personate,"* not knowing *"what they* [the great men] *do within / Where they attire, their mysteries of State"* (ll. 399-410). In this respect, see one of Smith's statements (above, pp. 40-41). For the shifting of the chorus' views, see above, pp. 139-40, and also the sentences immediately following.

In addition to what has been pointed out, note how the distinction between private and public place, first indicated in dialogue between Philotas and Chalisthenes and then applied to Philotas (I, i, e.g., 83-86, 102-4), is applied to Alexander by both Craterus and Alexander himself (III, i, 952-61). Likewise, a natural corollary of *"The usuall workings"* of a principal subaltern's ambition would be *"the frailty of greatnesse"* so intensified that it appears as *"the wrath of Kings."* In this respect also, the degeneration of the Macedonians, who have suffered from their course of conquest (V, i, 1767-69, 1830-34; ii, 1956-57), accords with the final thought that *"other heads"* will spring up to threaten Alexander and the security of state (V, ii, 2125-30)—and thereby censure of Alexander's severity (V, ii, 2119-24) is countered by the chorus that has just expressed that censure.

27. That is, by Chalisthenes (I, i).

28. "To the Prince," ll. 65-78. Such an attitude, aside from being conventional, is what one might expect from the author of *Musophilus* and gives an appreciable irony to Philotas' characterization of Chalisthenes as a vain, discursive book-man (I, i, 156).

29. *Philotas*, p. 36.

30. Greville, *Life of Sidney*, pp. 155-56, 151.

31. See Dixon Wecter, "Shakespeare's Purpose in *Timon of Athens*," *PMLA*, XLIII (1928), 707-21. Note, too, E. P. Kuhl, "The Earl of Essex and Liberalism," *PQ*, XXIV (1945), 187-90.

32. See Sidney's statements, above, chap. IV, nn. 46, 74.

33. It is interesting to note how Daniel's commonplace about height and ambition had been utilized by Walsingham in "A Discourse touching the pretended matche between the D[uke] of Norfolk and the Queene of Scots." Walsingham's process of thought, too, is a thoroughly conventional one, grounded upon the premise that Norfolk is great with the nobility "in respect of his alliance" and with the commons "in respect of a kinde of familiarity used toward them in publique sport, as in shootings and cock-fightings, a thing not to be discomended if it savoured not of an ambitious and aspiring intent." Thus, once more, is it pointed out—not about the affairs of Amphialus, nor about Daniel's or Shakespeare's play-worlds, but about likely events—how such worthy attributes show "perpetuall workings." These two qualities of Norfolk are "two gifts of God" and "being well employed by him whom God hath endued withal yield no small benefit to the commonwealth and Prince where he liveth; so on the other side, being abused through ambition, they breed to the Prince danger and the commonwealth disquietness." Any match between such a person and a woman like Mary, consequently, is likely to yield a fruit that would "needs taste of ambition, of all other the most dangerous fruit"; for about Mary, Walsingham writes as Sidney and other literary men did of some of their noble figures: with her, "the thirst of a kingdom can never be quenched until it hath hazarded the uttermost trial." Read, *Walsingham*, I, 72.

With such considerations, of course, one has moved from a fear of the many to what was considered one of the most frequent inciting causes of disquietude in a commonweal; and one finds oneself once more in that nebulous area between an obvious virtue that partakes of the heroic and an obvious ambition that partakes of an "honor" and a revenge suited to an agent of the Devil. Because of the states' attack on Leicester, Francis Needham believed that in the Low Countries the Earl was seeking only to serve his own turn and at the same time achieve "revenge"—an observation more unfavorable to Leicester, but substantially the same, for example, as that made by Buckhurst. Read, *Walsingham*, III, 250-51, 242. There should be no need here to elaborate upon a noble or royal honor and the necessity for its "reparation"—a fact, like all such facts in the complex of rule, at once platitudinous and capable of the most variable interpretations, both by contemporaries and by moderns. See III, 249-50. The Elizabethan government would attempt to utilize "honor" to play upon "the Grand Seigneur" of the Turks and to incite Parma, in conjunction with his son's proposed marriage to Lady Arabella Stuart, to set himself up as ruler of the Low Countries and break with Spain. Once more, though in different circumstances and with different emphases, one touches, nevertheless, upon that conventional picture into which Essex could be fitted easily.

34. Daniel's letter to Devonshire. *Philotas,* p. 38. For the abbreviated account, see p. 37.

## Chapter VI

1. I use *folio* to indicate the text as given in the 1623 Folio, but the number of lines is determined by the usual lineation of modern editors. Thus in the edition here used, aside from Act III, scene i, the lines which do not appear in Q1 are as follows. I, i, 166-79: the major part of a speech by Morton, pointing out to Northumberland that in his statement, "Let us make head," there was a "presurmise" of Hotspur's peril or death; yet he did say, "Go forth." I, i, 189-209: the major part of Morton's subsequent speech, pointing out that in contrast to the last attempt, the Archbishop of York now turns "insurrection to religion," enlarges his rising "with the blood / Of fair King Richard, scrap'd from Pomfret stones," and derives his quarrel and cause from Heaven to relieve a "bleeding land" under Bolingbroke. I, iii, 21-24: the major portion of a speech by Lord Bardolph, pointing out the need for Northumberland's definite support in "a theme so bloody-fac'd as this." I, iii, 36-55: the major portion of another of Lord Bardolph's speeches, being an analogy between building and insurrection. I, iii, 85-108: an entire speech of the Archbishop, urging that the "occasion" of the rebels' arms be published, but in the main, censuring the "giddy," "unsure," "vulgar heart" of the "fond many," who disgorged "royal Richard" but would now have him again. II, iii, 23-45: the major portion of Lady Percy's speech, describing Hotspur as a "miracle of men," imitated by "the noble youth" but unseconded in battle by Northumberland, whom she is urging not to join the rebels. IV, i, 55-79: the major portion of another speech by the Archbishop, pointing out how he has weighed the justice of the rebels' cause, which he supports. IV, i, 103-38: a portion of the dialogue between Westmoreland (20 ll.) and Mowbray (17 ll.), focusing, however, upon the trial by combat between Bolingbroke and Mowbray's father, in stopping which, Mowbray asserts, Richard caused his own death and all subsequent ills. See below, chap. VI, n. 3.

2. James G. McManaway, "The Cancel in the Quarto of *2 Henry IV*," *Studies in Honor of A. H. R. Fairchild,* ed. Charles T. Prouty, Univ. Missouri Studies, XXI (Columbia, 1946-47), 69-80. See also W. Craig Ferguson, "The Compositor of *Henry IV, Part 2, Much Ado About Nothing, The Shoemakers' Holiday,* and the *First Part of the Contention,*" *Studies in Bibliography,* XIII (1960), 19-29. Details concerning information in this paragraph, and the next seven, can be found in McManaway's article and in R. B. McKerrow, *A Dictionary of Printers and Booksellers* (London 1910), pp. 245-46, wherein are noted Simmes's difficulties in 1589 (arrested as one of the compositors of the Martin Marprelate press), in 1595 (having printed without license the popular *Grammar and Accidence*), and in 1599 (listed as one of fourteen forbidden to print satires and epigrams, and fined). On another occasion he was caught printing a ballad against Raleigh.

3. *The Second Part of Henry the Fourth,* ed. Matthias A. Shaaber, New Variorum Edition (Philadelphia, 1940), pp. 480-88.

4. Variorum, pp. 473-76.

5. McManaway, in *Studies in Honor of A. H. R. Fairchild,* p. 80. Because of the fact that the paper "proved a job lot," Miss Alice Walker believes that this attempt to solve the problem was "unavailing." This one consideration, however, should certainly be viewed with the others pointed out above. Although it does not strain the imagination that paper might remain unused, it is somewhat more difficult to envisage printed sheets being available for such

a cancel restoration after any appreciable period of time—especially when that restoration was not so advertised. *Textual Problems of the First Folio, Shakespeare Problems,* ed. J. Dover Wilson (Cambridge, 1953), VII, 94-95.

6. *Philotas,* p. 38.

7. The Augustinian concept of *rationes seminales* is here used figuratively, being transferred to human action. Thus Northumberland's falseness is a "seed"; note, e.g., how Aquinas' third division of *rationes seminales* are those "produced by universal causes." Walter Clyde Curry, *Shakespeare's Philosophic Patterns* (Baton Rouge, 1937), pp. 29-47 (i.e., "Tumbling Nature's Germens"). In *2 H IV* Warwick's "necessary form," and, even more, his "seeds" and "seed" (ll. 84, 90), bear the weight of the preceding examples and images used in the lyrical fusion of the immediate with a varying universal that is uncontrolled and uncontrollable, as far as man is concerned (ll. 45-56). Yet Warwick's speech also exists within the concrete, though conventional, context of "rank diseases" in the body of the kingdom "near the heart of it" and the comforting counsel of a slight treatment by opposites (ll. 38-44, 96-103). Somewhat paradoxically, then, these commonwealth difficulties can be controlled by a ruler who faces them, with his council, as "necessities"; and not simply the word *necessity* (ll. 73, 92, 93) but this culmination of such a connotative process reminds one of Hooker's thought (above, pp. 55-56). See also William Elton, "Timothy Bright and Shakespeare's Seeds of Nature," *MLN,* LXV (1950), 196-97.

At the same time, an audience is reminded, not of any current situation, but of Shakespeare's earlier play, and this jog to a regular theater-goer's possible recollection is remarkably congruent with Shakespeare's earlier dramatization. The repetition of Richard's words to Northumberland (*R II*, V, i, 55-59) is accurate; and, as it will be pointed out, in *R II* a Lancastrian emphasis on Bolingbroke as the hope of the people, and even as a child of destiny, had been reflected. In *R II* also, a clear stage picture of Bolingbroke kneeling to Richard had appeared. As a result, the lines of Henry here in *2 H IV* are much less of a discrepancy from what had been dramatized in *R II* than a fusion of different points in the dramatic order of the play, each accurate in itself. See also, e.g., Richard II's reference to "necessity" (V, i, 21).

8. Certainly the scene is an essential and cohesive part of *2 H IV*. It brings upon the stage for the first time in this drama a figure who has been referred to constantly, and by its elaboration of the first reference to the King's illness, expressed through the Prince and Poins, it moves to what will be emphasized in the epitasis and catastrophe, namely, the death of Henry IV and the accession of Henry V. Its grave lyricism obviously accords with the King's next and last scenes (IV, iv, v), wherein the old incident of Hal's taking the crown, drawn probably from *The Famous Victories,* fills out the culmination of a profligate-son motif (IV, v, 64-80), now transmuted to effective drama by its lyrical vigor. Furthermore, the language of Act III, scene i, continues words, images, and ideas connected with time, necessity, disease, and, to a lesser degree, the tide, which have appeared in earlier portions of the drama and will continue. Even in the last line of the first speech ("Uneasy lies the head that wears a crown"), the scene anticipates the crown imagery developed more fully with Henry IV's last appearance (IV, v); and there, too, it is connected with sleep and the heavy weight of rule. Although Henry's expression of guilt (IV, v, 184-87) moves beyond the worrisome memories of Act III, scene i, it moves into an emphasis upon Hal's successive right—a poetic process that is repeated (ll. 219-25).

9. That is, on the title page which also gives the actors their Jacobean name, "the Kinges Maiesties seruants": "THE / Tragedie of King / Richard the

Second: / With new additions of the Parlia- / ment Sceane, and the deposing / of King Richard, / As it hath been lately acted by the Kinges / Maiesties seruantes, at the Globe / By *William Shake-speare.* / (device) / AT LONDON, / Printed by W. W. for *Mathew Law,* and are to / be sold at his shop in Paules Church-yard, / at the signe of the Foxe. / 1608." Since only 170 lines are involved in the printing of the full scene in this quarto, which like the earlier ones is based otherwise on its immediate predecessor, one could not expect too many indications of the nature of the copy used by the printer. Yet the variations between Q4 and F1 point to copy derived from a theatrical performance, perhaps by means of shorthand "as it hath been lately acted." *The Life and Death of King Richard the Second,* ed. Matthew W. Black, New Variorum Edition (Philadelphia, 1955), pp. 370-71. The question of contemporary interest in *R II* is somewhat baffling, since the words of this title page might seem to contradict Augustine Phillips' statement at Essex's trial in February, 1601, to the effect that the actors considered the play "to be so old & so long out of use that they shold have small or no company at yt" (Variorum, p. 581). Yet, considering the years from ca. 1595-96 to early 1601, Phillips' statement might well be essentially true, especially in view of its circumstances, in that *R II* was no longer considered to be, by itself, a drawing card comparable to the newest plays.

10. They would have witnessed, in any event, the Flint Castle scene and the scene in which Richard censured Northumberland. Above, chap. VI, n. 7.

11. The title page of Q1 reads, in part: "Printed by Valentine Simmes for Androw Wise, and / are to be sold at his shop in Paules church yard at / the signe of the Angel."

12. G. B. Harrison mentions *R II* in this respect, a point which certainly should be repeated in this present context. *Shakespeare under Elizabeth* (New York, 1933), pp. 122-25. Harrison emphasizes, however, the wisdom of omitting anything that might be related to the succession, in view of Parsons' *Conference.*

13. *Ben Jonson,* I, 15-16. For the order of August 15 and the warrants of October 3, see I, 217-18. When one considers the likely date for the composition of *R II,* it seems surprising that editors do not call attention to this situation in 1597 at least as frequently as they call attention to a portion of Elizabeth's conversation with Lambarde in August of 1601.

14. The principal chronicles which were Shakespeare's sources are, of course, Holinshed, Hall, Froissart, Créton, and *Traïson.* In this instance, it may have been Froissart who led Shakespeare to omit Richard's journey to Conway before going to Flint; yet Shakespeare may have been influenced by a marginal note in Holinshed, which, in contradiction of the text, says that Richard stole away to Flint (Black, Variorum, p. 425). Through Holinshed from Créton, Shakespeare probably derived the name of Northumberland for Henry's messenger, a fact not given in Froissart. Even more important than such details, however, is the fact that in the chronicles, even in Holinshed alone, Shakespeare would encounter different interpretations of events conducive to variations in the interpretation of the characters involved. As a result, the words "pro-Richard" and "anti-Richard" seem inadequate for indicating Shakespeare's emphases here. I use terms which indicate three different attitudes in the heritage of sixteenth-century historians. Although such a simplification is bound to be inadequate also, in a very general way it can be said to correspond to the fact that fifteenth-century Lancastrian chroniclers represented Richard as an incompetent ruler, even a "wicked" tyrant, indulging in corrupt rule for personal advantage, and that they represented Bolingbroke as a just nobleman, the publicly acknowledged heir of Richard, a savior of England, a beneficent child of destiny.

Yorkist chroniclers then took an entirely different point of view. Being more interested in blackening the character of Henry than in exculpating Richard, they may portray Richard as the victim of an ambitious pretender but, at the same time, tacitly admit the corruption of Richard's government. Yet other chroniclers, especially French ones, viewed Richard as a martyr king, exploited by the shrewd politician Bolingbroke. It is not to be wondered at, then, that sixteenth-century English historians would reflect these conflicting traditions, some aspects of which could not be resolved because of their diametrical contradictions. Consequently, I here use "Lancastrian" to indicate attitudes favorable to Henry and "Yorkist" to indicate unfavorable ones, even though the particular form of expression might be closer to that of French chroniclers, for example; thereby "Richardian" can be used to indicate attitudes congruent with the concept of Richard the martyr king. For details of this heritage bequeathed to Elizabethan historians, see Louisa DeSausurre Duls, "The Complex Picture of Richard II Inherited by Sixteenth-Century Writers from Fourteenth- and Fifteenth-Century Chronicle Sources," unpublished Ph.D. dissertation, Univ. of North Carolina, 1962, and Richard Jerome Geehern, "Fifteenth and Early Sixteenth Century Interpretations of the Character and Career of King Henry IV," unpublished Ph.D. dissertation, Univ. of North Carolina, 1952.

15. *Edward II*, I, iv, 280-81.

16. DeWitt T. Starnes and Ernest William Talbert, *Classical Myth and Legend in Renaissance Dictionaries* (Chapel Hill, 1955), pp. 119-20.

17. See *Gorboduc*, II, i, 203-11 (e.g., "The youthfull heades of these vnskillfull kinges").

18. *Fabvlarum Ovidii Interpretatio, Ethica, Physica, et Historica, Tradita in Academia Regiomontana a Georgio Sabino, et in unam collecta et edita studio et industria T. T.* (Cambridge, Thomas Thomas, 1584) pp. 63-68.

19. V, i, 35-36.

20. Peter de la Primaudaye, *The French Academie* (London, 1618), pp. 455, 409-10. The material quoted is from the second book, the fifth day, chapter thirty-nine; see also the third day, chapter twenty-three. Translated into English, this second part appeared in octavo in 1594, although the translation of the entire work had begun its appearance in 1586. See also Rolf Soellner, "The Four Primary Passions," *SP*, LV (1958), 549-67.

21. In such revenge tragedies as *The Spanish Tragedy* and *Titus Andronicus*, the protagonist is at first passive as he suffers from deeds of villainy until he becomes "frantic" and speaks in a distracted, "mad," or even meaningless manner, not in Richard's logically lyrical one. At some point in the drama, however, he moves into effecting an active counter-stratagem. Such a structural movement is discussed in the study referred to in the preface; there also will be found analyses of the preceding plays.

22. Above, p. 29.

23. Above, chap. IV, n. 14.

24. Black, Variorum, p. 576; but see I. A. Shapiro, "Richard II or Richard III or. . . ?" *SQ*, IV (1958), 204-6.

25. Above, pp. 40-41.

26. *R II* falls into that structural movement in which a ruler is represented unsympathetically before his separation from power, but with his fall becomes an object of pathos. The same is true for Marlowe's *Edward II*. Such a movement, as well as the preceding play, is discussed in the study referred to in the preface. See below, p. 184.

27. E.g., II, ii, in which emphases relatively anti-Edward (ll. 1-14, 37-64) alternate with emphases relatively anti-noble (ll. 15-35, 65-72). A comparable process can be seen in III, ii and iii. See above, chap. VI, n. 26.

28. Black, Variorum, p. 278 (Q1, sig. H2, 16-18; also Q2, Q3).

29. In this instance it has seemed best to indicate Pope's insertion of *and*.

30. IV, i, 222-27, 269, and especially 272: "The commons will not then be satisfi'd." Such an interpretation of the commons' suit also accords with the lines that immediately follow its mention (ll. 155-57).

31. Although Shakespeare probably did not know the *Annales* and other Saint Albans histories, he may well have taken a hint from Holinshed, who after recounting the French version of the ambushing of Richard adds that "Some write . . . that . . . the king offered, in consideration of his insufficiencie to gouerne, freeli to resigne the crowne, and his kinglie title to the same, vnto the duke of Hereford" (Black, Variorum, p. 428). Holinshed omits the Lancastrian detail that Richard submitted with a "happy countenance"; but even if it had been included, it would accord neither with Shakespeare's process toward pathos for Richard nor with his depiction of woe throughout the play.

32. See above, chap. VI, n. 26. Oblique and direct comments about Henry's motives are left to Richard, and left within Richard's constant Yorkist frame of reference, which early in this drama would make even a sorrowful, exiled Bolingbroke a "high Hereford" (I, iv, 2).

33. Even within these relatively few lines (181-221), a number of interesting repetitions are apparent. The wavering of ll. 201-2 is congruent with the earlier tipping of the crown; while that which is intensified is, paradoxically, Henry's question (l. 200), in contrast with his statement (l. 190), for the question leads to the transfer of regalia and the temporary conclusion just noted. Bolingbroke's statement, however, had evoked a similar statement of willingness to abdicate and of Richard's sorrow (ll. 191-93). Then through Richard's sorrow, as earlier in the Flint Castle episode (III, iii, 133 ff.), Shakespeare turns once more in a Yorkist direction by renewing faintly the bucket imagery (l. 195) as the thought of Richard's speech moves to an oblique reference about the perpetuity of any ruling "contract" (ll. 198-99). At the same time, by such a development, which amounts to oblique censure of Henry, Richard's "loss of care, by old care done" (l. 196) is an equally oblique reference to his own past conduct, which will be recognized as censurable by Richard himself. Thus with a punning paradox ("ay"—"I"), Richard proceeds with the speech which leads to his strongly Lancastrian lines upon the completion of the transfer of regalia. Notice, too, the effect of the phrases accompanying the business with the crown and, to a lesser degree, with the scepter. The words "heavy weight" and "unwieldy" (ll. 204-5) connote York's "tired majesty," as well as the divine responsibility of rule and, with the latter, even the complex overtones of the earlier Phaëthon-Richard reference. At the same time, contradictory ideas are implicit, in "balm," "sacred state," "duteous oaths" (ll. 207-10)—contradictory in their implication of a prince's holy, regal permanence. Surely these lines, then, in their total effect show a fusion of disparate emphases, like the ending of the Flint Castle episode and the subsequent mirror incident.

34. In the preceding development one might also note how the idea expressed by Richard's words about "priest," "clerk," and "service" (ll. 173, 176) persist. He both deposes himself and represents himself as one who would direct another in this ceremony of abdication: thus the tipping of the crown (ll. 181-89). Richard's Christ imagery is discussed below.

35. Even in its details, this development, like the rest of the scene, is interesting and meaningful. Note Richard's "crimes," according to Northumberland (l. 223); "follies," according to Richard (l. 229); but finally "sins" (l. 275).

36. Steevens notes a reflection of the 139th *Psalm* (Black, Variorum, 274).

37. Erwin Panofsky, *Early Netherlandish Painting* (Cambridge, Mass., 1958), I, 203. See also Heinrich Schwartz, "The Mirror in Art," *Art Quarterly*, XV (1952), 97-118.

38. Although my emphasis varies somewhat from that of the authors, see Samuel C. Chew, *The Virtues Reconciled: An Iconographic Study* (Toronto, 1947), pp. 14-15; Peter Ure, "The Looking-Glass of Richard II," *PQ*, XXIV (1955), 219-24; John Erskine Hankins, *Shakespeare's Derived Imagery* (Lawrence, Kan., 1953), p. 141.

39. Chew, *Virtues Reconciled*, p. 15.

40. Above, p. 12.

41. Donne continues with the thought that kings have physicians about them and suffer from the fear of sickness "or the worst of sickness." "Are they gods? He that called them so cannot flatter. They are gods, but sick gods; and God is presented to us under many human affections as far as infirmities." His theme is that man's "matter is earth, his form misery." Yet in a manner not discordant with divine-right theories, nor discordant with the "sins" of Shakespeare's Richard, Donne also adds the conventional precept that the "deity" of kings "is better expressed in their humility, than in their height: when abounding and overflowing, as God, in means of doing good, they descend, as God, to a communication of their abundances with man, according to their necessities, then they are gods." *Works*, ed. Henry Alford (London, 1839), III, 529-30 (*Devotions upon Emergent Occasions*, "VIII. Meditation").

42. Chew, *Virtues Reconciled*, pp. 14-15.

43. IV, i, 290-98; as I take it, the appearance of sorrow, not the substance or the reality under the appearance, has destroyed the appearance, not the substance, of what should underlie a royal face. But once more Richard ignores the substance of his fall to intensify, instead, the grief of the victim, while expressing the idea that he has that within which passes show:

> 'Tis very true, my grief lies all within;
> And these external manners of laments
> Are merely shadows to the unseen grief
> That swells with silence in the tortur'd soul.
> There lies the substance . . . .

Such an interpretation agrees with those of Chambers, Deighton, Herford, Newbolt, Malone (Black, Variorum, pp. 275-76).

44. Similarly, when Richard's censure elsewhere becomes strong, the overtones, as with the earlier Phaëton reference, are apt to be contradictory. For example, the dominant image of Richard as a "mockery king of snow" before "the sun of Bolingbroke" (ll. 260-61) is, like the tear imagery of the Flint Castle episode (III, iii, 160-71), congruent with the idea of a *roy fainéant*—be it Arcadian or in the general tradition of chronicles by Lancastrians or dogma by Buchanan. Although in this particular instance, the lamenting force of the speech in which the image appears and the explicit lines of censure that follow (e.g., l. 263) tend to smother such an implication; yet the idea continues, at least obliquely, in the situation which Shakespeare then contrives so that Richard censures himself (ll. 273-75). After the mirror episode, moreover, by the simple reappearance of the topic of flattery (ll. 305-9), regardless of its use or its twisted misuse by Richard, that king might well have been linked in any audience's mind with previous matter in this stage-world, with nobles, as well as commons, who disliked and could not tolerate a "sea-walled garden" "full of weeds,"

> . . . her fairest flowers chok'd up,
> Her fruit-trees all unprun'd, her hedges ruin'd,

> Her knots disorder'd and her wholesome herbs
> Swarming with caterpillars.
>
> (III, iv, 44-47)

45. See also above, chap. VI, n. 44.

46. T. W. Baldwin, *The Organization and Personnel of the Shakespearian Company* (Princeton, 1927), charts between pp. 228-29, pp. 394 ff.

47. *The Works of Robert Armin, Actor,* ed. Alexander B. Grosart, Occasional Issues of Unique . . . Books, XIV (privately printed, 1880), p. 141 (the dedicatory epistle of *Phantasma, the Italian Taylor and His Boy*); see also p. xv.

48. Ambiguities from three of the lives in Plutarch and from Seneca would, thereby, have been intensified. See Robert Ornstein, "Seneca and the Political Drama of *Julius Caesar,*" *JEGP*, LVII (1958), 51-56.

49. Material in the following paragraph is discussed in more detail in the study referred to in the preface.

50. As, for example, in the Arcadians turning to Euarchus.

51. Above, chap. VI, n. 9; Black, Variorum, p. 246.

52. Here, too, one should note that, when Bolingbroke appears in the first of his three private scenes with Hal (*1 H IV*, III, ii), a false Hal-Richard identification and a false accusation that Hal is likely to be subservient to Hotspur lead to the vigorous denial that Henry desires, that an audience expects, and that specifies the exact form of both Hal's reformation and the catastrophe. Any emphasis upon stealing courtesy from heaven in order to win the love of the people is thus blurred by the development of the scene in this particular drama now unfolding before an audience. Even when a Yorkist statement of silent hypocrisy is given to Henry, it is still qualified, if not by a Lancastrian emphasis, yet by a strong theatrical one. *1 H IV*, V, iv, 44-58, needs no comment; but a process somewhat similar to that in the first scene appears in Henry's third private scene with Hal (*2 H IV*, IV, v, 90-225). Then a tormented cry for forgiveness precedes a filial acceptance of a "plain and right" possession, and when that cry is reflected in a prayer to the God of battles, the glory of Agincourt will open upon the stage (*H V*, IV, ii, 306-22).

53. See Myron P. Gilmore, "Freedom and Determinism in Renaissance Historians," *Studies in the Renaissance*, III (1956), 48-60.

54. W. W. Lawrence, *Shakespeare's Problem Comedies* (New York, 1931).

# Index

Abbot of Westminster (*Richard II*), 177, 180-81
Adair, E. R., 216 n. 122
Adkins, Mary Grace Muse, 225 n. 13
Aglionby, Edward, 83, 84, 215-16 n. 117
Ahud, 74, 78
Aikman, J., 210 n. 61
Albright, Evelyn May, 225 n. 13
Alexander the Great (*Philotas*), 130-32, 134-42
Alford, Henry, 235 n. 41
Allen, John William, 210 n. 60
Allen, Dr. William, Cardinal, 17, 67
Alston, L., 205 n. 35
Ambroise, Saint, 215-16 n. 117
Amphialus (*Arcadia*), 104-5, 107, 111-12, 116, 117, 229 n. 33
Andromana (*Arcadia*), 223 n. 70
Angelo (*Measure for Measure*), 122
Antigona (*Philotas*), 134, 135
*Antigone,* 43
Antigonus II, 73
Antiochus IV, 72-74
Antiphilus (*Arcadia*), 113-14
Antonio (*Merchant of Venice*), 195
Antony, Marc, 26
Antony, Marc (*Julius Caesar*), 195
Aquinas. *See* Thomas Aquinas
Arber, Edward, 225 n. 10
*Arcadia,* 91-94, 97-117
Archbishop of York (*2 Henry IV*), 146-47
Archytas, 213-14 n. 92
Aristotle, 7, 18, 21-24, 27, 35, 36, 40, 44, 51, 52, 56, 81, 93, 124, 186; *Epideictic Rhetoric,* 219 n. 43; *Politica,* 204 n. 31
Armin, Robert, 195; *Works,* 236 n. 47
Armstrong, E., 210 n. 60

Armstrong, William A., 224 n. 3
Arrowood, Charles Flinn, 210 n. 61
Arthington, Henry, 47
Arthur, Duke of Bretagne (*King John*), 197
Ascham, Roger, 23, 206 n. 8
Asplyn, Thomas, 46-47
Athaliah, 74
Attaras (*Philotas*), 136
Attilus (*Philotas*), 136
Augustine, Saint, 4, 15, 231 n. 7
Aumerle, Duke of (*Richard II*), 158, 166-67, 174, 176, 178-80, 194
Aylmer, John, 5, 18, 23, 49, 202 n. 7, 206 n. 8

Bacon, Francis, 66, 82, 106, 124, 225 n. 12; *Works,* 222 n. 44
Bagot, Sir William (*Richard II*), 178
Baldwin, T. W., 202 n. 11, 228 n. 23, 236 n. 46
Bale, John, 203 n. 17
Bancroft, Richard, Archbishop, 68, 212 n. 75
Barlow, William, 125-27, 151
Barrow, Henry, 46-48, 212 n. 76
Basilius (*Arcadia*), 104-8, 111, 112, 114-15, 235 n. 44
Batman, Stephen, 175
Baumer, Franklin Le Van, 205 nn. 35 and 36
Beale, Robert, 21, 92
Beaumont, Francis, 225 n. 13
Becon, Thomas, 23
Belon (*Philotas*), 136
Beza, Theodore, 210 n. 60
Bible, 3; Geneva Bible, 28, 29, 207 n. 25
Bill, William, 23
Birchet, Peter, 45-46
Black, Matthew W., 231-32 n. 9

238 INDEX

Blount, Charles, Lord Mountjoy, Earl of Devonshire, 143, 226 n. 14, 228 nn. 20 and 21, 230 n. 34
Bodin, Jean, 21, 24, 27, 28, 35-36, 39, 53, 61, 107, 116, 117, 124, 128-29, 215-16 n. 117; *Method for the Easy Comprehension of History*, 205 n. 2; *Six Books of a Commonweale*, 206 n. 9
Boleyn, Anne, 83
Bolingbroke. See Henry IV
Bond, John, 212 n. 81
Book of Common Prayer, 7, 8, 202 n. 10
Born, Lester K., 206 n. 5
Boucher, Jean, 108, 210 n. 60
Boyet (*Love's Labour's Lost*), 195
Bracton, Henry de, 53, 54, 204 n. 31, 215 n. 96, 216 n. 120
Bradforth, John, 218-19, n. 33
Briggs, William Dinsmore, 220 n. 6
Bright, Timothy, 231 n. 7
Brinsley, J., 14
Brown, Robert, 46, 215 n. 115
Brutus, Marcus Junius, the Younger, 40
Buchanan, George, 5, 39-40, 92, 93, 223 n. 68, 225-26 n. 13, 235 n. 44; *De Jure Regni apud Scotos Dialogus*, 210 n. 61; *History of Scotland*, 210 n. 61
Buckhurst, Lord. See Sackville, Thomas
Burbage, Richard, 195
Burghley, Lord. See Cecil, William
Burnet, Gilbert, 219 n. 41
Bushy (Bussy), Sir John (*Richard II*), 190, 191

Cade, Jack, 66
Cade, Jack (*2 Henry VI*), 196
Caenus (*Philotas*), 136
Caesar, Julius, 26, 30, 40, 208 n. 31
Caesar, Julius (*Julius Caesar*), 195
Calvin, John, 215 n. 115
Campbell, Lily B., 217 n. 2
Carlson, Edgar M., 215 n. 95
Carlyle, A. J., 201 n. 1
Carlyle, Bishop of (*Richard II*), 178, 180-82, 191, 193, 194, 197
Carlyle, R. W., 201 n. 1
Cartwright, Thomas, 6, 29, 47-48, 79, 202 n. 7, 207 n. 27, 212 n. 74
Cassius, Caius, 40
Cassius (*Julius Caesar*), 195

Castiglione, Baldassare, 66, 85
Catholic monarchomachial tracts, 39, 41, 51, 98
Cato the Elder, 38
Cebalinus (*Philotas*), 134-36
Cecil, Robert, Lord Cranborn, 143, 144, 153, 176, 203 n. 27, 228 n. 20
Cecil, William, Lord Burghley, 15, 16, 23, 46, 48, 65-68, 147, 151, 203 n. 25, 208 n. 32
Cecropia (*Arcadia*), 101-2, 108, 111, 112, 115, 223 nn. 67 and 72
Chalisthenes (*Philotas*), 131, 134, 141, 143
Chamberlain's Company, The Lord, 125, 144, 151-52, 156, 195, 231-32 n. 9
Chapman, George, 130
Charles I, King, 82, 225 n. 13
Cheke, Sir John, 23, 69, 206 n. 8
Chew, Samuel C, 235 n. 38
Chief Justice (*2 Henry IV*), 195
Children of the Queen's Revels, 130
Chrimes, Stanley Burton, 201 nn. 2 and 4
Christ, 191-92
Christian II, King of Denmark, 218 n. 26
Cicero, 8, 14, 35, 51, 124, 206 n. 5, 216-17 n. 126
Claudio (*Measure for Measure*), 122
Clichtoveus, Iodocus, 85
Clinias (*Arcadia*), 108, 123, 124, 145
Clitus (*Philotas*), 135
Coke, Sir Edward, 18-19; *Institutes*, 204 n. 32
Collier, J. Payne, 219 n. 46
Comes, Natalis, 169
Comines, Philippe de, 39, 85, 200
Commodus, Lucius Aelius Aurelius, 30
Confucius, 215-16 n. 117
Constable, Archibald, 202 n. 6
Contarini, Gasparo, 28, 35; *Commonwealth and Government of Venice*, 207 n. 20
Cooke, Anthony, 206 n. 8
Cooper, Lane, 219 n. 43
Cooper, Thomas, 212 n. 75; *Thesaurus*, 227-28 n. 16
Copinger, Edmund, 47
Cornwallis, Sir Charles, 82-83
Corrie, G. E., 202 n. 11
Cox, Richard, 206 n. 8
Craig, Hardin, 212 n. 78

## INDEX 239

Craigie, James, 207 n. 28
Cranmer, Thomas, Archbishop, 15, 68, 218 n. 27
Crasus, Marcus Licinius, 26
Craterus (*Philotas*), 134-36, 139-41, 144
Créton, 232 n. 14
Cundall, Henry, 195
Curry, Walter Clyde, 231 n. 7
Curtius, Quintus, 130, 136, 226-28 n. 16

Dametus (*Arcadia*), 114
Daniel, Samuel, viii-ix, 130-45, 146, 152-55, 177, 198, 210 n. 68, 229 n. 33; *Tragedy of Philotas*, 226 n. 14. *See also* the names of characters
Dante, 10, 202 n. 14
Davis, E. T., 211 n. 70
Day, John, 47
Dean, L. F., 205-6 n. 2, 224 n. 5
Deborah, 80-81, 85
Devereux, Robert, Earl of Essex, 65, 67, 125-28, 130, 133, 142-43, 146, 147, 151, 199, 224 n. 7, 229 n. 33, 231-32 n. 9
Devonshire, Earl of. *See* Blount, Charles
D'Ewes, Sir Simon, 203 n. 27
Dion of Syracuse, 40
Dionysius of Halicarnassus, 124
Dionysius the Younger, 40
Dixon, Richard M., 202 n. 9
Dogberry (*Much Ado*), 195
Doleman. *See* Parsons, Robert
Domitian(us), Titus Flavius, 30
Donne, John, 189; *Works*, 235 n. 41
Doran, Madeleine, 228 n. 22
Drake, Sir Francis, 66
Dudley, Robert, Earl of Leicester, 10, 15, 65, 66, 86, 93, 224 n. 6, 229 n. 33
Duls, Louisa DeSausurre, 232-33 n. 14
Duns Scotus, John, 4
Dymnus (*Philotas*), 135, 136
Eck, Jan van, 187

Edmund of Langley, Duke of York (*Richard II*), 158, 160-62, 166, 174, 177-80, 182-85, 194, 198
Edward II, King, 75, 225-26 n. 13
*Edward II*, 162, 164, 178, 233 nn. 26 and 27

*Edward III*, 121
Edward IV (*Richard III*), 195
Edward VI, King, 7, 63, 78, 206 n. 8
Egidio Colonna, 85
Eglon, 74, 77, 78
Elder, John, 217 n. 7
Elizabeth I, Queen, vii, 6, 8, 10, 14-18, 45-47, 49, 63, 65, 67, 68, 72, 78-88, 91, 96, 100, 115, 121, 125-27, 132, 142, 147, 151, 199-200, 204 n. 30, 204 n. 31, 206 n. 8, 215-16 n. 117, 225 n. 12, 232 n. 13
Elizabeth of York, Queen, 83
Ellis, Henry, 219 n. 46
Ellis, Robert Leslie, 222 n. 44
Elton, William, 231 n. 7
Elyot, Sir Thomas, 66, 202 n. 4; *Boke Named the Gouernour*, 208 n. 30
Ephestion (*Philotas*), 134-40
Erasmus, 14, 22-24, 82, 85, 86, 169; *Education of a Christian Prince*, 206 n. 5
Eron (*Arcadia*), 113
Escalus (*Measure for Measure*), 121
Essex, Earl of. *See* Devereux, Robert
Euarchus (*Arcadia*), 99, 103, 104, 107, 110-12, 114-16, 223 nn. 48 and 53
Exton, Sir Pierce of (*Richard II*), 194

Fabyan, Robert, 219 n. 46
Fairchild, A. H. R., 230 n. 2
Falstaff (*2 Henry IV*), 155
*Famous Victories*, 231 n. 8
Farnham, Willard, 203 n. 4
Fenner, Dudley, 68, 207 n. 27
Ferguson, Arthur B., 202 n. 4
Ferguson, W. Craig, 230 n. 2
Feuillerat, Albert, 220 n. 10
Ficino, Marsilio, 23
Field, John, 49
Figgis, John Neville, 201 n. 1
Finch, Henry, 48, 49
Fink, Zera S., 207 n. 20
Fisher, John, Saint, 5
Fitzwater, Lord (*Richard II*), 178
Fletcher, Dr. Giles, 157
Fletcher, John, 225 n. 13
Fortescue, Sir John, 4-5, 215 n. 96; *De Laudibus Legum Angliae*, 201 n. 4; *Works*, 205 n. 36
Fortescue, Thomas, Lord Clermont, 205 n. 36

## INDEX

Fowler, Thomas, 157
Fox, Harold George, 220 n. 2
Foxe, John, 69; *Acts and Monuments*, 217 n. 7
Francis, Duke of Alençon and Anjou, 39, 94-96, 98, 103, 117
French chroniclers, 160, 232-33 n. 14
Froissart, Jean, 232 n. 14
Frowde, Philip, 143
Furnivall, F. J., 202 n. 13

Garnier, Robert, 133
Geehern, Richard Jerome, 232-33 n. 14
George, Duke of Saxony, 78
Gierke, Otto Friedrich von, 201 n. 1
Gilbert, Allan H., 208 n. 30
Gilmore, Myron P., 236 n. 53
Glendower (*1 Henry IV*), 195
Gloucester, Duke of (*1, 2 Henry VI*), 196-97
Gorboduc, King, 68
*Gorboduc*, vii, 110, 170, 225-26 n. 13
Gough, J. W., 201 n. 1
Gratiano (*Merchant of Venice*), 195
Greene, Robert. See *James IV*
Greenwood, John, 47, 48
Greg, W. W., 225 n. 13
Greville, Sir Fulke, first Baron Brooke, 94, 132, 143; *Life of Sidney*, 220 n. 3
Grey, Lady Jane, 206 n. 8, 218 n. 27
Grindal, William, 23, 206 n. 8
Grosart, Alexander B., 236 n. 47
Grotius, Hugo, 214 n. 93
Guazzo, Stefano, 82
Guicciardini, Francesco, 200, 224 n. 5
Gynecia (*Arcadia*), 115, 223 n. 67

Hacket, William, 47, 224 n. 6
Haddon, James, 206 n. 8
Haddon, Walter, 23, 68, 206 n. 3
Hales, John, 6, 18, 79, 202 n. 7
Hall, Edward, 232 n. 14
Hankins, John Erskine, 235 n. 38
Harris, Mary Dormor, 219 n. 46
Harrison, G. B., 232 n. 12
Harrison, William, 21
Harsnett, Samuel, 128
Hart, Alfred, 150-51
Harvey, Gabriel, 23; *Letterbook*, 205-6 n. 2
Hastings, Sir Francis, 212 n. 81
Hatton, Sir Christopher, 16, 17, 46, 91, 205 n. 36, 221 n. 26
Hayward, Sir John, 126-28, 203 n. 17
Hazeltine, H. D., 201 n. 4
Hearn, Thomas, 219 n. 46
Heath, Douglas Denon, 222 n. 44
Helena (*Arcadia*), 112
Heminges, John, 195
Henry IV, King, 125-26
*Henry IV, First Part*, 236 n. 52; *Second Part*, 146-56, Variorum, 230 n. 3
Henry IV (*1 Henry IV*), 236 n. 52; (*2 Henry IV*), 147, 150-55, 236 n. 52; (*Richard II*), 157-200
*Henry V*, 236 n. 52
*Henry VI, First Part*, 196; *Second Part*, 196-97; *Third Part*, 170-71, 197
Henry VII, King, 83, 126
Henry VIII, King, 5, 19, 38, 63, 83, 86, 91, 94
Henry Stuart, Prince of Wales, 82, 141-42
Hercules, 74
Hereford, Duke of. See Henry IV
Herford, C. H., 224 n. 3
Hill, Charles Jarvis, 224 n. 2
Hinton, R. W. K., 201 n. 4
Hobbes, Thomas, 3
Hoby, Sir Edward, 176
Holdsworth, W. S., 201 n. 4
Holinshed, Raphael, 182, 217 n. 7, 232 n. 14, 234 n. 31
Holofernes (*Love's Labour's Lost*), 195
Homer, 12, 34
Hooker, Richard, 13-14, 20, 40-66, 68, 70, 82, 90, 91, 93, 95-99, 103-5, 108, 115-17, 122, 123, 128-29, 132, 154, 203 n. 17, 223-24 n. 78, 225-26 n. 13; *Laws of Ecclesiastical Polity*, 210 n. 63; *Works*, 217 n. 127
Horatius, 26
Hortentius, 26
Hotman, François, 52, 92, 94, 210 n. 60, 213 n. 89
Hotson, Leslie, 209 n. 49
Houck, Raymond Aaron, 210 n. 63
Howard, Thomas II, third Duke of Norfolk, 76
Howard, Thomas III, fourth Duke of Norfolk, 229 n. 33

# INDEX

Hubert, Sir Francis, 203 n. 20
Hudson, Winthrop S., 202 n. 5
Huguenot writings, 39, 51, 93, 96, 98, 213 n. 89. *See also* Hotman, François; *Vindiciae contra Tyrannos*
Humphrey, Lawrence, 5, 18, 202 n. 7, 212 n. 81

Iberia, King of (*Arcadia*), 113, 115
Infanta of Spain, 67
*Isle of Dogs*, 156-57

Jackman, Henry, 90
Jael, 74
*James IV*, 121
James VI, King of Scotland (James I of England), 17, 29, 39, 67, 82, 121, 225-26 n. 13; *Basilicon Doron*, 207 n. 28
Jehoash, 74
Jehu, 74
Jezebel, 74
John, King, 31-32, 126. See *King John*
John (*King John*), 197
John of Gaunt, Duke of Lancaster, 67
John of Gaunt (*Richard II*), 174, 190
John of Leyden, 46, 224 n. 6
John of Salisbury, 75, 218 n. 27
Jonson, Ben, 82, 123-24, 156-57; *Ben Jonson*, 224 n. 3; *Sejanus*, 130, 143
Joram, 74
*Journals of the House of Commons*, 207-8 n. 29
Judas, 191, 192
*Julius Caesar*, 195
Justinian I, 3; *Iustiniani Digesta*, 201 n. 1

Kalandar (*Arcadia*), 110
Kebel, John, 217 n. 127
Kemp, Will, 195
Kern, Fritz, 201 n. 1
Ketley, Joseph, 202 n. 10
Kett, Robert, 69
*King John*, 197
Kirk, Rudolph, 209 n. 46
Kirshbaum, Leo, 225 n. 10
Knappen, M. M., 202 n. 7
Knolles, Richard, 206 n. 9
Knox, John, 5
Kuhl, E. P., 229 n. 31
Kyd, Thomas, 233 n. 21

Lambarde, William, 126-27, 132, 151, 232 n. 13
Lancaster, Duke of. *See* Henry IV
Lancastrian chroniclers, 160, 232-33 n. 14, 235 n. 44
Laneham, Robert, 10, 15, 202 n. 13
Languet, Hubert, 92, 97, 98, 101, 102, 106, 210 n. 60
Lawrence, W. W., 236 n. 54
*Lear*, 154
Leicester, Earl of. *See* Dudley, Robert
Leland, John, 219 n. 46
Leonatus (*Arcadia*), 112
Lepidus, Marcus Aemilius, 26
Le Roy, Louis, 23, 33, 34, 51, 61, 108, 221-22 n. 31; *Aristotles Politiqves*, 206 n. 7
Lewkenor, Lewes, 207 n. 20
Lipsius, Justus, 209 n. 46
Loades, D. M., 218-19 n. 33
Louis XI, King of France, 30, 95
Lovejoy, Arthur O., 202 n. 14
Luciani, Vincent, 224 n. 5
Lumley, John, Baron, 126
Luther, Martin, 18, 53, 54, 78
Lydgate, John, 83
Lyndesay, Sir David, 85

*Macbeth*, 154
Machiavelli, Niccolò, 15, 28, 33-35, 54, 62, 85, 114, 116, 217 n. 127, 223-24 n. 78, 225-26 n. 13
McIlwaine, Charles H., 201 nn. 2 and 4, 215 n. 96
McKerrow, R. B., 230 n. 2
McManaway, James G., 147
Macrobius, 12, 23, 188, 189, 203 n. 16
Madden, Frederic W., 201 n. 1
Maitland, F. W., 205 n. 35
Major, John, 5, 24, 39, 75, 225-26 n. 13; *History of Greater Britain*, 202 n. 6
Marlowe, Christopher, 121, 143, 162, 178, 186. See *Edward II*
Marshal, William, 6
Marshall, John S., 210 n. 67
Marsiglio of Padua, 6, 202 n. 8
Marston, John, 130
Martin Marprelate, 46, 47, 230 n. 2
Martyr, Peter, 218 n. 27
Mary Stuart, Queen of Scots, 39, 67, 91, 100, 204 n. 31, 205 n. 36, 216 n. 118, 221 n. 26, 229 n. 33

## 242 INDEX

Mary Tudor, Queen, 6, 28, 41, 59, 69, 77, 78, 202 n. 9, 214 n. 93, 216 n. 118, 218-19 n. 33, 219 n. 41
Massinger, Philip, 225 n. 13
Mattathias, 74
Mayne, Cuthbert, 45
*Measure for Measure*, 121-22
Mendoza, Bernadino de, 24
Metron (*Philotas*), 135
Meyrick, Sir Gelly, 127, 128
Michel, Laurence, 226 n. 14
Middleton, Thomas, 225 n. 13
Mildmay, Sir Walter, 95, 96, 104, 221 n. 15
Milton, John, 56
*Mirror for Magistrates*, 124
Molina, Luis, 51, 213 n. 89, 214 n. 93
Mommsen, Theodore, 201 n. 1
Montaigne, Michel de, 12
More, Sir Thomas, 5, 28, 41
Morison, Sir Richard, 61
Mortimer, Roger, the Younger (*Edward II*), 162
Moses, 74, 211 n. 73
Mosse, George L., 201 n. 4
Mowbray, Lord (*2 Henry IV*), 146
Mowbray, Thomas, Duke of Norfolk (*Richard II*), 178, 179
Münzer, Thomas, 46
Mullinger, James Bass, 206 n. 8
Musidorus (*Arcadia*), 99, 100, 102, 103, 106, 107, 112, 116

Nashe, Thomas, 156-57
Neale, J. E., vii n. 1, 203 n. 27
Needham, Francis, 229 n. 33
Neilson, William Allen, 224 n. 2
Nero Claudius Caesar, 30
Nichols, John, 219 n. 42
Nichomachus (*Philotas*), 136
Noah, 72
Norfolk, Duke of. *See* Mowbray, Thomas (*Richard II*); Howard, Thomas, II; Howard, Thomas, III
North, Sir Thomas, 226-28 n. 16
Northumberland, Earl of (*2 Henry IV*), 147, 151-53; (*Richard II*), 158-59, 161-62, 164-67, 172-73, 175, 180, 182-86, 193-94, 195
Norton, Thomas, 18
Notestein, Wallace, 205 n. 33
Nowell, Alexander, 8, 14; Catechism, 202 n. 11
Numa Pompilius, 26

Octavius (Augustus), 26, 30, 208 n. 31
Ornstein, Robert, 236 n. 48
Ovid, 34, 169

Pamela (*Arcadia*), 101
Pandulphus, 32
Panofsky, Erwin, 235 n. 37
Parker, Matthew, Archbishop, 46
Parma, Alexander Farnese, Duke of, 229 n. 33
Parmenio (*Philotas*), 134-36
Parsons, Robert, 66-67, 78, 97, 129, 225 n. 13, 232 n. 12
Parthenia (*Arcadia*), 111
Paul III, Pope, 75
Pembroke's Company, 156
Penry, John, 47, 48
Percy, Henry, the Younger (*Richard II*), 158, 160, 178
Perdiccas (*Philotas*), 135
Petrarch, 15
Petrus Aloysius, Duke of Placenza (Piacenza), 75
Phaëthon, 169-73, 191
Phelan, Gerald B., 202 n. 9
Philanax (*Arcadia*), 100-1, 103, 104, 106, 107, 110, 111, 114
Philip II, King of Spain, 39, 59, 67, 69, 74, 77, 96, 216 n. 118, 218-19 n. 33
Phillips, Augustine, 126-27, 130, 195, 231-32 n. 9
Philoclea (*Arcadia*), 103
*Philotas*. *See* Daniel; names of the characters
Philotas (*Philotas*), 130-32, 134-42
Phrygia, Giants of (*Arcadia*), 223 n. 50
Phrygia, King of (*Arcadia*), 112-13
Pico della Mirandula, 23, 43
Pilate, 192
Plangus (*Arcadia*), 113, 115
Plato, 15, 16, 22, 23, 27, 29, 35
Plessis-Mornay, Philippe, Seigneur du, 92, 210 n. 60
Plexirtus (*Arcadia*), 112, 223 nn. 51, 60 and 62
Plutarch, 29, 85, 130, 236 n. 48; *Lives*, 226-28 n. 16
Pole, Reginald, 5, 75, 202 n. 5
Polidamus (*Philotas*), 136
Pollard, A. F., 205 n. 34
Pollard, A. W., 149-50
Polybius, 35, 52

# INDEX 243

Pompey, 26
Ponet, John, 7-8, 15, 23, 68-79, 96-98, 104, 117, 123, 129, 202 n. 9, 203 n. 17, 206 n. 9, 223 n. 62; Catechism, 202 n. 10; *Shorte Treatise,* 202 n. 5, 217 n. 8
Pontano, Giovanni, 200
Pontus, King of (*Arcadia*), 113, 114
Pratt, Josiah, 217 n. 7
Previté-Orton, C. W., 202 n. 8
Primaudaye, Pierre de la, 175; *French Academie,* 233 n. 20
Prouty, Charles T., 230 n. 2
Prynne, William, 207 n. 25
Puckering, Sir John, 17
Pyrocles (*Arcadia*), 99, 103, 106, 107, 109, 112, 115
Pythagoras, 35, 117

Quintillian, 219 n. 43

Raleigh, Sir Walter, 5, 33-34, 55, 57, 66, 230 n. 2; *History of the World,* 201 n. 3; *Works,* 208 n. 44
Read, Conyers, 203 nn. 25 and 26
Regiomontanus, 209 n. 49
Reynolds, Beatrice, 205 n. 2, 210 n. 60
Ribner, Irving, 224 n. 4
Richard II, King, 75, 122-23, 125-26, 146, 150, 155, 225-26 n. 13
*Richard II,* viii-ix, 125, 126, 128, 130, 144, 151, 155-200, 231 n. 7; Variorum, 231-32 n. 9
Richard II (*1 Henry IV*), 236 n. 52; (*2 Henry IV*), 152-54; (*Richard II*), 157-200
*Richard III,* 196
Richard Plantagenet, Duke of York (*2, 3 Henry VI*), 197
Richardson, H. G., 205 n. 35
Rogers, Daniel, 92
Rolfe, John C., 226-28 n. 16
Romulus, 26
Ross, W. D., 204 n. 31
Rothmann, Bernt, 46

Sabinus, Georgius, 233 n. 18
Sackville, Thomas, Lord Buckhurst, 229 n. 33
St. German, Christopher, 205 n. 36
Salisbury, Earl of (*Richard II*), 159, 165
Sandys, Edwin, 48, 207-8 n. 29
Sandys, Edwin, Bishop of Worcester and of London, Archbishop of York, 23, 46, 68, 212 n. 74
Sayles, G. O., 205 n. 35, 215 n. 96
Schwartz, Heinrich, 235 n. 37
Scipio, Africanus Minor, 72
Scott, E. J. L., 205-6 n. 2
Scott Pearson, A. F., 202 n. 7
Scroop, Lord (*Richard II*), 172
Scylla. *See* Sulla, Lucius Cornelius
Seneca, 228 n. 19, 236 n. 48
*Sermon of Obedience,* 9, 69
Servius Tullius, 26
Seton-Watson, R. W., 216 n. 122
Shaaber, Matthias A., 230 n. 3
Shakespeare, William, viii-ix, 45, 91, 121, 122-23, 130, 146-200, 203, n. 17, 209 n. 49, 225 n. 10, 229 n. 33, 233 n. 21; *Complete Plays and Poems,* 224 n. 2. *See also* titles of plays; names of characters
Shapiro, I. A., 233 n. 24
Shaw, Robert, 157
Shepard, Max Adams, 201 n. 4
Shirley, F. J., 211-12 n. 73
Sidney, Algernon, 41, 52
Sidney, Sir Philip, 36, 52, 85, 91-117, 122, 123, 197, 225-26 n. 13, 229 n. 33, 235 n. 44; *Complete Works,* 220 n. 10. See also *Arcadia;* names of characters
Simmes, Valentine, 147-52, 156
Simpson, Evelyn, 224 n. 3
Simpson, Percy, 224 n. 3
*Sir Thomas More,* 125, 149, 225 n. 13
Sisera, 74
Sisson, C. J., 212 n. 78, 224 n. 3
Skeels, Caroline A. J., 201 n. 4
Skelton, John, 85
Skivington, Richard, 157
Smith, Adam, 90
Smith, Nowell, 220 n. 3
Smith, Sir Thomas, 19-41, 43, 45, 50, 52, 53, 55, 59, 68, 89-97, 104, 115-17, 123, 128-29, 154, 176-77, 196, 198-99, 204-5 n. 32, 205 n. 36, 225-26 n. 13, 228 n. 26; *De Republica Anglorum,* 205 n. 35
Soellner, Rolf, 233 n. 20
Sostratus (*Philotas*), 136
Spedding, James, 222 n. 44
Spencer, Gabriel, 157
Spencer, Theodore, 203 n. 17
Spenser, Edmund, 33, 34, 92
Spes, Guerau de, 24

## 244 INDEX

Sprague, Arthur Colby, 210 n. 68
Starkey, Thomas, 76
Starnes, DeWitt T., 233 n. 16
Stirling, Brents, 208 n. 42, 212 n. 75
Stradling, Sir John, 209 n. 46
Strathman, Ernest A., 217 n. 1
Stourton, John, Lord, 221 n. 15
Strype, John, 205 n. 1, 216 n. 122
Stuart, Arabella, 65, 229 n. 33
Stuart, Esmé, 225-26 n. 13
Sulla, Lucius Cornelius, 26, 30
Surrey, Duke of (*Richard II*), 178
Sympathus (*Arcadia*), 110

Tacitus, 225 n. 12
Talbert, Ernest William, 219 n. 45, 233 n. 16
Tanner, J. R., 205 n. 34
Tarquin Superbus, Lucius, 26, 73
Telenos (*Arcadia*), 112
Thais (*Philotas*), 134, 135, 140
Theseus, 74
Thomas, Thomas, 171-72; *Fabvlarum Ovidii Interpretatio*, 233 n. 18
Thomas, William, 61
Thomas Aquinas, Saint, 6-7, 15, 210-11 n. 69, 231 n. 7; *De Regimine Principum*, 202 n. 9; *Summa Contra Gentiles*, 203 n. 24
Thomas of Woodstock, Duke of Gloucester, 67
Thompson, Faith, 208 n. 38
Thorne, S. E., 205 n. 36
Thorpe, Sir Robert de, 19
Thrasibulus, 40
Throckmorton, Job, 16-18, 207 n. 29
Tiberius, 63
Tillyard, E. M. W., vii, 202 n. 12
Timantus (*Arcadia*), 110-12
Topcliffe, Richard, 156-57
*Traïson*, 232 n. 14
Travers, Walter, 48
*Two Gentlemen of Verona*, 169
Tydeus (*Arcadia*), 112
Tyler, Wat, 66, 125

Ulph, Owen, 210 n. 59
Ure, Peter, 235 n. 38

Valentinian II, 215-16 n. 117
Valerianus, Giovanni Pierio, 209 n. 46

Vann, Richard T., 204 n. 30
Vincentio, Duke (*Measure for Measure*), 121-22
*Vindiciae contra Tyrannos*, 52, 92, 104, 210 n. 60, 213 n. 90, 214 n. 93
Vinogradoff, Paul, 205 n. 36
Vives, Juan Luis, 28, 82

Walker, Alice, 230-31 n. 5
Walsingham, Sir Francis, 21, 36, 39, 65, 92, 94-95, 203 n. 26, 225-26 n. 13, 229 n. 33
Warwick, Earl of (*2 Henry IV*), 147, 151-55
Wecter, Dixon, 229 n. 31
Wentworth, Paul, 92
Wentworth, Peter, 18, 67-68, 92, 95-97, 99, 104, 129, 204 n. 31, 207 n. 29
Westmoreland, Earl of (*2 Henry IV*), 146
Whitaker, Virgil K., 220 n. 6
Whitgift, John, Archbishop, 48, 204 n. 30
Wilbraham, Mr., 157
Wilcockes, Thomas, 49
William I, the Conqueror, 49, 77, 215 n. 98
William I of Orange, 92
Wilson, J. Dover, 150, 230-31 n. 5
Wilson, Thomas, 92
Wilton circle, 133, 143. See also Daniel, Samuel; Greville, Sir Fulke
Windsor, William, second Baron, 76
Withington, Robert, 217 n. 7
Wolfe, John, 127-28
*Woodstock*, 121, 124, 164
Wotton, Sir Edward, 21
Wright, Celeste Turner, 205-6 n. 2
Wyatt, Sir Thomas, the Younger, 68-69

Yelverton, Christopher, 92
York, Duke of (*Henry VI*). See Richard Plantagenet
York, Duke of (*Richard II*). See Edmund of Langley
Yorkist chroniclers, 160, 232-33 n. 14

Zeeveld, W. Gordon, 216 n. 123
Zelmane. See Pyrocles (*Arcadia*)

www.ingramcontent.com/pod-product-compliance
Lightning Source LLC
Chambersburg PA
CBHW021359290426
44108CB00010B/313